SECOND EDITION

CULTURALLY RESPONSIVE

Standards-Based Teaching

SECOND EDITION

CULTURALLY RESPONSIVE

Standards-Based Teaching

Classroom to Community and Back

Steffen Saifer
Keisha Edwards
Debbie Ellis
Lena Ko
Amy Stuczynski

A Joint Publication

CORWIN
A SAGE Company

education
northwest

For information:

Corwin
A SAGE Company
2455 Teller Road
Thousand Oaks, California 91320
www.corwin.com

SAGE Ltd.
1 Oliver's Yard
55 City Road
London EC1Y 1SP
United Kingdom

SAGE Pvt. Ltd.
B 1/I 1 Mohan Cooperative Industrial Area
Mathura Road, New Delhi 110 044
India

SAGE Asia-Pacific Pte. Ltd.
33 Pekin Street #02–01
Far East Square
Singapore 048763

Education Northwest
101 SW Main Street, Suite 500
Portland, Oregon 97204
503-275-9500
www.educationnorthwest.org
Info@educationnorthwest.org

Printed in the United States of America

Library of Congress Cataloging-in-Publication Data

Culturally responsive standards-based teaching : classroom to community and back/Steffen Saifer . . . [et al.]. — 2nd ed.
    p. cm.
"A Joint Publication of Education Northwest and Corwin Press."
Includes bibliographical references and index.
ISBN 978-1-4129-8702-8 (pbk. : alk. paper)

    1. Multicultural education—United States. 2. Race relations—Study and teaching—United States. 3. Minorities—Education—United States. I. Saifer, Steffen, 1951- II. Title.

LC1099.3.C848 2011
370.117—dc22   2010035762

This book is printed on acid-free paper.

10 11 12 13 14   10 9 8 7 6 5 4 3 2 1

Acquisitions Editor:	Dan Alpert
Associate Editor:	Megan Bedell
Editorial Assistant:	Sarah Bartlett
Production Editor:	Veronica Stapleton
Copy Editor:	Alison Hope
Typesetter:	C&M Digitals (P) Ltd.
Proofreader:	Dennis W. Webb
Indexer:	Gloria Tierney
Cover Designer:	Michael Dubowe
Permissions:	Karen Ehrmann

This project has been funded in part with federal funds from the U.S. Department of Education under contract number ED-01-CO-0013. The content of this publication does not necessarily reflect the views or policies of the U.S. Department of Education nor does mention of trade names, commercial products, or organizations imply endorsement by the U.S. government.

Contents

Preface

Culturally Responsive Standards-Based Teaching: Classroom to Community and Back describes how educators can use the knowledge and culture students bring to school in a standards-based curriculum that supports student success. We call this approach culturally responsive standards-based (CRSB) teaching. Unlike multicultural education—which is an important way to incorporate all the world's cultural and ethnic diversity into lessons—CRSB teaching draws on the experiences, understandings, views, concepts, and ways of knowing of the students in the classroom.

Through foundational research and snapshots of real-life classroom practices throughout the United States, this publication shows teachers and school leaders how CRSB

- engages all students in learning,
- builds relationships between the classroom and the outside world, and
- creates opportunities for families and community members to support student success in and out of school.

This resource guide also offers tools, resources, and references to help practitioners adapt and apply CRSB teaching in their own school environment. By using this material, the guide seeks to help teachers

- expand their understanding of their own culture, the students' cultures, and the ways culture affects teaching and learning; and
- develop strategies for incorporating these cultures into a rigorous, challenging, and effective curriculum that will enable students to meet state and local standards.

The guide does not write the CRSB curriculum. Instead, it forms a rich, fertile ground on which educators may create lessons that are unique (and responsive) to themselves and their students.

WHY THIS BOOK IS NEEDED

Across the nation, our schools are growing increasingly more diverse: culturally, economically, and linguistically. The National Center for Educational Statistics (NCES) reveals in its latest report on the Condition of Education that in 2007 forty-four percent of public school students were part of a racial or ethnic minority group, largely due to growth in the proportion of Latino students; 10.8 million school-age children spoke a language other than English at home, with Spanish being the most frequently spoken; and 46 percent of all fourth-graders were eligible for free or reduced-price lunch (Planty et al., 2009a, 2009b).

While these changes to the student population have been happening across the country, the distribution has differed greatly across regions. In 2007, for instance, the West was the only region where minority public school enrollment (57 percent) exceeded white enrollment (43 percent). One-third of all students in the West (33.5 percent) spoke a language other than English at home.

With these changes come additional challenges to schools. According to an earlier NCES report (Wirt et al., 2005), the percentage of children whose families had more risk factors (defined as living in poverty, non-English primary home language, mother's low educational level, or single-parent household) were less likely to have mastered more-complex reading and mathematics skills by Grade 3 than were children from families with fewer risk factors. In grades 4 and 8, white and Asian/Pacific Islander students had higher average scores than did Native American, Latino, or black students in both reading and math, with the level of poverty in the school negatively associated with student achievement in both grades. In addition, language minority youth lagged behind their counterparts who spoke only English at home on most education (and economic) indicators, including school enrollment, grade retention, high school completion, postsecondary enrollment, and highest educational level attained—with those speaking Spanish faring less well than those speaking other non-English languages.

A number of studies suggest low school performance might be linked, in part, to the lack of congruence between the cultures of the students' families and communities and the cultural norms embedded in the expectations, policies, procedures, and practices of schools (Bensman, 1999; Bowman & Stott, 1994; Cummins, 1986; Delpit, 1995; Entwistle, 1995; Ladson-Billings, 1995). In addition, a recent examination of 80 research studies and literature reviews (Henderson & Mapp, 2002) found a positive and convincing relationship between family involvement and benefits for students, including improved academic achievement, higher grade point averages and scores on standardized tests, enrollment in courses that are more challenging, more classes passed and credits earned, better attendance, improved behavior both at home and at school, and better social skills and adaptation to school—holding across families of all economic, racial or ethnic, and educational backgrounds, and for students of all ages.

In a report to the U.S. Department of Education, the Regional Advisory Committee for the Northwest stated that the overriding regional challenge is to close the achievement gap between white students and students of other cultural and racial groups. When considering the achievement issues, specific challenges were identified that included addressing language, culture, and diversity among students and developing strategies to engage the community, especially families, in effective and meaningful ways (Northwest Regional Advisory Committee, 2005).

One of the most powerful ways to strengthen family and community partnerships for successful student learning is to change instructional and curricular practices so they are more culturally responsive. Drawing on the knowledge, skills, and experiences of students and the support of family and community members enriches the curriculum and builds family and community support, broadening learning experiences for all students.

DESIGN AND APPLICATIONS

The format of this publication and the materials contained in it were designed with the help of a cadre of users. Teachers, administrators, youth workers, curriculum coordinators, in-service trainers, and professors at colleges of education field-tested this guide. Some used it as a stand-alone document to support their teaching practices, and some used it with a variety of professional development supports, including one-to-one facilitation, technical assistance within professional learning teams, and group professional development either on site or through an online course. These field-testers and reviewers provided invaluable feedback that has shaped the development of these materials. They also helped in designing several options for the guide's intended use as a professional development tool and as a resource to support teaching practices.

The vast majority of the educators who contributed to the ideas in this publication, particularly those highlighted in the snapshots, are from the Pacific Northwest. This is because the first edition of the book was developed with funds from the U.S. Department of Education provided to the Northwest Regional Educational Laboratory (now Education Northwest) for work specifically within a five-state region: Alaska, Idaho, Montana, Oregon, and Washington. However, we strongly believe that most of the ideas in these snapshots are generalizable across diverse contexts and locations. Although a school in rural Alaska may seem to have nothing in common with an inner-city school in Baltimore, they actually have a number of remarkable similarities: high dropout rates, many disenfranchised minority youth, most of the teachers from a culture other than the students', difficulty recruiting and maintaining highly qualified teachers and administrators, pressure from the state and the district to improve test scores, facilities in need of improvement, service to low-income communities with high substance-abuse rates and inadequate social supports, and, most important, great potential to harness the strengths and culture of the students for their academic and life success.

Culturally Responsive Standards-Based Teaching: Classroom to Community and Back is intended for use by K–12 teachers, youth workers, curriculum coordinators and developers, principals, administrators, preservice teachers, and instructors at colleges of education. It can be used in professional development trainings or as a resource for individual teachers in the classrooms. CRSB teaching is an approach that asks educators to engage in a process of continual reflection and improvement. As such, this guide is organized to take the educator through the steps of such a process, with each chapter building on those before it. The reader is encouraged to tailor the concepts and tools to his or her specific role, setting, students, families, and community. Tools and examples ("snapshots") are formatted differently and listed in the table of contents so they can be found easily. Because effective reflection begins with authentic inquiry, many of the tools contain thought-provoking, open-ended questions.

List of Snapshots

List of Tools

Acknowledgments

This book was a collaborative effort made possible by the assistance of many individuals within the Northwest Regional Educational Laboratory (now Education Northwest). The writing team is grateful to the following individuals for their invaluable contributions: Diane Dorfman, Rändi Douglas, Elke Geiger, and Kendra Hughes. The support of Eve McDermott and Steve Fleishman is greatly appreciated.

Special thanks go to Rhonda Barton, Denise Crabtree, Linda Fitch, Michael Heavener, Gwen McNeir, Eugenia Cooper Potter, Bracken Reed, Cathy Swoverland, and Patti Tucci, for editing and design assistance.

We acknowledge and appreciate the generous contributions from the following practitioners and researchers in the field who provided valuable input and feedback through interviews, field-testing, and reviews: Shauna Adams, Judy Barker, Carrie Bartos, Paul Bartos, Carrie Bodensteiner, Lori Bogen, Denise Buckbee, Julie Cajune, Jioanna Carjuzaa, Reid Chapman, Angela Rose Cheek, Myra Clark, Janet Collier, David Cort, Barry Derfel, Lilia Doni, Dan Dunham, Dawn Dzubay, Larry Ericksen, Karen Exstrom, Kathy Fuller, Ann Gardner, David Greuenewald, Verenice Gutierrez, Tania Harman, Camille Harris, Rosa Hemphill, Matt Henry, Billie Hetrick, Jane Hilburn, Cynthia Irving and Freestyle staff, Laurie Kerley, Judy Kirkham, Wanda Kirn, Diana Larson, Amy Lloyd, Jennifer Loyning, Carole Luster, Shirley Marchwick, Wanda McCulough, Marcene McDonnell, David McKay, Elaine Meeks, Linda Mettler, Valorie Miller, Darren Morse, Tamara Mosar, Frank Newman, Evangelina Orozco, Libby Owens, Tiffany Parish, Deborah Peterson, Marcy Prager, Lynne Sadler, DeNae Simms, Michelle Singer, Jill Spaulding, Libi Susag, Patricia Tate, Sue Thomas, Elise Tickner, Tamara Van Wyhe, Marney Welmers, David R. Wetzel, and Stephanie Windham.

Finally, we would like to acknowledge the School-Family-Community Partnerships team's advisory committee members for their great advice regarding the needs of students, parents, schools, and community members in the area of education: Terry Bostick, Irene Chavolla, Elizabeth Flynn, Dell Ford, Debbie Gordon, Betty Klattenhoff, Lily Martinez, Peggy Ames Nerud, Paula Pawlowski, Barbara Riley, and Paul Sugar.

PUBLISHER'S ACKNOWLEDGMENTS

Corwin gratefully acknowledges the contributions of the following reviewers:

Denise Carlson, Curriculum Consultant
Heartland Area Education Agency
Story City, IA

Bruce Clemmer, Director I
Clark County School District, English Language Learner Program
Las Vegas, NV

Thelma A. Davis, Principal
Robert Lunt Elementary School
Clark County School District
Las Vegas, NV

R. John Frey, Assistant Principal
Columbus High School
Columbus, NE

Suzanne Javid, Education Consultant
SCJ Associates, LLC
Bloomfield Hills, MI

Rachel Mederios, ELL Teacher
Jefferson Elementary School
Boise, ID

About the Authors

Dr. Steffen Saifer has been the director of the Child and Family Program at Education Northwest since 2000 and an adjunct faculty member at Portland (Oregon) State University since 1996, where he has taught graduate courses in education. His areas of work and expertise include cultural-historical activity theory, the role of play in human development, and school–family partnerships. Saifer has worked extensively in Russia and Eastern Europe, where he has assisted in education curriculum reform. Recently he has been assisting to implement a graduate program in early childhood development at BRAC University in Dhaka, Bangladesh (cofunded by the Open Society Foundation and BRAC University). He is the author or coauthor of numerous publications, including *Practical Solutions to Practically Every Problem: The Early Childhood Teacher's Manual* (2003) and *Education and the Culture of Democracy: Early Childhood Practice* (1996).

Keisha Edwards is a trainer for the Oregon Parent Information and Resource Center (Oregon PIRC) at Education Northwest. Her primary work is to design and deliver meaningful learning experiences to educators and families on educational equity, cultural competence, and effective strategies to engage diverse families as allies in the school change process. In this role over the past five years, Edwards has facilitated more than 300 workshops, trainings, and coaching sessions with diverse audiences. As a result, she strongly believes that a new discourse, personal reflection, and deep dialogue across differences will soon be the most powerful and preferred strategies to transform school culture. Edwards is the author or coauthor of several publications, including *Everyone's Guide to Successful Project Planning: Tool for Youth* (2000) and *Beyond the Oregon Trail: Oregon's Untold Racial History* (2003).

Debbie Ellis is the project director for the Oregon State Parental Information and Resource Center (Oregon PIRC) at Education Northwest. Her area of work and expertise focuses on school–family partnerships, educational equity, and early childhood parent education. Ellis coordinates a statewide conference for educators and parents focusing on school–family partnerships, educational equity, and academic achievement. She assisted in the development of a statewide parent leadership curriculum to help underrepresented parents navigate the school system and help their children achieve in school, and is developing multimedia training for families to understand the key transitional periods in their child's education. She has worked as a teacher, family advocate, and parent educator, and is the author or coauthor of numerous publications, including *See Poverty, Be the Difference: Discovering the Missing Pieces for Working with People in Poverty* (2007) and *Partnerships by Design: Cultivating Effective and Meaningful School-Family Partnerships* (2002).

Lena Ko is an advisor in early childhood education and school–family–community partnerships at Education Northwest. She has more than 20 years of experience training and coaching educators, coordinating professional development and technical assistance in model early childhood teaching centers, and consulting and doing technical writing for various education agencies, interagency groups, and early childhood programs. She has worked to help develop a statewide family resource center project, and has worked on several federal grant initiatives to help communities improve outcomes for children and families. Her primary areas of research include early childhood curriculum and professional development and training, kindergarten readiness, culturally responsive teaching and learning, and school–family–community partnerships in education. Ko received her master of science degree in human development and family studies with an emphasis on early childhood development from Colorado State University. She has experience working with culturally diverse populations in unique settings, including children with special needs at a therapeutic preschool. As a bicultural learner and trained education equity advocate, she is passionate about the role of the school meeting the diverse needs of all learners. She has coauthored an Education Northwest publication on a school process called the School-PASS (School Practices for All Students' Success) that focuses on assessing and preparing for the needs of new and diverse students.

Amy Stuczynski is currently working with the Human Services Research Institute evaluating the use of family team meetings by public child welfare agencies. She began her career as a social worker for a community-based service organization for African American youth and families in Madison, Wisconsin. She later joined Education Northwest where she wrote about language, literacy, and culture for six years. Amy holds a master's in social work from the University of Wisconsin-Madison.

1

Culturally Responsive Standards-Based Teaching

All the evidence shows that unless we change the culture of schools, nothing changes. That is—no matter what curriculum we introduce, or how many structural changes we make to the organization—if we do not transform the beliefs, the norms, and the relationships . . . nothing will change.

—Pedro A. Noguera (2003)

The nature and quality of public education in the United States is currently one of the hottest topics in our nation. It sparks scorching headlines in local and national media, such as "Calling Out America's Worst Schools," "NAACP Protests Strategies to Close Achievement Gap," and "In Search of Educational Leaders." It has the power to ignite so much blame, shame, anger, and disagreement within and between its diverse constituents that on some days the heat generated seems literal. The issue—one that entwines the American dream with social challenges such as privilege, generational poverty, immigration, economic inequality, and 200 years of racial and social inequities—is so confounding and compelling it has been on our nation's front burner for more than two decades.

During the past 20 years, U.S. school districts of all sizes have experienced unprecedented increases in cultural and linguistic diversity. Walk into almost any school or classroom in the nation and you will experience a cross cultural zone where ethnicity, class, gender, language, national origin, and other cultural factors are vibrant and alive in the sights, sounds, smells, and textures of the building and its occupants. Even if students, families, and the school staff look similar to each other on the outside, districts are experiencing newly expanded perceptions of diversity. "Invisible" diversity—such as socioeconomic status, family structure, citizenship, sexual orientation, spirituality, learning styles, and family histories—bubbles just beneath the surface. Take, for example, the Community Unit School District 200, just west of Chicago. The majority of its 14,000 students are Caucasian, yet students served by the district's ELL program speak more than 35 languages.

The increased diversity found in U.S. public schools mirrors the changing "face" of America, and can be experienced as a benefit or as a challenge. Unfortunately, most districts—with limited financial, human, and other resources—struggle to meet the needs of their increasingly diverse learners. As a result, schools across our nation are faced with a persistent "academic achievement gap."

> The U.S. Department of Education defines "achievement gap" as the difference in academic performance between different ethnic groups. Glen Singleton, coauthor of *Courageous Conversations About Race: A Field Guide for Achieving Equity in Schools,* (2006) intentionally defines the gap as "a racial achievement gap that exists between Black and Brown students and their White and Asian counterparts." Other experts may factor in gender or socioeconomic discrepancies, or focus on the difference between what a student is capable of achieving and his or her actual level of performance.

The causes for the achievement gap are profoundly complex (Chubb & Loveless, 2002; Haycock, 2001; Johnston & Viadero, 2000; McCombs, 2000). Poverty, mobility, language, homelessness, institutional racism, unequal distribution of resources, low expectations for students from culturally diverse backgrounds, teacher quality, and cultural incongruence between home and school are all contributing factors.

The complex root causes that underlie our nation's achievement gap require multifaceted strategies and diverse key stakeholders working effectively together. Fortunately, culturally responsive standards-based (CRSB) teaching utilizes many of the strategies that researchers say are necessary to teach students with diverse needs who are from diverse backgrounds.

Many community organizations, districts, and state departments of education across the United States—including Boston Public Schools, Partners in School Innovation (San Francisco), the North Carolina Department of Public Instruction, the National Center for Culturally Responsive Educational Systems (Phoenix), and the Center for Culturally Responsive Urban Education (Denver)—are adopting CRSB teaching as a research-based strategy to raise the academic achievement of culturally and linguistically diverse students.

> Check out how policy makers and educators across the country are implementing CRSB teaching as a powerful strategy to "close the achievement gap"!
>
> - Boston Public Schools http://www.bostonpublicschools.org/files/GapPolicy.pdf
> - Partners in School Innovation http://www.partnersinschools.org/program/theory.html
> - North Carolina Department of Public Instruction http://www.ncpublicschools.org/schooltransformation/community
> - The National Center for Culturally Responsive Educational Systems http://nccrest.org/
> - Center for Culturally Responsive Urban Education http://cruecenter.org

LEARNING FROM STUDENTS' LIVES

The way to improve education and society is to make schooling more central to family and community, while making family and community more central to schooling.

—Urie Bronfenbrenner (1985)

Fourth-grader Danika reflects on a poem she has just written:

I am from Lea-bo and Mercachoo,

Fur balls with big ears and paws.

Noses always moving,

In tag they're always zooming

There's never a dull moment.

. . . I am from Harry Potter and Agatha Christie,

Battered broomsticks and little gray cells.

I am from music,

My fingers dancing on black and white keys,

Bach, Beethoven, and Mozart.

. . . I am from the forest.

Rain beading evergreen branches with dew like jewels,

Great trees shielding me from the rain.

The everlasting peace that can cure any sickness.

. . . I am from sushi, charsiubau and Jolly Ranchers

Camping at Wallowa Lake among the deer,

Playing Honeydukes candy store with Misha, Trillium, Alexis, and Maya

And speaking Mohawk, "Sekon!," with my dad.

. . . I am from life.

A swirl of metaphor, simile, and meaningful descriptions of personal experiences and family personalities passes through her mind, inviting a deeper understanding of her world. Danika will recite her poem to her class, and her classmates will think about and write down suggestions for titles for her poem—part of the "Where I'm From" process. The suggestions may reflect a particular line or idea from the poem that caught their attention. They'll soon have a chance to share their own "Where I'm From" poems and family stories that ultimately will be bound in a beautiful hand-crafted book. In the writing and editing process, the students develop a sense of pride about their lives and learn more about their personal histories and cultures, as well as those of their classmates—many of whose families are recent immigrants from all over the world. (More information on the Family Story Book project at Atkinson Elementary is found in Snapshot 3.1 on page 52 "Family Story Book.")

In a different school, a high school English teacher works with students on a project that inspires them to do their best work: a document that adheres to demanding publishing parameters for an authentic audience. Students research, write, publish, and sell a book about a much-loved tradition in their rural community—the Thanksgiving Day football games between two rival high schools. They interview family and community members who graduated from both high schools between 1906 and 1973 about their days as a player, cheerleader, or fan. In all, the students collect 120 oral histories and supplement them with articles and photographs from old yearbooks and newspapers. Together, students create a valuable historical document and build community support and enthusiasm for the school. (For more information, see Snapshot 5.7 "Project of the Year Books.")

These are just two examples of some of the powerful ways teachers are integrating culturally responsive teaching with a standards-based curriculum to engage all students in learning. This type of teaching looks slightly different in every setting because it is dependent on the children and youth you are working with— their lives, families, and communities. Because of this personalization, it can benefit all students.

CULTURALLY RESPONSIVE AND STANDARDS-BASED TOGETHER

CRSB teaching is the integration of two important aspects of education: culturally responsive teaching and standards-based teaching. Much has been written about culturally responsive teaching and standards-based teaching separately, but it is the integration of the approaches that is critical to the goal of high achievement for all students. Culturally responsive teaching addresses the needs of students by improving motivation and engagement (Ginsberg & Wlodkowski, 2000), and standards-based teaching provides all students with the opportunity for rigorous, high-level learning. CRSB teaching means doing both, together.

CRSB teaching values students' culture, draws on that culture as a strength in their education, and challenges them with a rigorous, relevant curriculum. CRSB succeeds in part because it fosters deeper, stronger school–family–community partnerships; these partnerships have been shown to improve academic achievement (Boethel et al., 2003; Henderson & Mapp, 2002). CRSB teaching strategies foster such partnerships because they bring family and community culture into the classroom and school in meaningful ways. When curriculum content and methods incorporate local norms, behaviors, objects, and practices, students and families feel a direct link between home life and school life. When teachers value and use the strengths of local cultures, they send a positive message that can improve the school's relationships with family and community members.

Snapshot 1.1 "Project FRESA" more fully illustrates how two teachers collaborated on a project that embodies all the important aspects of CRSB teaching. Project FRESA (*fresa* is Spanish for strawberry) focused on the local strawberry crop and its impact on students, who are primarily the children of immigrant farm workers. The project helped students meet state standards in language arts, math, geography, and technology, while at the same time developing their critical thinking skills and combating racism.

Snapshot 1.1

PROJECT FRESA

Mar Vista Elementary School, Oxnard, California

Grade levels: 3 and 5

Subject areas: Language arts, math, geography, and technology

Highlights: Project FRESA is an interdisciplinary, multimedia project created to help students meet standards by building on the relationship between their own lives and the strawberry fields that surround and sustain their local community.

"We believe that education can be used to transform lives in a positive way," says Michelle Singer, a bilingual teacher at Mar Vista Elementary. That's just what happened when Singer began using what was important in the lives of her students as a basis for her curriculum.

In one assignment, Singer asked students to find out how long their family members had worked in the neighboring strawberry fields, and then plot the data.

"I showed one of my students how to find the graphs and charts on the Internet that we had done in our math class. After school, the girl went home, got her grandfather, and took him to the public library to show him the chart . . . and his place on it. (He is the person listed on Figure 1.1 with the most years—35, to be exact!) In all his years, this man had never set foot in a library before. This is one of the things that we hoped would come from this project," says Singer. "That people would do things they normally would not do . . . that they would value things they did not value before!"

Incredible transformations like this began in 1999 when Singer and fellow Mar Vista teacher Amada Irma H. Perez were selected to be part of the California Association for Bilingual Education's Telementor Project. The training was designed to help teachers develop a technology project that included a standards-based curriculum, antiracist/antibiased education, community learning, and second language acquisition.

Mar Vista Elementary is set in a rural area of Ventura County, just north of the Santa Monica/Malibu area. Of its 699 students, 77 percent receive free or reduced-price lunches, and 75 percent are limited English proficient.

Perez and Singer designed Project FRESA around what was common in the lives of their students. The students are primarily immigrants from Mexico, and most speak both English and Spanish. The teachers knew that most of the students and their families had a personal connection to the strawberry fields that surround the school. In fact, all the students in Perez's third-grade class and all but two of the students in Singer's fifth-grade class had a friend or family member who was associated in some way with the fields.

To examine issues related to the strawberries and the implications of fieldwork for their families, environment, and local economy, students interviewed family members, conducted research, and collected historical and geographical information. They used technology to share their findings with their classmates, families, and community in stories, poems, graphs, charts, and drawings (such as Figure 1.2).

Long before Perez and Singer began Project FRESA, they practiced many of the strategies needed to make this project successful.

(Continued)

(Continued)

Figure 1.1 Graph Depicting the Number of Years Family Members Worked in the the Fields

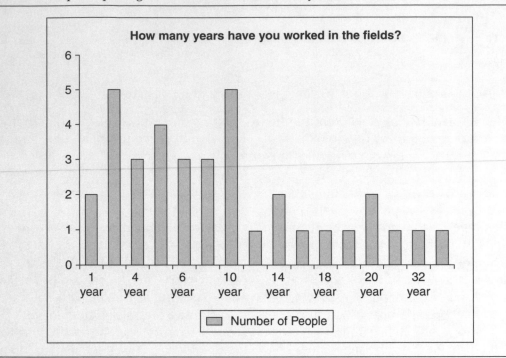

Source: Information gathered by students and compiled by teachers Michelle Singer and Amada Perez.

Both teachers demonstrated respect and high expectations for their students, and reported that the students are all hardworking, intelligent, and dedicated. These teachers are driven by the belief that their teaching should honor students' lives; they believe that their role is not to be the one knowledgeable person who imparts wisdom to their students. Rather, they know that a classroom is filled with teachers and learners. They enjoy being the facilitator sometimes, but also appreciate the opportunity to learn from their students.

The administrative staff is completely supportive of Singer and Perez's work. This enables the teachers to incorporate numerous philosophies that are central to the project—such as critical pedagogy and antiracist education—into their teaching. From the beginning, their superintendent and special projects director were aware of the project and how it was linked to standards. The administrators were eager to see how Perez and Singer connected it to the lives of the students, and encouraged and celebrated their work. Also, the district,

in Singer's words, "encourages creative risk taking."

One of the teachers' concerns was finding time for the students to do the necessary project work while still covering all the standards that must be met. They rethought the way time was being used. For example, students had a regularly scheduled "buddy time" meant for peer mentoring. The teachers decided to use this time for cross-age collaborative work. Determined to do whatever was needed for the project to work, the teachers were available to the students before and after school, during lunch breaks, and at recess so students would have time to reflect, write, and respond.

Project FRESA also has been used as a curriculum example in a beginning education course at a university, showing teachers how to integrate the Internet into the classroom. Many teachers write to Perez and Singer to ask their advice about projects. Often the two teachers let their students answer the questions and guide others through the Project FRESA website.

The kids also give other teachers suggestions on how best to do this work with their students. For instance, they advised one kindergarten teacher to "be patient with the younger students. It may take a little more time for some of these younger students to grasp it."

Project FRESA is an ongoing project, but each year students are engaged in different ways and the project has a different focus. One year the focus was on dialogue with other teachers and classrooms in the United States and abroad via e-mail. For example, the students shared information with a class in a part of India that grows strawberries; it was an exchange that opened up the world. Mar Vista students discovered many differences between their lives and those of their peers:

- Students often work in the fields in India, while parents and other family members are the main workers in California.
- The strawberry fields in India are much smaller than the fields in California.
- The workers dress much nicer in India than they do in California.

The teachers believe that their classroom structure, combined with an engaging curriculum, leads to a higher percentage of students on task, motivated to be in class, and engaged in their own learning.

Figure 1.2   Student Drawing of a Strawberry Stand

Standards-Based Teaching

The primary drive behind the standards movement is to provide all students with the opportunity for rigorous, high-level learning. Federal requirements demand—and all educators expect—that students will achieve to their full potential. CRSB teaching is always grounded in state and local standards and the student achievement goals of the school and students. When discussing standards, we mean academic standards that are explicit learning expectations, usually written by the district or state. These are referred to as content standards, performance standards, or benchmarks.

Project FRESA is based on state standards such as California's fifth-grade history standard on immigration. The students trace their own family's story—discussing why their family came to this country and what they found here. Besides meeting the standards, the students learn more about themselves and their families. They frequently find that their families came to the United States for a better life for their children.

TAKING ADVANTAGE OF TEACHABLE MOMENTS TO MEET STANDARDS

How well do you know the academic standards that your students need to meet this year? From the set of standards-based learning goals that are planned for the entire year, do you have flexibility about when certain learning goals are to be met? Sometimes, CRSB teaching means moving activities around to take advantage of teachable moments. Teachable moments happen all the time when incidents or events arise that capture students' interest. Teachers need to make decisions about when to use these moments to teach something different from what they had originally planned.

At the beginning of the school year, the Project FRESA teachers had an opportunity to address the standard for writing a persuasive letter. After a guest speaker talked about the negative effects of the pesticides used in the fields where students' parents worked, the students wanted to do something about the issue. The teachers rescheduled the curriculum and activities around writing persuasive letters, which had been planned for the end of the year. Students wrote letters to the governor asking him to look into the use of pesticides, as well as the harmful effects of pesticides, and to consider creating standards for their safe use. The timing of this activity made more sense at the beginning of the year because it was more relevant to the students at that point and was connected to something real in their lives.

Further information on using standards for curriculum planning can be found in Chapter 5; also see the standards section in the resources list on page 216.

Culturally Responsive Teaching

Culturally responsive teaching infuses family customs—as well as community culture and expectations—throughout the teaching and learning environment. By providing instruction in a context meaningful to students and in a way that values their culture, knowledge, and experiences, culturally responsive teaching fosters student motivation and engagement. In Project FRESA, students study statistics and probability, but instead of using generic charts and graphs, they create timelines and graphs with data they collect from their family members. This is an example of standards-based mathematics that is hands-on, includes the students and their families, and connects them to meaningful learning.

Culturally responsive teaching is built on a foundation of knowledge and understanding of your own and your students' family and community culture, which is critical to the process of teaching and learning. Learning about all the cultures represented in the classroom can seem like a daunting challenge, but the success of many teachers shows that it is worth the effort. Becoming culturally responsive is an ongoing process that evolves as we learn more about ourselves, our world, and other cultures. To become culturally responsive, look at your own culture—especially if it is part of our country's dominant culture—from the worldview of others; have an open mind to what you don't understand; and be ready to learn new ways of looking at and doing things. (For tools designed to help you become more culturally responsive, see Chapter 3.)

What Is culture?

Culture can be defined as a way of life, especially as it relates to the socially transmitted habits, customs, traditions, and beliefs that characterize a particular group of people at a particular time. It includes the behaviors, actions, practices, attitudes, norms, values, communication styles, language, etiquette, spirituality, concepts of health and healing, beliefs, and institutions of a racial, ethnic, religious, or social group. Culture is the lens through which we look at the world. It is the context within which we operate and make sense of the world. Culture influences how we process learning, solve problems, and teach.

Everyone has a culture, though most of the time our own culture is invisible to us. It is frequently thought of as the way things are and becomes the norm by which we measure all others' behavior. In *The Diversity Kit: An Introductory Resource for Social Change in Education* (Ahearn et al., 2002), the authors write, "Nonetheless, one's beliefs and actions are not any more natural or biologically predetermined than any other group's set of beliefs and actions" (p. 5).

Cultural groups are not homogeneous. They represent different geographical locations, histories, and experiences. Minority cultures express varying degrees of assimilation to the dominant Anglo culture in this country. Cultures change over time, and vary across class and gender, even between families and individuals. The music we enjoy, how we spend our leisure time, what we talk about, and what we eat are examples of individual differences within the same cultural group. "Professionals who think of cultures as they were generations ago, who romanticize cultures, or who fail to see cultures as complex, dynamic, changing systems will quickly fall short of the goal of effective services," writes Cross (1995–1996).

This guide looks at culture very broadly. It includes all the aspects of students' lives that could engage and motivate them to learn and to do their best work; these aspects include—but are not limited to—family culture, community culture, youth culture, and pop culture. Teachers can start by thinking and learning about their students'

- differences in ways of thinking, feeling, and expressing pleasure, distress, and concern;
- similarities in the cares and concerns of an individual or her family;
- country of origin, history, practices, health, beliefs, and language; and
- frames of reference—religion, valid ways to express oneself, and acceptable and unacceptable behaviors.

KEY POINTS TO REMEMBER ABOUT CULTURE . . .

- Culture is complex, dynamic, and ever changing.
- All humans are cultural beings. We all have several primary cultural identities that "shape" us. Sometimes our culture is "invisible," even to ourselves, and can be difficult to describe. Important cultural identities in U.S. culture are race (including skin color), class, gender, language, religion, and national origin.
- Culture, which includes values, beliefs, histories, stories, and traditions, shapes the lens with which we view the world, and moves and motivates us.
- When diverse cultures come together it creates a "cross-cultural zone" that is filled with a wide range of emotions, perspectives, values, beliefs, and history, both personal and community.
- Key elements and emotions in the cross-cultural zone include identity development, acculturation, acculturation stress, cultural privilege, historical mistrust, historical guilt, fear, anger, learning, and curiosity.
- Our ability to negotiate the dynamic in the cross-cultural zone can make or break relationships, and hinder or help learning.
- Since our culture moves and motivates us ("makes us tick"), it is central to our understanding of each other and to the learning process.

Building bridges between teachers and students begins with simple questions: Who are these kids? What's important to them? It takes time to learn the answers to those questions and to know how they understand themselves, each other, and you—their teacher. It takes practice to ask yourself and your students questions, and it requires a safe and secure space to explore those questions and to share the answers.

Why focus on culture?

The dominant U.S. culture is reflected in all aspects of most schools, from the curriculum to the way teachers interact with students to how teachers communicate with families. Many of the lowest-performing schools have a student-family population that differs culturally from that of the school, whether racially, ethnically, socioeconomically, or in some other way. For example, many classrooms emphasize individual responsibility and achievement, competition, and teacher-led learning. Some cultural groups, such as some Asian groups, Native Americans, and Alaska Natives, may be unaccustomed to this style of learning, and instead place a higher value on group work that fosters shared responsibility. Such differences may thwart learning in the typical American classroom.

Researchers have found that disparities between the cultural values and patterns of communication of the home and of the school may undermine children's enthusiasm for learning and their belief in their own capacity to learn by the time they have reached the age of eight (Cummins, 1986; Entwistle, 1995). Some students believe that schooling can be detrimental to their own language, culture, and identity (Ogbu, 1993). This clash between a student's home culture and school culture—which is often an unrecognized, hidden clash—can have a huge impact on that student's ability to learn and achieve.

When youth, family, and community culture are included in the classroom, students feel a sense of belonging, see purpose in learning, and are motivated to do well. School relationships with families and communities improve. As Cleary and Peacock (1998) report, "Schools that acknowledge, accept, and teach a child's cultural heritage have significantly better success in educating students" (p. 108).

ESSENTIAL ELEMENTS

CRSB teaching promotes six essential elements that are embedded in and woven throughout the teaching:

- It is always *student centered*.
- It has the power to *transform*.
- It is *connected and integrated*.
- It fosters *critical thinking*.
- It incorporates *assessment and reflection*.
- It builds *relationships and community*.

These elements are just good teaching practices that can be used by all teachers. Throughout this guide, we focus on these elements; they are described briefly here and in more depth in later chapters.

Becoming Student Centered

CRSB teaching is always student centered. Content is taught through individualized learning that is connected to goals and standards. CRSB practices promote authentic learning that is relevant and meaningful to students, and connect learning in the school to what the students know and are learning outside the classroom. Teaching becomes more student centered when

- students' lives, interests, families, communities, and cultures are the basis for what is taught;
- students are involved in planning what they will learn and how they will learn it;
- the social, emotional, and cognitive strengths and needs of the students are recognized by their teachers and reflected in individualized learning plans; and
- instruction is built on the students' personal and cultural strengths.

The teachers who created Project FRESA use a student-centered philosophy to inform every aspect of their teaching. They take the time at the beginning of the year to get to know the students and their families. The teachers then create activities that examine issues that are important to their students and that relate classroom lessons to their daily lives. Throughout the year, students are regularly encouraged to be active participants in their own learning and to make many decisions in the classroom. For instance, the class brainstorms rules at the beginning of the school year that serve as general rules for all students to follow. If a student finds it hard to stick to a rule, the class makes specific suggestions about the rule.

Other ways teachers can make lessons more student centered are to

- study family or community history, using it to study other historical ideas;
- relate lessons to students' personal, family, or community cultures;
- speak (and value) students' home languages;
- allow students to suggest topics that grow out of their interest in the community, as well as personal and group interests;
- invite students to write about their own lives, and about things and people who are important to them; and
- use literature written by people whose culture reflects that of the students.

See Chapter 3 for more information on student-centered teaching.

Promoting Transformational Teaching

CRSB practices can transform teaching and learning by valuing and building on the knowledge all students bring to class. Transformation happens in the following ways:

- The role of the teacher is transformed from instructor to facilitator by allowing students' experiences, perspectives, and interests to help shape the curriculum.
- The curriculum is transformed as the subject matter is examined from many different perspectives, in ways that promote growth and discovery.
- The participants' perspectives are transformed as they begin to value and respect things and people that they may not have valued or respected before.

For example, one goal of Project FRESA is to give students the opportunity and language skills to voice their daily reality. Discussing their collective experiences with farm labor gives students a new sense of value. Because of their dialogue and reflection, students often take social action that leads to positive changes throughout the school and community. Transformation happens as the students and school staff members alter their value systems and their behavior.

Other ways teachers can make their teaching transformational include

- helping students to recognize the strengths and significance of their culture, family, and community, and to see their own lives and perspectives as subjects worthy of study;
- studying curricular concepts from the point of view of students' cultures, comparing them with the way concepts are presented in textbooks;
- helping students to critically examine and challenge the knowledge and perspectives presented in the curriculum and textbooks, and to address inaccuracies, omissions, or distortions by bringing in multiple perspectives;
- encouraging students to take social action by doing things like contacting government representatives or educating the community on issues; and
- providing opportunities for community members to see students in a new and positive light—through meetings, presentations, and exhibitions—thus increasing their support for the school.

See Chapter 3 for more information on transformational teaching and learning.

Connecting and Integrating CRSB Practices

CRSB teaching should not be an "add-on" or separate activity, but rather an approach that is connected and integrated with what is happening in the rest of the classroom and school community. CRSB teaching is connected and integrated when

- learning is contextualized and builds on what students already know, allowing them to comprehend new information more easily;
- interdisciplinary work is used to illustrate the relationships among different subjects and their applicability; and
- the work encourages students and teachers to connect with other students, teachers, administrators, families, and community members.

For example, the interdisciplinary nature of Project FRESA means that lessons cross boundaries of language arts, math, geography, and technology. Consequently, students are better able to see how they can use different disciplines to help solve problems in the real world. The project's design also ensures that the teachers work collaboratively and that the students in the two classes work as "buddies."

Other ways teachers can connect and integrate the curriculum include

- discussing how subject matter is related to students' lives and why the information is important to them;
- connecting projects with other activities that the school promotes;
- linking study to local issues and events by allowing students to investigate, measure, calculate, and write about those issues;
- incorporating a variety of standards to be learned within each task, from basic skills to cultural awareness and interpersonal skills; and
- sharing information with other students, teachers, classrooms, and parents.

See Chapters 5 and 7 for more discussion and examples of connected and integrated teaching and learning.

Fostering Critical Thinking

As you make the curriculum more relevant to students and draw in their families and community, you bring depth and breadth to learning. You also help students develop one of the most important abilities of a well-educated person: to think critically. Critical thinking is a fundamental part of learning, involving high-level thinking processes such as decision making, logical inquiry, reasoning, artistic creation, and problem solving. CRSB teaching creates opportunities for students to build critical thinking skills by using these skills in real-life situations and understanding how to apply them in other contexts.

Practices that promote critical thinking include these:

- Teachers pose questions that probe student thinking.
- Students monitor their own level of understanding and become self-directed, self-disciplined, and self-corrective.
- Teachers and students approach learning in different ways.

Project FRESA gives students the opportunity to ask questions, voice opinions, analyze information, and communicate their understanding of their reality in a meaningful way. Students learn and use critical thinking skills to explore their role in society and to examine complex ideas about social and educational justice. These skills develop in concert with more-complex ways of writing and with higher-order reasoning. After Mar Vista Elementary students wrote a persuasive letter to the governor about the side effects of pesticide use, they used the governor's reply to further hone their thinking skills. They analyzed the governor's response, talked about his point of view and purpose, and discussed the politics they found in his letter.

Other ways to promote critical thinking skills are

- involving students in the planning of a project;
- asking students to reflect and report on why they chose their topic of interest, how they researched it, how they completed their task, what they found out about the topic, and how they liked studying the topic;
- persuading students to formulate, share, and debate their opinions;
- encouraging students to examine the perspective put forth in the text, question it, and discover any alternative perspectives (which also promotes transformational learning); and
- teaching students to recognize stereotypes.

See Chapter 5 for more information on fostering critical thinking.

Incorporating Assessment and Reflection

Assessment and reflection, for both the teacher and the student, should be ongoing and infused throughout the curriculum. In CRSB teaching, a variety of authentic assessment measures are used to monitor progress throughout the year and to make midcourse adjustments. In addition, students and teachers develop and pose rich questions to reflect critically on lessons learned. As students and teachers practice assessment and reflection, both groups better understand their own teaching and learning styles and make academic, personal, and cultural connections. They become more skillful in evaluating and improving their own performance and thinking.

Examples of how teachers can encourage assessment and reflection include

- having students define an identified need, then create a plan to address the problem;
- assessing students through multiple, authentic means—reports, portfolios, and presentations—and by a variety of people (teachers, students, and community members);
- helping students to create the rubric by which they will be assessed;
- encouraging students to use journals to set personal goals and reflect on what they have learned; and
- having students reflect on their progress and make adjustments as needed.

See Chapter 6 for more information on assessment and reflection.

Building Relationships and Community

CRSB teaching builds and supports relationships and community. When you recognize family and community members' knowledge and experiences as strengths that are valuable to a child's education, you are valued and respected in turn by students, staff, families, and community members. CRSB teaching fosters partnerships because family and community members are reminded that they have something to offer the school and that they can have a significant positive impact on the quality of their children's education. CRSB teaching builds relationships between individuals and among groups as people learn what others have to contribute. They learn to rely on each other, work together on concrete tasks that take advantage of their collective and individual assets, and create promising futures for youth and the community.

Teachers can build relationships by

- getting to know their students, students' families, and the community they serve—using what they learn to help inform what is taught;
- communicating with parents about what they are teaching and how parents can be involved;
- helping students to meet and get to know other people in their community; and
- using multiple avenues to include families in what is done in the school.

As with all relationship building, it can take time to gain families' trust and participation, particularly when it is necessary to overcome decades of exclusion or poor school–community relations. When Project FRESA students first approached their family members, some encountered resistance. Families wanted to know why the students were asking questions and how the answers would be used. Once the parents understood the purpose of the project, they became very supportive and actively participated. New connections were established and bonds were strengthened among the students, parents, and community. Now that they see their work being viewed with a new understanding and respect, parents and other family members feel valued and seem more comfortable coming into the school and talking with the staff.

Other ways teachers can build relationships with families and community members include

- making an event that is extremely important (and exciting) to the community a subject of study;
- bringing outside resources into the school;
- inviting family and community members to speak to the class or share a special skill;
- involving students in making presentations to the community;
- talking to community leaders about what they consider appropriate and critical subjects to be taught; and
- learning about the students' cultures by spending time with people of that culture, reading books, attending community events, and learning the language.

See Chapter 3 for more information on building relationships.

Snapshot 1.1 "Project FRESA" tells the story of how two teachers worked together to bring CRSB teaching and the essential elements to two classrooms in their elementary school. Snapshot 1.2 "Listening to Community Voices" provides a picture of how one district worked on a comprehensive initiative over a long period of time in order to bring all the essential elements of CRSB teaching to their entire district.

Snapshot 1.2

LISTENING TO COMMUNITY VOICES: CREATING SCHOOL SUCCESS

Chugach School District, Prince William Sound, Alaska

Grade level: Pre-K–12

Subject areas: All

Highlights: This long-term, comprehensive, and very successful districtwide school reform effort, which was developed with the community, paid great attention to being culturally responsive and setting high standards.

How can a school district in crisis become one where student performance exceeds state and national norms? How can a school that once caused community discontent become a source of pride? How can an unstable district become a stable district that attracts and keeps quality staff?

For one school district, the journey began with a process of reinvention and two years of extensive preparatory work before they could implement a system of change that would provide performance-based, individualized education for all students. With the help of the Northwest Regional Educational Laboratory (NWREL, now Education Northwest), the Chugach School District (CSD) took on the Alaska Onward to Excellence (AOTE) training as a way to provide their team members with the skills to build trust with community members, empower community engagement, and be supportive of the change. Bob Crumley, Chugach's superintendent, says, "Without the NWREL and their AOTE process, Chugach's education system as we know it today would not have happened."

In 1994, the CSD decided it was not adequately serving students nor preparing them for the future:

- Scores on the California Achievement Test were the lowest in the state.
- Only 10–20 percent of students were reading at grade level, with the average student reading three grades below grade level.

- Most students had difficulties experiencing any success after high school: in 25 years, only a few high school graduates completed a postsecondary education.

In order for students to succeed, district officials decided they had to tear down everything and rebuild a new school system that would improve the way they served students and their families.

District Realities

There are not many districts like the CSD. Although it has only 249 students, the students are geographically scattered over 22,000 square miles of south-central Alaska. Most students live in isolated and remote areas only reachable by plane. Half of the students in the district are Alaska Native from traditional Native communities.

There are only 40 faculty and staff members to serve the district's widely dispersed student population. Eighteen are based at three community schools, one manages a school-to-work program in Anchorage, and the rest are either visiting teachers or specialists who work with home-schooled children or who supply education support services. There is an average 14:1 student:teacher ratio—purposefully kept small because the district believes that is best for students.

Because the district's educational programs range from preschool to postsecondary education—serving students up to age 21—all teachers work with students of various ages, and all teach multiple subjects. Education occurs 24 hours a day, seven days a week, with instruction taking place in the community, in the home, at school, and in many workplaces.

Building Relationships and Community

From the outset, the district's overhaul was undertaken collaboratively. Parents and family members, students (both past and present), staff members, community leaders, and business partners all joined in the effort. The CSD believed that the first step in the process was to find out what the community really wanted its schools to do, so they started by listening to and valuing everyone's voice. Their collaboration yielded a common mission and core vision that included their shared values and beliefs:

> The students of CSD will grow to become successful healthy adults with all the necessary tools to make a good future for their lives.

In order to accomplish this vision, the stakeholders created the following list of goals based on their common values and beliefs:

1. Students will demonstrate effective written and verbal communication to a variety of audiences.

2. Students will effectively use critical thinking and problem-solving skills in making daily decisions.

3. Students will demonstrate a positive attitude that includes self-confidence, leadership, and a sense of humor (character development).

4. Students will learn to set priorities and achieve personal, family, and community goals.

5. Students will possess the skills and attitudes to adapt to an ever-changing environment.

6. Students will understand, preserve, and appreciate their own language and culture and the heritage of others.

7. Students and community will incorporate modern technology to enhance learning.

8. Students will develop the civic responsibilities and the social and academic skills necessary to make a successful transition to life after school, whether in a rural or in an urban environment.

9. Students will possess the work ethic that enables them to be self-directed, determined, dependable, and productive.

Throughout the process, everyone is empowered to be a leader. Students are encouraged to take responsibility for their own learning. Although students, faculty, and resources are widely dispersed, CSD achieves a unity of focus by holding quarterly stakeholder meetings and annually gathering community input on CSD performance and goals.

Basing Curriculum on Standards

From all the conversations at their meetings, the stakeholders realized they could not reach their vision within the regular school curriculum. Instead, a standards-based system of "whole-child education" that emphasizes real-life learning situations was pioneered. With the aim of helping students reach their full potential as individuals and as members of their communities, a continuum of performance-based standards was created for 10 content areas:

1. Mathematics

2. Reading

3. Writing

4. Social sciences

(Continued)

(Continued)

5. Science

6. Technology development

7. Personal/social/health development

8. Career development

9. Cultural awareness and expression

10. Service learning

Many of the basic academic skills are similar to the regular curriculum and statewide standards. Because the CSD listened to what its community members really wanted, though, it developed a system that goes above and beyond the state standards and focuses on "education for the whole child." The district identified standards such as personal/social/health development as among the most important, because if the students don't show improvement there, they won't be successful academically.

Creating a Student-Centered/ Whole-Child Educational Approach

The CSD "threw away seat time" as the most appropriate means to educate the child, and implemented and refined an innovative standards-based system with an individualized, student-centered approach that has the flexibility to accommodate the personal learning styles and rates of all students. Within this system, students work at their own developmentally appropriate pace.

Through multiple means, each student is assessed to determine his current functioning, instructional learning styles or patterns, and strengths and weaknesses. For each child, a student learning profile (SLP) is developed from information gained and updated every three years. Teachers use the SLPs to determine such things as whether a student learns best through visual instruction, hearing, or physical aids that can be manipulated. SLPs are key inputs into

learning plans tailored to the strengths, weaknesses, developmental stage, and circumstances of each child. As teachers prepare these individualized instructional strategies, students and parents participate in setting goals for demonstrating mastery of the 10 content areas at the student's level.

Building in Assessment and Reflection

From the beginning, all the stakeholders—especially business partners—emphasized that accountability should be built into the educational system and embedded in the district's performance goals. Consequently, students must be able to demonstrate measurable proficiency in the 10 content areas.

CSD worked with the Alaska Department of Education and Early Development to secure a waiver so they did not have to use the traditional Carnegie units (or credit-based graduation requirements) and grade levels. CSD students still must meet the state benchmark testing requirements and pass the High School Graduation Qualifying Exam. Demonstrable proficiency with specific minimum graduation levels of mastery in each of the 10 content areas—and not the number of credit hours earned—was set as the essential condition for graduation. Students are evaluated through a variety of formal and informal assessments. These assessments are designed to determine whether students can apply skills and knowledge in real situations.

Keeping students and parents apprised of the educational process was very important to all stakeholders, so CSD created an assessment system that both parents and students can understand. Expectations are clear, and progress toward meeting them is documented in a running record of assessments completed in all content areas. Teachers, students, and parents regularly consult these student assessment binders. Upon graduation, students are given their assessment binders, which serve as proof of skill mastery.

Student assessment binders are but one of several CSD tools designed to accommodate individual differences in learning and to foster school system accountability. The Aligned Information Management System (AIMS) also helps students and parents to be aware of their progress. This online database has all the current information about the students. Parents and students can access secured information from home at their convenience. Through consistent communication among staff, students, and parents, all parties are involved in helping to set educational goals, implementing plans at home and in the community, and taking part in ongoing assessment. Because of this consistency, students, parents, and community members have a thorough understanding of the evaluation system.

Making It Connected and Integrated

Integrated learning and multisensory approaches to teaching are key elements of CSD's "whole-child" education. The aim of these approaches is to help students make real-life connections and recognize the value and usefulness of what they are learning. CSD uses a variety of districtwide tools for developing integrated-learning teaching units. Each year, the district staff meets to develop thematic units for the upcoming school year. Resulting lesson plans and student projects transcend content areas, so subjects are not taught in isolation.

CSD's Anchorage House epitomizes this approach to contextual learning. Students begin participation in this residential program starting at the junior high level; the program provides them with four distinct opportunities throughout their secondary education to apply their learning skills in an urban community. The students travel from their often-isolated communities to Anchorage, where they live in a house purchased by the district. With plenty of support and supervision, the students learn everything from how to use

mass transit and ATMs to what careers and educational opportunities are available in the city. During the last two phases, which may span from several weeks to 10 months, students participate in internships or other workplace programs as they take responsibility for managing their daily activities.

Transforming Lives

All the hard work continues to pay off for the students and staff of CSD. Transformations can be seen in all stakeholders. Students are proud of their achievements, and so are their families. Family and community members feel more connected to the schools, and teachers have pulled together like never before. Proof of these transformations can be seen in test scores and graduation rates:

- Dramatic increases in results on the California Achievement Test from 1995 to 1999.
  - Reading scores increased from the 28th to the 71st percentile.
  - Math scores increased from the 54th to the 78th percentile.
  - Language arts scores increased from the 26th to the 72nd percentile.

- Scores surpassed the state average in the four subject areas tested in Alaska's High School Graduation Qualifying Examination.
- Thirty-one of seventy-five graduates have gone on to postsecondary educational institutions from 1995 to the present.

What this transformation has meant for staff has also been tremendous. Staff turnover averaged 55 percent from 1975 to 1994, but since the implementation of the new system, faculty turnover rate has fallen to an average of 7.5 percent. The district offers 30 days of faculty training each year to better implement changes and to work within

(Continued)

(Continued)

the system more effectively. The district also provides flexible working conditions, which allow for sharing or rotating jobs and creating a relief team of experienced teachers. Teachers within the district have formed their own organization, the Prince William Sound Teachers' Association. Since they are a team, they believe that everyone should share the same rewards, so they rejected a salary plan proposed by the district with a pay-for-performance system that rewards individual and districtwide accomplishments. Instead, they asked that everyone receive the same, averaged amount.

Due to the collaborative approach, the district has created a new environment for learning where all community members have embraced their rights and responsibilities as stakeholders in the future of the students.

For more information on the CSD and their standards-based system, visit www.chugach schools.com.

The CSD received the 2001 Malcolm Baldrige National Quality Award in the area of education. To read the write-up by the National Institute of Standards and Technology, visit www.nist.gov/public_ affairs/chugach.htm

IMPLEMENTING CULTURALLY RESPONSIVE STANDARDS-BASED TEACHING

In our work with teachers, we have found that beginning the CRSB process usually includes the following steps:

1. Think about the various ways you can effectively bring your family and community culture into the classroom. Ask yourself, What self-exploration do I need to do? How does my own cultural framing affect the way I see my students and their families?

2. Think about what more you need to know about your students before you begin. Ask yourself, What are my students' cultural backgrounds and perspectives? What are the various things they and their families value? How can I tap into the cultural strength of my students' family and community cultures? How can I make sure I am not operating on stereotypes?

3. Consider how you build relationships and community in your classroom. Ask yourself, What activities or actions can help me and my students get to know one another better and learn from each other? How can I show students, families, and community members that their cultural framing and knowledge are valuable?

4. Start small and then build up to larger activities and projects. Ask yourself, How can I bring a "cultural responsiveness" to current lessons and activities? In other words, How can I expand lessons or activities to make sure they are student centered, transformational, and that they build relationships? Ask yourself, How can I help students see and consider various points of view and understand ways that concepts apply in other contexts?

5. Find allies—in students, teachers, parents, community members, administrators, and others. Ask yourself, What other teachers in the building currently practice or would support CRSB teaching? How are my CRSB lessons connected to other initiatives or projects in the school? How do my CRSB activities connect to our building or district mission? It helps to have support!

Figure 1.3 Continuum of Options and Opportunities for CSRB Teaching

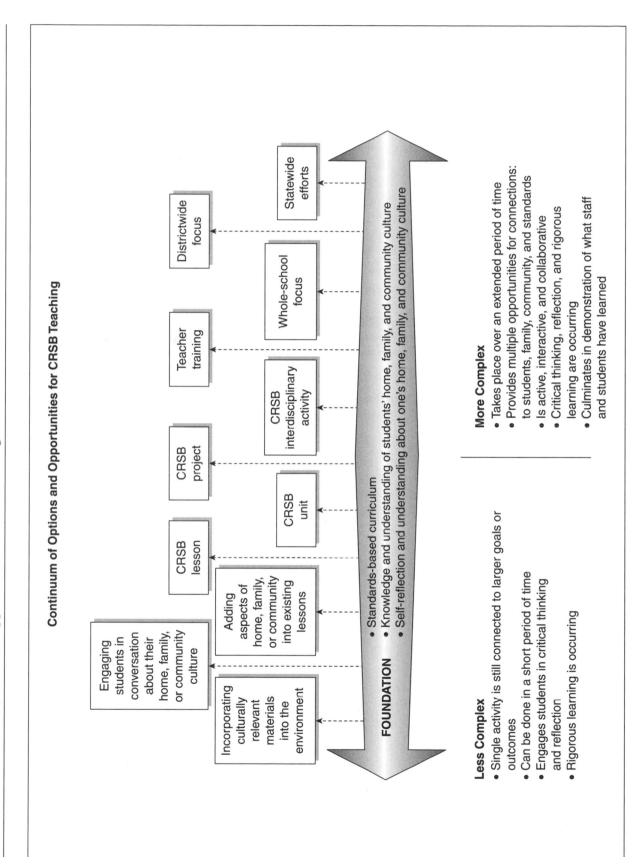

Continuum of Options and Opportunities for CRSB Teaching

Engaging students in conversation about their home, family, or community culture

Incorporating culturally relevant materials into the environment

Adding aspects of home, family, or community into existing lessons

CRSB lesson

CRSB unit

CRSB project

CRSB interdisciplinary activity

Teacher training

Whole-school focus

Districtwide focus

Statewide efforts

FOUNDATION

• Standards-based curriculum
• Knowledge and understanding of students' home, family, and community culture
• Self-reflection and understanding about one's home, family, and community culture

Less Complex

• Single activity is still connected to larger goals or outcomes
• Can be done in a short period of time
• Engages students in critical thinking and reflection
• Rigorous learning is occurring

More Complex

• Takes place over an extended period of time
• Provides multiple opportunities for connections: to students, family, community, and standards
• Is active, interactive, and collaborative
• Critical thinking, reflection, and rigorous learning are occurring
• Culminates in demonstration of what staff and students have learned

CONTINUUM OF OPTIONS AND OPPORTUNITIES FOR CULTURALLY RESPONSIVE STANDARDS-BASED TEACHING

There is a broad array of options and opportunities for implementing CRSB teaching in your classroom or program. Figure 1.3 (page 21) shows the variety of options and where they fall along a continuum: from informal and brief to formal and elaborate. The continuum moves from less-complex areas such as engaging students in dialogue about their family or community culture to more complex areas such as interdisciplinary units centered on family or community connections. Note that both of the examples in this chapter fall at the more-complex end of the continuum. Throughout this manual, you will be able to read about simpler, less-complex ways to adapt your standards-based lessons and activities to make them more culturally responsive. The rest of this book will take you through various points on the continuum, describing them in more depth and providing examples and tips for implementing them.

REFLECTION QUESTIONS

1. What is your personal response to CRSB teaching? What does it mean to you?

2. What are the different types of cultures that you see among your students, families, and colleagues? In what small ways could you incorporate one of these cultures into your existing lesson(s)?

3. What are the important aspects of your own culture(s) that impact who you are? How does this affect how you relate to and interact with the culture(s) of your school, your students, and their families?

4. Do you know any teachers—or have you read about any or seen any in films—that engage in CRSB teaching? Describe the things they do that are culturally responsive and tell how you could use some of their strategies in your classroom.

5. Describe an activity you have seen or done that is culturally responsive but not standards-based and one that is standards-based but not culturally responsive. How might you alter these activities to make them both standards-based and culturally responsive?

6. What are some specific standards that Project FRESA appears to address? What state or district standards can you draw from to create a similar project?

7. How has youth culture changed since you were a student? How does it compare to the current youth culture of your students?

8. Were there any conflicts between your family culture and the culture of your school when you were a student? How did that impact your learning? What are some conflicts between the culture of the school you work in or with now and your students' cultures? How do you think that is impacting their learning?

9. Think back on a powerful and positive learning experience you had as a student. In what ways were some of the essential elements of CRSB teaching a part of that experience?

10. How are any or all of the essential elements reflected in your current teaching practices?

11. Are there any "elements" in addition to the ones listed that you think are necessary to ensure CRSB teaching?

12. What are some examples of CRSB activities you have seen at the beginning, middle, and end of the continuum of options and opportunities?

2

Taking Stock of Current Classroom Practices

Effective teachers are familiar with the populations of students in their classes. They explicitly acknowledge the diversity of their students, valuing their strengths and knowledge.

—Michael S. Knapp (1995)

Integrating culturally responsive standards-based (CRSB) practices into your teaching requires some deliberate thought and reflection. A great place to start is to take stock of your current practices and aptitudes: What is your curriculum? What kinds of CRSB practices are you already implementing? What knowledge do you have, and what would you like to learn? This chapter will help you document your current practices and define professional goals for yourself.

CRSB curriculum draws on theories about curriculum that emphasize responsiveness to particular people, in a particular place, at a particular time (Jones & Nimmo, 1994). Teachers are encouraged to be careful observers of students' interests and to develop concrete learning experiences based on them. Teachers should continually revise their curricula in response to what is actually happening in the daily life of the students in the program.

These theories emphasize that teacher–child relationships and dialogue should be focused on the work or learning that is occurring (rather than on routines, rules, conduct, and performance). Teachers recognize that individuals create or construct their own new understandings through the interaction of their prior knowledge (which is culturally based) and the new ideas they come into contact with (Brooks & Brooks, 1993). Thus, the teacher's role is to translate information into a format appropriate for the individual learner and her state of understanding, encouraging students to direct their own explorations.

Judy Barker is a teacher of special education in a rural Oregon high school. Her reflection takes stock of her current ideas and classroom practices and reflects on how she can move forward. This teacher's reflection shows her continuous process of getting to know and understand her students while helping them to learn writing and other skills. She describes her changing ideas of family influences and cultural responsiveness.

Tool 1 "Taking Stock of Current Classroom Practices" will help you examine your current practices and reflect on your interactions with diverse groups of people, the educational opportunities provided in your classroom, and the community supports available to you.

REFLECTIONS OF A HIGH SCHOOL SPECIAL EDUCATION TEACHER

Judy Barker

One of the ways in which we introduce lessons in our classrooms is to draw on personal experiences from the beginning. When we first introduced the unit on families, we talked about our personal experiences with our own families. A photo display on the board introduced the students to the members of my own family. Photos included my husband, sons, pets, summer vacation, grandchildren, parents, teddy bear collection, wedding photos, car, and so on. The photos elicited a lot of oral language experiences from the students as they asked questions. Many of my students have met both of my sons, and were interested in seeing more-recent pictures of them. It was a way to begin to develop comfortable discussions.

As the unit continued, it was obvious that my home life, background, and culture are vastly different from those of my students. But we continued to share, comparing the similarities and contrasting the differences. The one thing that is obvious is that each of us has a strong bond to our own family. No matter how much dysfunction or struggle we have been through, every single person defended his own family, while learning to be able to identify some of the weaknesses therein. That cut right through all cultural borders.

Included in our writing skills lessons is the concept that a story contains more than just one sentence. We have begun by providing examples of one sentence, then expanding on the same idea for nine more sentences ("My family has _____ members"). We will continue until all those are completed, then prepare a final draft that will be used for the storyboard presentations, which probably will be next fall.

Our culmination project is to make a storyboard to display in the school for each student. We are hoping for the display to not only become a magnet for families to come to school, but also to provide a "glimpse" for the other members of our staff into the window of special education and life skills.

For sure, my personal cultural understanding of the Hispanic [Latino] and Native American students was extremely limited. I had not been exposed to their culture much, except second hand. An experience for me that was particularly rewarding was to participate in a traditional meal and powwow on the reservation. Many of my students and families attended. In addition, I was invited to attend a flute performance, a drumming and healing ceremony, and a ceremonial sweat in a sweat lodge. Even though I had not participated in such activities before, it was interesting to compare rituals of my culture and faith with theirs (baptisms, special family prayers, holiday traditions, rites of passage, celebrations), and to note the similarities. I brought in photos of special family celebrations to share with the students. I have been struck by how much the early teachings from my family continue to influence me and my life. Even though all of my family members died when I was young, those memories are vivid. At first I think I was struck by the blinders that I felt my students were looking through. It is easier now to realize that the traditions of their immediate environment are extremely powerful. It is what shapes and will continue to shape their lives.

(Text resumes on page 33)

┌─ **TOOL 1** ───

╔══╗
║   **TAKING STOCK OF CURRENT CLASSROOM PRACTICES**   ║
╚══╝

Use the following tool to think about your current practices and aptitudes. Scan your environment and currently planned curriculum. Explore what's already happening that is culturally responsive and standards based, and use that to determine what you would like to see happen.

You may not have an answer for all the questions, which is OK, because culturally responsive standards-based teaching is an ongoing process depending on you, your students, your school, and your community. This is not a test—it is merely a tool to help you grow in your CRSB practices.

Part 1: Getting to Know and Interact With Diverse Groups in the Community

Reflect on the practices you currently use to get to know your students and their community. Think about your response to differences and similarities in backgrounds and environments between school and students' homes. Describe your students' backgrounds and community or school demographics (including ethnic or cultural groups represented, whether they live in rural or urban communities, economic status, percentage ESL, languages spoken, etc.).

_____

_____

_____

What else would you like to know about your students and their home backgrounds?

_____

_____

_____

What are ways you currently get to know your students and their families (open houses, parent conferences, family interviews, story sharing, writing assignments, etc.)?

_____

_____

_____

What cultural celebrations do you participate in?

_____

_____

_____

(Continued)

(Continued)

How do you currently respond to differences and similarities between your own culture and students' cultures?

_____

_____

_____

Describe the environment of the school and classroom, especially aspects that reflect your students' lives. To do this, scan the classroom and take note of what's on the walls, the set-up of the desks, and information that is present for both students and adults. For example, are there any student pictures, your own family pictures, student work, posters, family-made artifacts, literature and hands-on materials from the cultures represented by students, or other visuals that reflect students' lives?

_____

_____

_____

Describe how the environment may invite students to explore culture or to share their background experiences.

_____

_____

_____

Describe your supports, colleagues, and partners.

_____

_____

_____

Whom do you collaborate with outside the school?

_____

_____

_____

Who are your mentors, guides, and inspirations?

_____

_____

_____

What do you think are the potential strengths within yourself or the school, or both?

_____

_____

_____

Part 2: Recording Essential Elements in Your CRSB Teaching

What activities are you currently doing that can be described as CRSB teaching? Chapter 1 introduced six essential elements of CRSB teaching. The bulleted points under each element below review the definitions and give examples. The questions that follow provide a way to document your current activities as they reflect those six essential elements. (This activity can be interesting to do with a fellow teacher: try answering questions for each other to learn about your peer's observations.)

Essential Element: Becoming Student Centered

- What is taught is derived from students' lives, interests, families, communities, and cultures.
- Teachers involve students in planning what they will learn and how they will learn it.
- Teachers recognize the social, emotional, and cognitive strengths and needs of the students and meet them where they are.
- Instruction is built on students' personal and cultural strengths.

Describe how your curriculum is developed. What parts are prescribed? What parts do you have control over? Has it been planned based on the lives of students?

_____

_____

_____

Describe any activities that are designed to use your students' interests or connect to their cultural, personal, family, or community experiences.

_____

_____

_____

How did the activities described above connect to student interests, accommodate different learning styles, allow for student input in the planning, or focus on student strengths?

_____

_____

_____

Essential Element: Promoting Transformational Teaching

- Teachers change their role from instructor to facilitator by allowing students' experiences, perspectives, and interests to help shape the curriculum.
- Teachers help students examine critically and challenge the knowledge presented in the curriculum, examining the perspective from which the texts were written.
- Teachers and students see their own lives as subjects worthy of study, examining the strengths and significance of their culture, family, and community, while respecting each other's language, knowledge, and skills.

(Continued)

(Continued)

Describe any activities designed to help students examine the strengths and significance of their culture, family, or community.

_____

_____

_____

Describe any activities designed to help students critically examine the knowledge and content that is presented to them.

_____

_____

_____

Essential Element: Connecting and Integrating CRSB Practices

- Learning is contextualized and builds on what students already know, allowing them to comprehend new information more easily.
- Teachers use interdisciplinary work to illustrate the relationships among different subjects and their applicability.
- The work connects students and teachers with other students, teachers, or family and community members.

Describe any activities you have done with students that were hands-on, project-based, or community-based learning.

_____

_____

_____

List or describe activities that connect to students' past experiences, involve students in real-world applications, and relate to life outside the classroom.

_____

_____

_____

List collaborative activities you do across subjects or classrooms, or with other teachers.

_____

_____

_____

Describe how you integrate the standards into your curriculum.

_____

_____

_____

Essential Element: Fostering Critical Thinking

- Teachers pose questions that probe student thinking.
- Students monitor their own level of understanding and become self-directed, self-disciplined, self-monitored, and self-corrective.
- Teachers and students approach learning in different ways.

What activities have been done to promote critical thinking skills and what skills have been developed?

_____

_____

_____

What activities asked students to monitor their own understanding of learning goals?

_____

_____

_____

Essential Element: Incorporating Assessment and Reflection

- Teachers help students define their educational needs and create a plan to address the issues.
- Teachers assess students through multiple, authentic means and enlist others to help assess students (teachers, students, and family and community members).
- Teachers and students work together to create rubrics by which students are assessed.
- Teachers encourage students to use journals to set goals and reflect on what they learn, making adjustments as needed.

In what ways do students reflect on their learning? Describe how you provide time for reflection.

_____

_____

_____

Describe ways you have used assessment to inform your instruction.

_____

_____

_____

What classroom-level assessments have you used, and how have students been involved in planning the assessment process?

_____

_____

_____

(Continued)

(Continued)

Essential Element: Building Relationships and Community

- Teachers strive to get to know their students, students' families, and the community they serve—using what they learn to inform what is taught.
- Teachers communicate with parents about what they are teaching and how parents can be involved—using multiple avenues to include families in what is done in the school.
- Teachers help students to meet and get to know other people in their community.

In what ways have family and community members had opportunities and "entry points" for connecting with the curriculum?

_____

_____

_____

What community resources or connections have been accessed?

_____

_____

_____

What activities help students to better know each other, their families, and their communities?

_____

_____

_____

Now that you have reflected on your activities using these questions, go back and look at your accomplishments and where you can build on them. List ideas for ways to further integrate the six essential elements into your teaching.

_____

_____

_____

Part 3: Self-Reflection

The following short survey is designed to help you look at the skills and aptitudes that are necessary to successfully implement CRSB teaching. Throughout the guide you will see these questions repeated in descriptions of CRSB teaching. These skills and aptitudes develop with time and should be continually refined based on your specific context and students.

Rating scale: S = Strength, D = Developing

Culturally Responsive Standards-Based Teaching	S	D
I understand the cognitive, social, and emotional development of my students.	☐	☐
I have high expectations for all students in my classroom or program.	☐	☐
I focus on my students' strengths rather than on their problems or negative behaviors.	☐	☐
I develop relevant and rigorous learning activities for my students including use of community history, culture, and language.	☐	☐
The learning activities I design for students support our school and community learning standards.	☐	☐
I know how to effectively motivate and engage all students in my classroom or program.	☐	☐
I can effectively assess my students' skills, interests, and goals and help them to do the same.	☐	☐
I involve students in decision making at all levels of the class or program.	☐	☐
I understand the home, family, and community cultures of my students.	☐	☐
I understand my own culture well and how that culture affects my teaching.	☐	☐
I can effectively work with the cultural differences that arise between me and my students.	☐	☐
I feel comfortable engaging my students in critical dialogue about family and community culture, both individually and in groups.	☐	☐
I effectively communicate with my students and their families.	☐	☐
I collaborate with other teachers and staff to continually improve my teaching.	☐	☐

(Continued)

(Continued)

Part 4: Strengths, Assets, and Goals

Take a few minutes to read what you have recorded so far. Look at the strengths and supports you bring to developing a CRSB classroom and set some goals for further growth.

What strengths do you have when it comes to including student culture in classroom activities?

_____

_____

_____

What assets can you draw on from your environment, students, other teachers, administration, community, school, and so on?

_____

_____

_____

One step I can take right away to infuse my students' home, family, or community culture into the classroom is . . . .

_____

_____

_____

Describe hurdles and challenges you can see for CRSB teaching and learning.

_____

_____

_____

Which areas would you like to explore next? What goals would you like to make?

_____

_____

_____

FINDING TIME AND RESOURCES

Educators are faced with time and resource constraints. It can be helpful to remember that CRSB teaching is an approach that grows over time. The challenge lies in finding creative ways to integrate aspects of students' backgrounds with standards-based content. Many teachers do a little bit of this all the time, tailoring how they introduce new lessons based on students' prior knowledge and interests.

Many teachers believe they have to develop large, complex projects in order to bring students' family or community culture into the classroom and successfully implement CRSB teaching practices. However, effective CRSB teaching can happen by starting with the standards-based curriculum already in place and making minor changes to existing lesson plans. These small changes can have a large impact, resulting in meaningful, personal, and real-world connections for all students.

Here are some tips to make the most of your time and to help you find resources:

- Start from where you are. Sometimes it only takes one meaningful activity to have a lasting impact on a student.
- Consider ways to emphasize depth over breadth. It's more meaningful and a better investment of time for you and your students to cover fewer things well than many things less well.
- Collaborate with colleagues and family or community liaisons in your efforts. Find colleagues to work with to test new ideas, assess effects, and adjust strategies.
- Think about how parents, support staff, aides, tutors, or after-school programs can play a part in a new project.
- Use asset mapping (Dorfman, 1998) as a tool for linking with community and family resources from outside your immediate pool.
- Involve students in developing learning goals, lesson plans, and methods for demonstrating knowledge and sharing it with the community.
- Communicate with school administrators to show them your achievements and garner more support. Begin a discussion at your school on how to provide more time for planning and professional development.

Laurie Thurston, a high school English teacher, uses simple protocols to address the issues of students arriving late to her classroom or missing a day of school. It is a positive approach in response to a common issue among students from poverty, and it requires minimal time and effort to establish and maintain on the part of the teacher.

She has a wall chart that reads as follows.

✓ Check the table for materials and handouts from the day you missed.
✓ Take a seat & check today's agenda.
✓ When (if) there's a break in class, check with the "Go To" Guy or Gal for directions & notes, etc. . . .

If you are late . . . welcome!

✓ Give Laurie your pass.
✓ Get any materials set out.
✓ Read the agenda for the day.
✓ Wait for direction quietly—either I or another student will get you caught up . . .

All of her students know the "rules" to follow if they arrive after the tardy bell, and the coveted leadership position of "go to" person rotates regularly. Students agree that Ms. Thurston's tardy process decreases absences and fosters respect. One senior reflected,

> Ms. Laurie understands that sometimes our home lives might interfere with us getting to school on time. I have a lot of home responsibilities, including my sick grandmother. Sometimes my mother has to work at 5 a.m. and my grandmother is difficult. Being called out by teachers for coming late equals more stress. Now I don't have to choose. In Ms. Laurie's class, I might be 10 minutes late and it's no big deal for me to jump in and be on track.

Snapshot 2.1 "Molecules—With a Twist of Culture" is from a high school science teacher who adds a cultural aspect to an end-of-the-year chemistry project she has been doing for years. Because her class includes students from the local community as well as from a residential boarding program, she believes that adding this little "twist" adds more relevance to her lesson. The local students are a combination of European Americans and Asian Americans. Boarding students come from Asia, Europe, the Middle East, and Africa. Some are proficient in English, while others have limited English skills.

Snapshot 2.1

MOLECULES—WITH A TWIST OF CULTURE

Oregon Episcopal School, Portland, Oregon

Grade levels: High school, primarily sophomores and juniors

Subject areas: Mainly chemistry, but includes math, reading, research, writing, oral presentation, and technology

Highlights: In the project, students do research, create a model, write a paper, and give a presentation on a molecule of their choice—including personal, social, or environmental implications or impacts of their molecule.

Creative extension: Five chemistry classes at the Oregon Episcopal School (OES), with two teachers, pursued this project this year. In past years, they had also tried an interstate collaboration with a teacher from Washington State so students could present their projects to each other and communicate over the Internet if they were studying the same molecule; but end of year schedules made it difficult to coordinate.

An "Aha!" Moment in the Lab . . .

"After having started the three-week unit on molecular modeling, one student—who was panicking about putting together the information on her molecule—came in after school for help," begins Rosa Hemphill, a science teacher at OES for the past 13 years.

"She had chosen to model oxycodon, a morphine analog. As she built the physical model, she began identifying the functional groups and to recall some of the chemistry she already knew.

"After a while, her dad came into the lab to see what she was doing. He wanted to know about the functional groups in the molecule, and she was able to explain some of their chemistry. WOW!!" exclaims Hemphill. "He asked her what polarity meant and what its effect would be. They took digital photos of her physical molecule model to place in her PowerPoint presentation, carefully double-checking to make sure the plastic bonds made up of little purple, white, and gray bonds were correct. Ultimately, her dad told her they had a close relative with a medical condition who had successfully used the chemical to control his severe pain. All of a sudden, the chemical model she was working on became more important. They discussed adding the idea of culture and family background to her presentation by mentioning the relationship between the molecule and her relative's medical condition.

"Afterward, it struck me that this was one example of how the connections with family can provide the impetus for a student to really work on and benefit from assignments like this one," Hemphill reflects.

Molecular Modeling Project

For the end-of-the-year Molecule Project, students are asked to choose a chemical molecule about which they want to learn more. The directions call for researching the industrial, medicinal, and historical uses of the molecule, along with its chemical properties. As part of the instructions, students are to draw Lewis structures for their molecules and then build them in a computer-based molecular modeling program (Figure 2.1). They then apply what they have learned during the school year to explain the chemistry of that one molecule and to put together a PowerPoint presentation to share a "picture" of their molecule, its properties, and its real-world impacts. The project takes two to three weeks of class time.

As part of their presentations, students give their reasons for wanting to study the particular molecules they have chosen. The presentation also includes evidence of understanding how to calculate molecular

Figure 2.1 Model of a Molecule

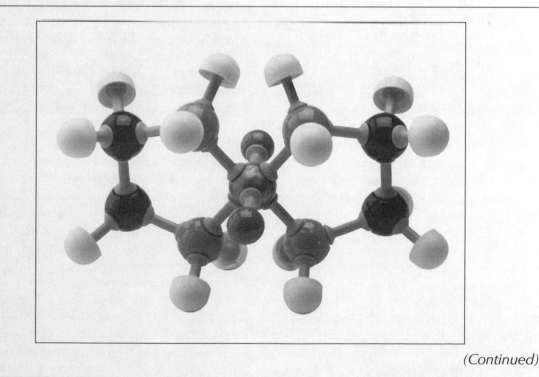

(Continued)

(Continued)

mass, identify molecule type, determine if it is an acid or a base, calculate the heat of reaction, estimate its solubility, and relate the nanoscale properties of the molecular model to the real-world properties of the chemical.

Oregon science standards that are covered in this modeling project include these:

- Explain atoms and their base components (protons, neutrons, and electrons) as a basis for all matter.
- Distinguish between examples of chemical changes and physical changes.
- Recognize that heat energy is a by-product of most energy transformations.
- Recognize that the historical development of atomic theory demonstrates how scientific knowledge changes over time.

Hemphill had three additional learning goals for her students during this project:

- To synthesize information from the course by applying it to one molecule
- To understand the role technology and science play in our lives
- To understand how chemistry can be applied to students' lives, communities, and cultures

Just a Little Change

"One might think that the teaching of science is fairly culture-free since certain science materials, tools, and skills are recognized and used universally. However, the cultural background students bring to their science class affects the words they use, the expectations they have of the process, and how they see the results. A student can understand new concepts more easily if she is presented with a tieback to experiences from her background, which includes her cultural experience.

"This year, the Molecule Project again involved students selecting a molecule of their choice to study, model, and present— on the basis of their own interests. But I tweaked it a bit to bring in the possibility of cultural responses from students," Hemphill explains. "I asked them to consider if (or how) their molecule may impact their culture or community." This small change allowed students to bring their interests and their backgrounds, both personal and cultural, into their studies about chemical bonding in the molecules and added "real-world" properties to the chemicals they chose.

Some students, including several of the international students who related the cultural connections of their molecules to their home countries, picked up on the suggestion. Two mainland Chinese students modeled morphine. Their reason for studying the molecule was the devastation brought to China by the Opium Wars. Another student studied chloracetophenone (CN) tear gas because it was used in his country, Korea, to quell student uprisings.

Several students studied molecules that made up the medicines they or a relative had taken. One girl had been given oxycotin (oxycodon molecule) as a painkiller after a boating accident in which she injured her back. One Japanese student wanted to find out how nitroglycerin, an explosive, could be taken by his grandmother in Japan for her heart. Two American students studied lactose because of high levels of lactose intolerance found in Asian and African lineages. Some students studied the chemicals present in foods or plants, such as nightshade, that are used medicinally by different cultures. One student looked at the effect of "essential herbal oils" used in her country on bacteria and found that they are indeed antibacterial—which strengthened her faith in the cultural lore of her country.

A key finding for Hemphill was that international students seemed more likely to bring their cultural background into this project than were students from local cultural groups. "I suspect that mainstream students may think that if they are not international students they may not have a cultural reference point," explains Hemphill. "One of my lessons, then, is that I must come up with a way for American students to indicate the cultural impacts of their chosen molecules."

REFLECTION QUESTIONS

1. Which tools or parts of the tools in this chapter were most helpful to you? Why? Which were the most challenging? Why?

2. Reflecting on the essay by Judy Barker, the special education teacher, what are some similarities between your own family and the families of your students? What are some of the differences?

3. What do you think will be your biggest challenges in implanting a CRSB curriculum? How do you see yourself overcoming these challenges?

4. What information, resources, skills, or allies do you need to teach in a CRSB way?

5. What is one small thing you can do right away to be more culturally responsive?

6. Reflecting on Snapshot 2.1 "Molecules—With a Twist of Culture," what are some other ways that science or math activities can be culturally responsive?

7. Critique the Molecules project. What went well and what might the teacher have done differently?

3

The Foundation for Culturally Responsive Standards-Based Teaching

We live in a country with a rich mix of cultures. We must do all we can to teach ourselves and help those around us to respect diversity.

—Janet Gonzalez-Mena (2005)

There are several important foundation skills that underlie culturally responsive standards-based (CRSB) teaching and create inclusive and unbiased classrooms and schools. The first asks educators to engage in reflective self-analysis to examine their own attitudes toward different ethnic, racial, gender, and social class groups (Banks, 2008; Delpit, 1995; Phillips, 1988). The second asks educators to develop the capacity to know each of their students well, which includes knowing their families. Educators then need the ability to take this information and use it to build on and connect students' personal and cultural strengths to various academic content areas.

This chapter presents tools for developing these skills. It is an ongoing and dynamic process and requires the practitioner to see through the eyes of a learner. The ability to use students' home, family, and community culture to enrich the curriculum evolves as we learn more about ourselves, our world, and other cultures. Once you have spent time getting to know your cultural self, your students, and their families, you can use the information to take stock of your current practices and build onto them a CRSB environment and curriculum. The following excerpt from Janet Gonzalez-Mena offers one woman's thoughts about her own cultural self.

SOME THOUGHTS ON CULTURAL PLURALISM

Janet Gonzalez-Mena

As a white, middle-class American with mostly Anglo-Saxon heritage (my Spanish surname comes from my husband), I was surprised to discover that I have a culture. I, like everyone else, move within a cultural framework every minute of every day. My framework influences the way I think and act and how I perceive, handle, and interact with people and materials. I move within my cultural framework as unconsciously as I move within the physical world I live in. I don't think about my culturally determined actions, postures, or ways of dealing with people—they're automatic.

When I meet someone who obviously doesn't move in the same cultural framework that I do, I'm jarred. Because my way seems right, even normal, I tend to judge others based on my perspective. But being a polite person who tries to get along with people, I do what I can not to notice. Because my way is normal to me, it seems rude to make an issue of the fact that someone else is "not normal." And because I have a whole society behind me giving me the message that "my people" are the standard by which everyone is judged, I can afford to keep on ignoring what I choose to.

But can I? What does this attitude do to me? It shields me from reality. It gives me a slanted perspective, a narrow view. What does it do to people who are different from me to have those differences defined as abnormal and then ignored? What does it do to someone to ignore some integral aspect of his or her identity?

I have a strong desire to quit ignoring differences and begin not only to notice them but also to celebrate them. I want to look at differences as sources of strength, not abnormalities or weaknesses. I don't expect to change all at once—in fact, I've been working on this shift of perspective for a number of years. Revising one's view can be a slow process.

Source: Excerpted from: Gonzalez-Mena, J. (2005). *Diversity in early care and education: Honoring differences* (4th ed.; pp. 9–12). Boston, MA: McGraw-Hill. Reproduced with permission of The McGraw-Hill Companies.

GETTING TO KNOW YOUR CULTURAL SELF

In the reflection process—or "cultural self-assessment"—the individual examines his own cultural background and upbringing, analyzes how his "cultural view" influences the way he sees the world, and strives to understand how his cultural view influences the way he understands his students and their families.

One of the primary challenges of cultural self-assessment is the ability to recognize that everyone has a culture. For many people, culture may seem "invisible." Our society often relates culture to things we can easily identify: racial and language differences, ethnic foods, religious practices, and so on. To help identify one's culture, it is useful to include such things as family structure and traditions, connection to education, and socioeconomic background. As we reflect on our cultural experiences, it is important to remember that cultural upbringing and worldview are innately connected to what we value and see as "normal."

There are many ways to begin a cultural self-assessment, including reflecting on your own life story, having conversations with fellow teachers about their cultural experiences, and comparing and contrasting their stories to your own. Libi Susag, a physical education teacher from a middle school on the Fort Peck Reservation in Poplar, Montana, offers a reflection describing her struggle to understand the concept of culture, how her culture influences her work, and how her own culture relates to that of her students. She contemplates her progress and tells of ways she has used this new understanding to develop a culturally responsive unit for teaching traditional Native American games.

AN EYE-OPENING JOURNEY TOWARD CULTURAL AWARENESS

Libi Susag

Culture is a difficult concept . . . one that has been tough for me to grasp. My difficulty in defining my own personal culture has been a struggle, even a source of contention with family members as I began probing the "whys" and "how comes" of my unknowing.

My best attempt at a definition for culture is this: Culture is the smoke that hangs over a fire. You know it's there, you can actually see it. Too much of it affects you in various ways, and yet you still cannot reach out and grab hold of it. From that struggling point of view I have journeyed forward to explore others' cultures, in hope of discovering a better understanding of my own.

One of my biggest "ahas!" came during a drive to a rodeo. My driving companion (a fellow teacher and rodeo companion), although old enough to be my mother, was raised in a very similar way to me. As she talked about her family, she shared memories about her grandmother's attitude toward her grandfather—always very negative. It was quite obvious she felt she had married beneath her. Her grandmother had always hoped to travel, but she wasn't able to because of her family's financial situation (during the Depression). Her grandmother had a high school diploma, which was many more years of formal education than her husband, who had completed only the third grade. She married him knowing he would prove to be a good provider and a kind man.

As she continued to share about her family, her story began to flicker an "aha!" light for me. I asked if her grandmother was a German immigrant. My friend said yes, and also shared that "immigrant" was her grandmother's favorite put-down. If someone was dirty, grubby, or poorly clothed, her grandmother would scoff at them and say, "Clean yourself up, you look like an immigrant." I began to realize I had perceived culture as something everyone proudly wore on his or her sleeve, but that is not always so. I began to remember my own grandparents and parents talking about the Depression and war eras, and how they

(Continued)

(Continued)

were taught to hide who they were and where they came from, for fear of mistreatment. To be known as an immigrant or to display your differences could result in a very negative experience. I have come to realize that, for some, an entirely new value system and culture of assimilation has developed in this melting pot country. Some people don't proudly show their origins and heritage and instead shroud them in layers of history and avoidance.

This new "aha" has helped me immensely in my teaching. I teach on an Indian reservation, where one would assume that people are surrounded by culture, and the students would be extremely aware of their own culture and heritage. Surprisingly enough, I have found that my students know very little of their backgrounds. Many students know they are Indian but cannot tell you from which tribe they are enrolled members. Elders say that the Native Americans are losing their heritage. They are very correct, and have a variety of reasons to be concerned. In my students I see their lack of interest in cultural history, yet they are consumed with "gangish" fashions, rap music, and Doritos-eating/Mountain Dew–chugging social values.

While trying to implement culturally responsive teaching, I have been amazed at how much I have begun to notice cultural things in my school surroundings and in areas that I have never paid attention to, like television and media advertisements. Currently the educational push in my school is to include Native American culture in every subject area. I have been challenged about how to accomplish this in my physical education and health classrooms. While attending an education conference, I learned about teaching Native games to children. I thought it was a good fit for me and I also thought it might help my students begin to understand and value their culture, and give them a connection to something larger that they might have never known existed.

So I made arrangements for our school to host the International Traditional Games Society. The society spent two days teaching and sharing games with our middle school students. Preparing the students for this Native Game unit was a step-by-step process. I discussed culture with my students as it applied to our health classes, surveyed my students to learn more about their backgrounds, and made connections between our Floor Hockey unit and the game called Shinny they would eventually play. (For more about the Native Games unit, see Snapshot 5.1 "Rediscovering a Lost Heritage.") The unit was highly successful. The students increased their own awareness of culture, even if it took some digging to get them to realize a connection.

This reflection started on a journey (to the rodeo). Now, in conclusion, I can say my journey is not over. Many questions still have not been answered for me. However, because I have completed a few milestones on my journey, the path that lies ahead is a little bit easier for me to follow.

Tool 2 "Getting to Know Yourself" and Tool 3 "Self-Assessment on Culture, Self, and Systems" are designed to help you better understand your cultural self. Feel free to break the reflections into smaller pieces and complete them at your own pace. This type of self-reflection is a very personal journey; it's not necessary to share your responses with anyone unless you're comfortable doing so.

TOOL 2

GETTING TO KNOW YOURSELF

This survey was designed to help you reflect on your own educational experiences and cultural heritage, to consider how those experiences influence the way you view the world, and to realize how they influence the way you teach.

Getting to Know Yourself as a Student

What were your educational experiences as a youth? How would you describe the schools you attended? What were you successful at, and why? What did you struggle with, and why? What was your most memorable grade or stage in school? Why?

_____

_____

_____

As a youth, how did your family culture support your school success?

_____

_____

_____

Did your family culture ever clash with school culture? If so, in what ways and how did it affect you?

_____

_____

_____

Did you have a favorite or powerful teacher? If yes, what made him or her your favorite? If not, describe the kind of teacher you would have liked to have had.

_____

_____

_____

Getting to Know Yourself as a Teacher

Why did you choose teaching as a career?

_____

_____

_____

(Continued)

(Continued)

What are your favorite subjects to teach? Why? Are there subjects that you do not like to teach? Why?

_____

_____

_____

What is your biggest reward in teaching? What is your biggest challenge?

_____

_____

_____

How would your students describe you as a teacher? How would their families describe you?

_____

_____

_____

What have you learned about yourself (as a student and as a teacher) that can be used to enhance your teaching, motivate your students, or make your curriculum more meaningful?

_____

_____

_____

Getting to Know Your Cultural Self

What was your cultural situation growing up? Think about where you lived, your class or socioeconomic status, ethnic or cultural background, religious or spiritual tradition, and gender. How did all these things influence you?

_____

_____

_____

Describe your cultural situation today. How do you identify racially or ethnically? Who is your family? What is your socioeconomic class? What spirituality do you practice? Where do you live and why do you live there?

_____

_____

_____

How do you see ways that your "cultural self" influences your teaching?

_____

_____

_____

── TOOL 3 ──

SELF-ASSESSMENT ON CULTURE, SELF, AND SYSTEMS

This self-assessment is designed to help you think about the cultural skills and aptitudes necessary to successfully implement CRSB teaching. Read each of the statements and rate yourself, then complete the reflection questions that follow. This exercise will help you think about the areas where you are very capable and the areas where you need improvement, and will help you set learning goals. Before you begin the assessment, remember that it is not a test and there are no wrong answers: it is merely a tool to help you grow in your CRSB teaching practices. Assess yourself periodically to check for growth.

Rating scale: D = Developing, M = Meeting, E = Exceeding

Culture, Self, and Systems	D	M	E
I understand my own cultural heritage and background.	☐	☐	☐
I feel comfortable sharing my cultural background and perspective with my students.	☐	☐	☐
I recognize the norms and values of the dominant culture.	☐	☐	☐
I understand how U.S. history and institutions such as the media, families, and the formal education system influence the way people perceive one another.	☐	☐	☐
I understand power dynamics with regard to race, culture, and ethnicity.	☐	☐	☐
I understand the concept of privilege and recognize the dynamics of oppression.	☐	☐	☐
I recognize institutional biases.	☐	☐	☐
I understand how personal assumptions and biases work.	☐	☐	☐
I am aware of how socioeconomic factors affect educational expectations and opportunity for my students.	☐	☐	☐
I understand the role that culture plays in our society.	☐	☐	☐
I can negotiate cultural differences.	☐	☐	☐
I strive to be culturally responsive to my students and in my classroom.	☐	☐	☐

Reflections on my knowledge about culture, self, and systems:

What strengths do you have related to "culture, self, and systems" that will enable you to bring your students' home, family, or community culture into your classroom?

_____

_____

_____

Which competency areas need improvement?

_____

_____

_____

What could you do to improve in those areas (e.g., read a particular book, take a workshop or course, get a mentor, observe other teachers, practice reflection)?

_____

_____

_____

Choose one area for improvement and make a plan of action to address it.

_____

_____

_____

Developing Cultural Responsiveness

Developing cultural responsiveness requires many things, including self-reflection, interaction with diverse groups of people, educational opportunities, community support, desire, and time. According to research (Cross, Bazron, Dennis, & Isaacs, 1989; Klug & Whitfield, 2003), culturally responsive teachers hold a set of skills and knowledge that includes the following:

- Valuing diversity: Demonstrating respect for other ways of interacting with the world by seeking knowledge about different cultures, withholding judgment, and moving beyond just "tolerance."
- Having a capacity for cultural self-assessment: Being aware of our own cultural framing in order to understand how others define themselves.
- Being conscious of the dynamics inherent when cultures interact: Paying attention to the feelings in the pit of our stomach, confronting our prejudices, and refining our perceptions.
- Embedding cultural diversity and responsiveness into all aspects of the school or classroom: Recognizing that schools operate under a certain culture, and acknowledging the need to make that culture more inclusive. Searching for ways to make the classroom a blend of school and home cultures for the benefit of students.
- Implementing different interactions and behaviors in response to cultural diversity: Understanding the "double consciousness" students go through when home and school cultures are at odds with one another. Obtaining a willingness to adjust our own teaching style to reach all children.

BUILDING RELATIONSHIPS WITH STUDENTS

As educators consciously build and strengthen relationships with students and their families, their efforts foster trust, shared responsibility for education, and mutual support. If you ask students why a class or subject is their favorite, they will often tell you that they have a personal connection with the teacher. In fact, many teachers have seen a turnaround in students' classroom behavior and academic performance after getting to know students on a personal level through activities such as personal interviews (Nieto, 2003).

In the next reflection, teacher David Cort from Tulalip Elementary School in Marysville, Washington, shares how he acknowledges and values students' rich culture in the classroom and why he feels it is important to do so. (More about Tulalip Elementary School can be found in Snapshot 7.1 "Tulalip-Based Curriculum and Lushootseed Classes.")

TREASURING EVERYONE'S RICH CULTURE: ONE TEACHER'S THOUGHTS

David Cort

As a teacher, I'm so fortunate because I have students coming in every day who have this wonderful culture that they're eager to share with me. It's something totally new for me, and it's a beautiful, rich culture. So, I'm grateful every day that students are willing to share this gift with me. Of course, I want to be respectful of their culture. We have to make sure that students are being guided by their elders and their parents so that any time they bring cultural content to the classroom, they have permission from their families to do so. I've found in my experience that families are almost always very generous, and they are happy to have their young people sharing these cultural experiences that are important to them.

I'm attracted to being and teaching in a setting that is so obviously culturally rich. But, wherever I've taught, I would value and treasure the special experiences and especially the cultural heritages that students would bring to my classroom, whether that's on an Indian reservation, in South Central LA, or anywhere else. One of the delights of teaching is helping students bring out those special experiences, that culture, that they have to share. In that way we all enrich each other within the classroom. And, of course, I have a beautiful cultural heritage to share, too, about my European American ancestry, my Irish roots. I help my European American students value their own cultural heritage over the ocean in Europe. I think it helps European American kids to be more accepting of other cultures when they realize that they, too, have a beautiful, rich heritage to treasure.

One thing I have discovered is that oftentimes the things that strike me as most alien are the things that are most worth paying attention to because they reveal a different cultural perspective on the world. Those things that may be the most difficult for me to appreciate or get a grasp of I try to see as showing a difference in worldview. For example, with Lushootseed [native language throughout most of western Puget Sound] literature, repetition is a highly valued art form. When European American anthropologists began working with Native storytellers, sometimes they would take out the repetition and the circular forms of narration. To them, from their Western tradition, it seemed tedious and unnecessary, but in fact it's precisely that difference that shows us that this is something special and unique about this literature that we should try to understand and value.

Our math textbooks oftentimes tend to value standard units of measurement over nonstandard units of measurement. When we're confronted with traditional cultures where the measurement is in nonstandard units like the distance between your middle finger and the tip of your thumb, it makes us reevaluate our own value system. It makes us question if it's true that standard units are really more valuable. Or, is it the case that nonstandard units are just as valuable? We have to understand the different contexts in which we use standard and nonstandard units of measure.

To do this type of teaching is more work in the sense that you don't have a textbook to go by. But, if you're working in a class where a number of your students aren't benefiting from the textbook anyway, then as a teacher you're naturally motivated to put in that extra work and find a curriculum that will resonate with your students, one that meets our Essential Learnings (Washington state standards) of course, but that does so in a way that excites and motivates our students if the textbook won't do that. I think all teachers would do that and put in extra work to find ways to reach their students.

My words of wisdom? Well, I suppose I could say something. I am European American, and if I go into a community with a different culture and a different heritage I need to go very humbly as a learner, and seek out guidance from elders who can help me learn from their community. I know I've certainly been corrected along the way and I have appreciated and valued that. It has helped me grow as a person. All of us know that when you go into another culture, you are bound to make mistakes and commit cultural faux pas. You just try to be as humble and gracious as possible and when you make those inevitable errors, then you try to learn from them and move on. I wouldn't have continued doing the work that I'm doing except that I've had so much encouragement and affirmation from people in the community around me. And, even if I make mistakes from time to time, people tell me to let it roll right off my shoulders and move on, that they appreciate my work and they want me to keep doing what I'm doing.

The first step in really getting to know students may entail a shift in thinking for some practitioners from being the "sage on the stage" to the "guide on the side." It means changing the teacher's role from one where he imparts knowledge to his students and directs the learning in the classroom to one where he recognizes the social, emotional, and cognitive strengths and needs of students and "meets students where they are"—while maintaining high academic standards. Teachers who strive to build powerful relationships with students do the following well:

- Regard students' ways of speaking and thinking as resources, not as problems
- Involve students in the construction of their own knowledge—helping students discover their learning needs, take responsibility for learning experiences, and plan for meeting educational goals
- Create opportunities in the classroom for students to discuss their goals and aspirations, share what they want to learn about, and find ways the school can help them
- Listen to students as they discuss ideas together
- Promote candid discussion about topics relevant to students' lives, and challenge students to solve real-life problems—stretching students beyond the familiar
- Develop a large "bag of tricks" to get to know their students and families well

This chapter is designed to help build that "bag of tricks." Tool 4 "Getting to Know Your Students Better" can be a starting point to discover ways to establish a meaningful connection with your students.

TOOL 4

GETTING TO KNOW YOUR STUDENTS BETTER

These questions were designed to help you think about each student in your class, consider the influences in her life that affect her learning, and see how you can use this information to enhance learning. You don't have to answer all the questions at once, nor fill in the form for every student at one time. Keep completed sheets as an ongoing record of what you already know and still need to learn about your students. You can also use the questions as an interview guide, asking students to provide the needed information.

What is this student's dominant learning style? Does this student know about his or her learning style?

_____

_____

_____

What are three strengths or positive things you can say about this student?

_____

_____

_____

What does the student do outside school for fun and relaxation (pets, extracurricular activities, hobbies)? How can I use these things to make learning more meaningful?

_____

_____

_____

What do I know about this student's home/family/community culture? For instance, what languages are spoken in this student's home? Who lives in the home with this student? What do the student's parents do for a living?

_____

_____

_____

What is my biggest challenge in teaching this student?

_____

_____

_____

What do I need to know to create a rigorous and meaningful learning environment for the student? What types of staff interactions and curriculum experiences would he need to be successful?

_____

_____

_____

QUICK ACTIVITIES TO HELP YOU GET TO KNOW YOUR STUDENTS AND BUILD COMMUNITY

Poetic Introductions

Ask students to use the format below to create poems that describe themselves. Have students share their poems with one another and find a creative way to display the work in the classroom.

- Name
- Child of (parent, guardian, or family name)
- Lives in (name of community)
- Connected to (share five cultural aspects of self, such as ethnicity, food, language, religion, practices, traditions, etc.)
- Values (share three things that are important)
- Repeat name and child of (parent, guardian, or family name)

Getting-To-Know-You Venn Diagram

Gather students in groups of three. Supply a prepared three-circle Venn diagram for each group. Students talk in their groups about themselves and the things they like to do. After a brief discussion, the students decide on three ways in which they are all alike; they write those things in the intersecting areas of the diagram. Then each student writes in her circle three facts that are unique to her. This activity helps students recognize and appreciate similarities and differences in people.

Cultural Boxes

In this activity, each student selects a container of a reasonable size from home that represents some aspect of his culture, personality, or personal interests, such as a football helmet or a mask. Ask students to fill their object with other items that represent themselves—for example, family photos, CDs, a food staple, or a historical family artifact—and bring their containers to school. Students can use the objects as prompts to write or speak about their cultural self. Model the activity and encourage creativity by going first: it's important for students to see the whole you, too.

Snapshot 3.1 "Family Story Book" illustrates how a classroom assignment helped students and teachers get to know each other and their families.

Snapshot 3.1

FAMILY STORY BOOK

Atkinson Elementary School, Portland, Oregon

Grade level: 5

Subject area: Writing

Highlights: By writing personal poems and family stories, students and teachers learn about each other's lives and cultures.

Stephanie Windham's students at Atkinson Elementary School, located in southeast Portland, Oregon, have much to be proud of as they near the end of their Family Story Book project. This year, students wrote a story based on those told by their families, as well as a poem titled "I Am From." Each student chose one piece to take through the revision and publishing process.

The project is rigorous: "All the writing assignments during the year lead up to it. It demands more than most students have ever been asked to produce," says Windham. One student described her experience:

To me, writing is unlike anything else. It gives you a way to express your thoughts, feelings, and concerns. In this project, we had the opportunity to combine our writing skills with the information we learned about our families. . . . When we first started, I felt like I had nothing to work with, and sometimes I even felt like giving up on the story. But I decided to continue because I wanted to accomplish as much as I could in my last year at Atkinson. This book took six weeks to make, and a frustrating six weeks it was. Rewriting and revising the same story over and over again made the story seem dull and boring. When we had the finished product, we realized that all the time and effort was worth it.

Developing a Sense of Pride About Their Families and Their Lives

For many students, the project has been a transformational experience. While improving their writing skills and learning about the genre of story writing, the students have developed a sense of pride about their lives. Windham explains that one of her goals has become to "help students see their families as a source of pride and comfort." The students come from all over the globe, including China, Vietnam, Pakistan, the former Soviet Union, and countries in Latin America. By writing their own stories and hearing their classmates' stories, students have gained a global perspective and learned more about their families' histories and cultures.

Initially, Windham's goal was to find a way to get students to interact. The class did several activities to share aspects of their lives—for example, bringing an artifact from home or mapping where their family came from. Windham says, "After these activities they were just more of a community—they saw things that they shared. I said to myself, I need more of these kinds of things to help them appreciate that they are in a class full of wonderful kids that have a lot to contribute to their views of the world."

These activities led her to the idea for the Family Story Book. The project is completed in about six weeks, with students working every school day for 60 to 90 minutes.

While the work may not start until the spring, the anticipation and preparation begins in the first month of school. To immerse students in the genre, Windham shares copies of class books from the past few years, reading family stories written by former students. During the year, she also reads stories from the *Chicken Soup for the Soul* series and other short-story collections. During this reading time, students learn about the purpose of telling stories, and practice skills such as identifying the conflict in a story. They also discuss where the former students might have gotten their family stories. Then they recall their own family's storytelling habits—thinking about the family stories they have heard over the years, and taking notes on who tells the stories, whom they are about, where they take place, and what happens in the stories.

Perfecting Skills

During writing time in the classroom, Windham and her students were able to learn from the school's resident professional writer, Chris Weber. Weber spends 45 minutes in the classroom three to four times a week for most of the year, helping students develop their writing skills. During the book project, he visits daily. In one lesson, Windham and Weber demonstrate interviewing techniques for the students. They discuss the difference between closed and open-ended questions and model effective note taking. Some students are encouraged to use tape recorders during the interview. Students also are encouraged to return to the interviewee after the initial interview to ask more-detailed questions. When they've had sufficient preparation, students write a letter to a relative asking for specific interview times and form a list of questions.

As a new element this year, Windham introduced the "I Am From" poem, which she found in Linda Christensen's book (2000) *Reading, Writing, and Rising Up.*

Christensen describes a process for helping students create their own poems modeled after George Ella Lyon's poem, "Where I'm From." The class reads the poem and discusses it. They brainstorm their favorite foods, family sayings, celebrations, items found around their homes, people important to them, and places they like to visit. The brainstorming sessions lead to rich classroom conversation and sharing as Windham encourages students to dig deeper. As one student recalled, "We told a part of our life and Ms. Windham would say, 'How do you feel about it?' And, I think that was the hardest part, because sometimes you wouldn't know how you felt about things until you wrote them down."

These conversations built a foundation for lessons on using all five senses in writing, creating similes and metaphors, and crafting descriptive language. Then, after their discussions, the class analyzes each line to discover the details the author included: where she played, what foods she associated with growing up, expressions her family used. After the analysis, the students have a much clearer guide for creating unique, personal poems. They write about memories, objects, and experiences that illustrate who they are. Some of the resulting poems are humorous, some are about a specific place or event, but all richly illustrate the students' lives.

Students chose either their poem or family story to take through the revision and editing process for the class book (Figure 3.1). Once the children had the raw material for their stories or poems, they made outlines and wrote first drafts. There are several layers of revision that occur, each dependent on peer teamwork. Early in the year, Windham teaches students how to share their work, provide positive feedback, and maintain an atmosphere of trust. Laughing at or belittling someone is forbidden. Windham does the next level of editing.

(Continued)

(Continued)

Figure 3.1 Photo of Family Story Books

Windham uses the categories established by the Oregon Statewide Writing Assessment guidelines to assess the writing: ideas and content, organization, sentence fluency, conventions, voice, and word choice. Because the work will be published, students need to pay attention to punctuation and spelling, which can be a special challenge for Windham's English language learners. Windham has found that focusing on subject matter that excites her students' imaginations and generates enthusiasm will circumvent roadblocks caused by dread of writing and confusion over rules of grammar.

Creating Lasting Impressions

When the stories and poems are completed, Windham helps students make their books, using Japanese bookbinding techniques. In the end, each student has an anthology of the class's work, with each page telling a different story. When they take their book home at the end of the year, the children also take home all of their rough drafts, providing evidence of the writing process they traveled.

While Windham's intent is to focus her students' attention on the positive and uplifting aspects of their family histories, she noticed that the students frequently want to choose themes emphasizing hard times, the death of a family member, car accidents, or fights. While she understands the motivation behind these stories, she encourages students to think about how everyday experiences can be worth recording. She reads stories describing memories from her own childhood, rich in emotion and sensory detail. She has seen how this technique helps students see strengths in their families: "My students can relate to these stories on so many levels: a child's point of view, loneliness, 'when I'm big,' treats, grandparents, sharing. I can see it in their faces and the discussion afterward is always full of positive statements about similar experiences in their own families."

It is a powerful feeling to produce a work of art that creates a lasting impression—not just for the students, but also for their families. Students' families over the years have been extremely enthusiastic about the project. Windham enlists family members to assist with typing stories. The project creates an element of excitement among family members. When Windham gets siblings of prior years' pupils in her class, one of the first questions parents will ask is whether students are going to create the Family Story Book again this year. The stories, often about a parent, grandparent, aunt, or uncle, become family treasures. Family members, especially those unfamiliar with American schools, gain confidence and a better understanding of the education their child is getting. As an example, one father of a Russian student made a point to contact Windham after the project in order to tell her, in his struggling English, "It is good you teach this, having children come to ask their parents questions. You are teaching the right things."

The students are proud to have a finished product they have worked on for so long. They are excited about the information they have learned about their families, and eager to share it with their peers. Windham says, "It may be a lot of work, but the kids really do treasure it. It's one of those things where you spend the entire year trying to get the kids to remember all kinds of things like fractions—you cannot pick and choose what they will remember. But, the [Family Story Book] project is always remembered. It's always something that the kids come back and say something to me about. It's well worth all the work."

For Windham, the book project has been a culminating writing project that encourages students to celebrate who they are. On the last day of school, after desks and lockers are cleared out, Windham and her students have a pajama party with snacks and sleeping bags. One last time, they read to each other their stories and poems without feedback or comments, "it's just what it is."

Teachers elsewhere have used the "I Am From" poems described in Snapshot 3.1 "Family Story Book"—frequently at the beginning of each school year as a getting-to-know-you activity—with amazing results:

- Sixth-grade teacher Jennifer Tolton, at Blue Creek School in Billings, Montana, has students write "I Am From" poems in October. She shares the results with family members at the fall parent–teacher conferences. Tolton, who is new to the school, states, "It took some time for parents to really feel comfortable with a new teacher with their kids. The 'I Am From' poems made conversation with the parents really relaxed, because we were going over these funny things that the kids were interested in that surprised them. Sharing the poems made all the difference."
- Tamara Van Wyhe, a language arts teacher from Kenny Lake School in Copper Center, Alaska, also uses the "I Am From" poems to get to know her students and their families. "It is such a safe way to experience poetry," Van Wyhe explains. "Plus, it requires so much thought about what really matters in one's life and what the things are that have truly shaped the students into the individuals they have become."

CONNECTING WITH FAMILIES AND THE COMMUNITY

School staff may find it difficult to connect with families and the community to learn about local cultures. Some teachers live in one community and come into a different community to teach. Sometimes the students and their families live far from the school. Terry Cross (1995–1996, pp. 2–3), founder and director of the National Indian Child Welfare Association, suggests the following steps to learn more about a culture or community:

- Spend more time with strong, healthy people of that culture.
- Identify a cultural guide—that is, someone from the culture who is willing to discuss the culture, introduce you to new experiences, and help you understand what you are seeing. You can find bridges across cultures using translators, cultural liaisons, facilitators, tour guides, and hosts; some ESL teachers and paraprofessionals act as cultural brokers for immigrant or minority families and students throughout the curriculum.
- Spend time with the literature. Reading articles by and for persons of the culture is most helpful. Along with the professional literature, read the fiction. This is an enjoyable way to enter the culture in a safe, nonthreatening way. Find someone with whom you can discuss what you have read.
- Attend cultural events and meetings of leaders from within the culture. Cultural events allow you to observe people interacting in their community and see values in action. Observing leadership in action can impart a sense of the strength of the community and help you identify potential key informants and advisors.
- Finally, learn how to ask questions in sensitive ways. Most individuals are willing to answer all kinds of questions if the questioner is sincere and motivated by the desire to learn and serve the community more effectively.

Some additional activities to get to know your students and their families include visiting homes (see page 61), conducting home surveys, holding potlucks, creating family picture boards, planning cultural fairs, connecting with school or community family resource centers, and sharing family photo albums that students have created using their own disposable cameras. Snapshot 3.2 "Using Students' Writing to Build Relationships and Community" explores one language arts teacher's use of several strategies to get to know her students and to connect to their families and the community.

Tool 5 on page 59 "Self-Assessment on Student, Family, and Community Engagement and Connections" is designed to help you think about the skills and aptitudes you need to build healthy relationships with students, families, and communities.

Snapshot 3.2

USING STUDENTS' WRITING TO BUILD RELATIONSHIPS AND COMMUNITY

Kenny Lake School, Copper Center, Alaska

Grade levels: Junior and senior high school

Subject area: Language arts

Highlights: Using poetry as a means to get to know your students and their families

Rich symbolism paints a vivid picture of the relationship between a young woman and her mother in the poem "Broken House." The piece is so descriptive and powerful that the reader can see the strife between the two women, hear the sounds of their struggle, and feel the author's pain over the destruction of a family and their home.

Such honesty and personal insights from a 17-year-old student make the reader wonder what the teacher did so her students feel comfortable enough to write that way.

Tamara Van Wyhe, a language arts teacher, knows the importance of a trusting relationship in promoting good writing. "Students know I want them to reveal their true selves in their writing—who they really are, not what others want them to be or might see them as. They know I value their honest voices, so they write very openly."

Van Wyhe teaches junior and senior high school students at Kenny Lake School, a rural K–12 school in Copper Center, Alaska, which is nestled between the Copper and Klutina rivers about 200 miles northeast of Anchorage. With only about 120 students, who are both Alaska Native and Caucasian, the teachers at Kenny Lake get to know their students well. Van Wyhe tries to learn as much as she can about all of her students and works hard to create a safe learning environment where students can use their experiences to better understand themselves and their relationship to the world, encouraging them to use these experiences as a basis for their writing.

"Broken House," by Tonia Goodlataw

We took apart the house, section

By section, hating how easy it was

To break, how quickly everything fell down.

The breaking of the key became

The breaking of the door, which made

The frame crumble to the floor.

We tried to patch it back together,

But what was broken could not be fixed.

We held nothing but heartache

In our slivered hands. We did this as

The boys watched and learned,

Watching every action turn into

A reaction. We let them holler

While we ripped and shredded,

Putting each piece in a secret closet,

Just letting it pile up. While

Everyone looked away, my mom and

I sat and watched everything shatter, a Family now was broken.

Building Relationships and Community

Van Wyhe has found that writing can help build positive relationships between students and their families, between the school and the community, between her and her students, and between her and her students' families. Through her students' writings, Van Wyhe has developed a greater understanding of the strengths of their families and how they support their children's learning. This new knowledge has even changed the focus of her parent newsletter—moving away from "Look what the school is doing for your child" to "Thank you for all you are doing to help your child learn."

"In my classroom, we write a lot about how family, culture, and community influence who we are because the rural Alaskan environment shapes students in such powerful ways," Van Wyhe explains. After reading *The Education of Little Tree* by Forrest Carter, the students create personal timelines and write about learning experiences that occurred outside school. The students think deeply about what they learn from others, often realizing that those "others" are usually family members, elders, or community members.

Always looking for ways to include parents and the community, Van Wyhe shares the students' writing in an annual anthology. Students from all grades submit favorite pieces they have written throughout the year. Then a student committee chooses pieces for inclusion, edits the writing, and designs the layout and cover, thereby creating a unique compilation that both is meaningful to the students and provides a place to apply skills required as part of Alaska's language arts standards. Poems from the book are read aloud during the annual "Arts

(Continued)

(Continued)

Night," which is one of the most popular school events. Many community members purchase copies of the anthology during Arts Night and have students autograph their work. The PTA shows how proud they are of the students' accomplishments by sponsoring the project and ensuring that each published author receives a copy of the anthology. (Figure 3.2 shows the cover of the anthology for the 2003–2004 school year, which contains the poem "Broken House.")

In addition to bringing the community into the school, Van Wyhe brings the school into the community. The public library hosts a monthly "First Friday" event where community members recite their own material or read something that has particular meaning to them. Van Wyhe takes students to these events to share their work. Students and community members learn from each other as they interact on a regular basis at these meetings.

Van Wyhe believes it makes a significant difference if education—especially language arts—is real and meaningful to the students. She writes, "If, as Robert Frost suggested, being a poet 'is a condition, not a profession,' then I believe it is important to encourage students to try their hands at writing verse. If being a poet is 'a condition' that allows one to capture experience and make sense of life, then it seems to me all students should graduate with a full understanding of the benefits of this learned 'condition.' It is my sincere hope that all the student writers at Kenny Lake School will leave this place suffering from the wonderful condition known as 'being a poet,' regardless of what it is they are writing."

"I am a poet!" Those four simple words—not a question, nor a hesitant statement, but a declaration—appear in one eleventh-grade student's journal. It serves as a testament to the power of Van Wyhe's teaching. By writing about memories, tears of pain, and shouts of joy, Kenny Lake students capture their experiences, strengthen their relationships, and make sense of their lives.

Figure 3.2   Anthology of Student Poetry

TOOL 5

SELF-ASSESSMENT ON STUDENT, FAMILY, AND COMMUNITY ENGAGEMENT AND CONNECTIONS

Read each of the statements on the self-assessment and rate yourself. Then complete the reflection questions that follow. Think about the areas where you are very capable and the areas where you need improvement, and set learning goals. Before you begin the assessment, remember that it is not a test and there are no wrong answers: it is merely a tool to help you grow in your CRSB practices. Assess yourself periodically to check for growth.

Rating scale: D = Developing, M = Meeting, E = Exceeding

Student, Family, and Community Engagement and Connections	D	M	E
I understand and am sensitive to changing definitions of family.	☐	☐	☐
I know the cultural backgrounds of my students.	☐	☐	☐
I know the norms and values of the cultures of my students and their families.	☐	☐	☐
I can identify the cultural strengths, supports, and barriers for each of my students.	☐	☐	☐
I feel comfortable bringing my students' home, family, and community culture into the classroom teaching practices and curriculum.	☐	☐	☐
I communicate clearly, effectively, and in culturally appropriate ways with my students and their families.	☐	☐	☐
The lessons, activities, and learning materials used in my classroom will help my students to better understand and negotiate cultural differences.	☐	☐	☐
My classroom lessons and activities foster an abundance of meaningful relationships among and between people (i.e., myself, students, parents, community members, other teachers in the building).	☐	☐	☐
My classroom lessons and activities foster an abundance of meaningful relationships among and between systems (i.e., the student/family and school, the school and community, the family and community).	☐	☐	☐
When I plan lessons that have strong student, family, or community connections, I involve students, families, or community members in lesson development.	☐	☐	☐
I find ways to connect my classroom lessons and activities to larger school, district, or community initiatives that are related to culture and cultural competence.	☐	☐	☐

(Continued)

(Continued)

Reflections on my knowledge about student, family, and community connections:

What strengths do you have related to student, family, and community engagement and connections that will enable you to bring your students' home, family, or community culture into your classroom?

_____

_____

_____

Which competency areas need improvement?

_____

_____

_____

What could you do to improve in those areas (i.e., read a specific book, take a workshop or course, get a mentor, observe other teachers, practice with reflection)?

_____

_____

_____

Choose one area for improvement and make a plan of action to address it.

_____

_____

_____

Home Visiting: Getting To Know Students and Connecting With Families

Home visiting is a powerful strategy for both fully understanding your students and connecting with their families. Many teachers do home visits beyond the primary grades, and most are enthusiastic about the positive impact visits have on all aspects of teaching and learning in the classroom and at home. Many students act differently at home than at school—so seeing students in their own homes helps teachers get to know their true personalities, learning styles, interests, and strengths.

Kyle and McIntyre (2000) state, "Knowing the students' outside interests, families, and home routines, and then using this information to connect in meaningful ways, can have huge rewards in helping to construct happier, healthier, and smarter kids." Teachers often use the information discovered on home visits as the basis of curriculum topics or for selecting books for the students to read.

Through home visits it is possible to see how a family's culture is uniquely manifested. Values, interaction styles, and parenting approaches all become evident. Seeing and using the style of verbal and nonverbal interaction—or discourse—that you observe in the home can be a very important way to connect and communicate with a student. Kyle and McIntyre (2000) report on a teacher who realized during a home visit that her indirect communication style ("Are you ready to open your books and read?") contrasted sharply with the direct communication style of the family ("Sit down and eat"). She realized that what she had interpreted as noncompliant behavior had been a miscommunication, leading to a misunderstanding. Consequently, she changed the way she spoke to the student (and many other students) in the class.

The prospect of conducting home visits can present many concerns for teachers. However, knowing a few key strategies for conducting successful home visits will allay most of those concerns. For instance, finding time for home visits is one challenge faced by many teachers. Among the solutions that teachers have used are conducting parent conferences during home visits, and using staff development time or faculty meeting time for these visits.

Another concern expressed by some is not speaking the home language of the student's family and not having the resources to pay for a translator. Many families have a relative or friend who they can rely on for translation. Although some ask the student to act as translator, it is best to find an alternative solution. When children act as translators, it often disrupts the balance of power in the household.

A positive attitude is one critical factor for successful home visits: Be open and interested in learning about the student and family, and consider family members to be the experts on their child. Engage in discussion and dialogue; share some of your own experiences (i.e., parent–teacher relationships forged for your own children), and be positive. Look for family strengths and uniqueness. Be open to the family's suggestions and questions. Be flexible and try not to get locked into an agenda.

The most successful home visits are voluntary. Family members need to know that these visits are purely optional. Family members also like to know the purpose in advance—for example, to answer any questions or concerns the family may have about school, or to get to know the family and student better. Whenever possible, send a list of discussion topics ahead of time or provide them over the phone. Although many families feel more comfortable talking with teachers on their own turf than on the school's turf, some prefer to meet at school or in a neutral place.

Arrange for the home visit ahead of time, but not more than three weeks in advance. Ask to come at a time when you can meet as many immediate family members who are significantly involved with the student as possible, including parents, siblings, grandparents, aunts, uncles, and cousins. Keep the time of the visit short—about half an hour—but be prepared to spend more time if everyone feels comfortable. Therefore, do not schedule a visit with another family immediately after this visit. Call the family the day before to remind them of the scheduled visit, and again just before going to their home to make sure the time is still convenient for them.

"Families 'own' the teacher when they come to their house," Lynne Shlom Ferguson, principal of Arleta Elementary School in Portland, Oregon, explained in an interview. Many of Arleta's early primary teachers do home visits in August. By the time the children arrive in September, they know their teacher and they see photographs of themselves on the wall along with the goals that they have set for the year (with assistance from their families and teacher). Ferguson believes this sense of deep connection between families and teachers—which she calls "ownership"—is a "huge variable" in the success of the school. Although 73 percent of the students are from low-income families and 25 percent of the students are ESL, Arleta has been rated as a "strong" school by the Oregon Department of Education for the previous several years. In spring 2003, 82 percent of third- and fifth-grade students met or exceeded state benchmarks in reading.

Districtwide support of home visiting is rare in these times of tight budgets and basics-only education. However, districts in Sacramento, California; Columbus, Ohio; and Kansas City, Missouri, have all attempted to put in place a districtwide initiative regarding home visiting (Delisio, 2008). In almost all cases, the impetus comes from a community group interested in forging stronger home–school ties as part of a larger reform effort. It is often funded by a foundation or other "outside" funding and is rarely sustained for long. This is in spite of near-universal acclaim for its value from school staff and parents.

Jo-Lynn Nemeth, principal of McCoy Elementary School in Kansas City, Missouri, strongly believes that home visits are an essential element of any school reform effort. "It's something schools could and should do if they are serious about improvement, increasing attendance, and increasing parent conference attendance. . . . It's the best relationship builder you can have. We now have 90 percent attendance at parent conferences" (Delisio, 2008).

Resources on Home Visiting

Many excellent resources on home visiting are available from the following sources:

Education World (specifically district-level home visit initiatives; www.educationworld.com/a_admin/admin/admin342.shtml)

Center for Home Visiting, University of North Carolina (www.unc.edu/~uncchv)

North Central Regional Educational Laboratory (www.ncrel.org/sdrs/areas/issues/envrnmnt/famncomm/pa41k6.htm)

Parent Teacher Home Visit Project (www.pthvp.org)

Tool 6 "Home Visiting: Getting to Know Students and Connecting With Families" provides suggested discussion points and factors to observe.

— **TOOL 6** —

HOME VISITING: GETTING TO KNOW STUDENTS AND CONNECTING WITH FAMILIES

Before the Visit

- Talk about home visits with all your students in class and explain what you hope to get from them. This allows the students to prepare.
- Arrange for the home visit with the family about three weeks prior to the visit.
- Set up a family board to post family pictures and stories from home visits.
- Explain the purpose (verbally and in writing) and length of the visit.
- Provide a list of some questions or discussion points.
- Call the day before as a reminder.
- Call just before going to make sure it is still convenient for the family.

Remember

- Your purpose for visiting is to get to know the families and students better.
- Home visits should be voluntary for all families.
- Families are the experts on their student.
- Provide a translator if you do not speak the language.
- Look for ways to weave the themes that come out of home activities, interactions, and stories into the classroom activities.
- Observe how the family provides for learning activities such as reading, studying, playing, and discussing. Think about how you can use this information to inform your curriculum and homework assignments.

Discussion Points

- What are your child's strengths, interests, hobbies? Ask for more information about anything that you notice in the environment that reflects the family's values or interests.
- What are family activities that you use to teach your child?
- What should I know about your child to teach him or her well?
- How does your child play and communicate with other children? Adults?
- What are your goals for your child this year? What are your aspirations for your child?
- What would you like to know about the school or classroom?
- What is the best way to communicate with you? How often would you like to communicate?
- How can we best work together to benefit your child?
- What are some of the challenges or concerns you have regarding your child?
- What are some challenges or concerns you have regarding the school?
- Are there any helpful resources, materials, or ideas that I might be able to get for you?
- What are some ways you can assist the school or our classroom? Do you have particular skills, knowledge, or abilities that you would like to share?

After the Visit

- Send a thank-you note to the home and include in it all the things you learned and hope to do with the class as a result of your visit.
- Within a week, send home any follow-up materials promised or a note explaining when the family should receive them.

POWERFUL RELATIONSHIPS CAN BE TRANSFORMATIONAL

By getting to know students and families on a personal level, and bringing that information into the curriculum, teachers are better able to facilitate transformational teaching and learning.

Through transformational teaching and learning, students and instructors experience a change in their points of view, and begin to value and respect things and people they may not have valued or respected before. Students learn more about themselves and others and see their place in the world. Because teachers use the lives and cultures of the students, their families, and the community as subjects worthy of study and create learning opportunities from everyone in the class (not solely from what is in textbooks), the students consider themselves, family members, and fellow students as sources of information and knowledge. Teachers and students are given opportunities to understand how cultural experience is integrated into an individual's life.

In transformational teaching and learning, the role of the teacher is transformed from instructor to facilitator when the curriculum is created with students' input and is shaped by their experiences, perspectives, and interests. When teachers shape the curriculum around the students and their lives, students are able to make authentic connections and to construct meaning. Students are more likely to become active participants in their learning and take responsibility for the types and depth of knowledge gained. And because the curriculum is based on "real-life issues," it provides ways to integrate and organize learning across subject areas and enhances the transfer of knowledge from one academic task to another, from subject to subject, and from school to outside life.

The curriculum is transformed as the subject matter is examined from many different perspectives—especially the students' perspectives—in ways that promote growth and discovery. When the curriculum includes critical thinking, students can see themselves and others equally, accurately, and more realistically represented. They question established practices and assumptions. Through an examination of the historical experiences and contemporary issues of multiple cultural groups, students come to understand that they have the right to ask questions and that they ultimately have the power to change society. Thus, students experience culture not only as a point of affirmation and celebration, but also as a source of influence and power.

Snapshot 3.3 "AASK What You Can Do for Your Community" describes how one Oregon school created a tutoring program to transform the lives of its middle and high school students and the lives of the elementary students they tutor. Careful attention to bridging the cultural divide between the tutors and their students is one factor that has made the program a success. Following the snapshot is Tool 7 "Self-Assessment on Transformational Teaching and Learning" (page 69), which is designed to help you think about the skills and aptitudes related to transformational teaching and learning that are necessary to successfully implement CRSB practices.

Snapshot 3.3

AASK WHAT YOU CAN DO FOR YOUR COMMUNITY

Oregon Episcopal School, Portland, Oregon

Grade levels: 3–5, tutored by middle and high school students

Subject areas: Mainly reading, writing, and math

Highlights: This tutoring program has a special focus to increase the English skills, academic achievement, and resiliency of elementary students with limited English proficiency, while providing middle and high school students with an opportunity to teach and serve in their own community.

Creative extension: Because of its success, AASK is now working with some of the same students after they have moved on to middle school. AASK has also expanded its tutoring base by partnering with a local public high school to provide more mentors for students.

Giving Back to the Community

In his inaugural address in 1961, President John F. Kennedy challenged the American people with these words: "Ask not what your country can do for you—ask what you can do for your country." Oregon Episcopal School (OES), a private school in Portland that is more than 140 years old, asks the same of its staff and students. The school's mission is to prepare students with promise for higher education and lifelong learning and to enhance their intellectual, physical, social, emotional, spiritual, and artistic growth so that students realize their power for good as citizens of local and world communities. Two guiding principles that help OES realize its mission are to

- facilitate contributions to society by undertaking programs of outreach and service to others; and
- build community, relying on the contributions of students, faculty and staff, families, parents, alumni, trustees, the parish congregation, and the community at large.

Believing that community involvement is necessary to carrying out this mission, OES formed a partnership with Vose Elementary School that provides opportunities for academic achievement and enrichment, skill development, personal growth, and multicultural competence for all participants.

What Is AASK?

AASK stands for "Aardvarks Advocate Skills and Knowledge." (The aardvark is the OES mascot; see Figure 3.3.) During the school year, AASK provides trained tutors from the middle and high schools for one-to-one tutoring with students at Vose Elementary School. Twice-weekly sessions after school, lasting 50 minutes each, focus on increasing skills in reading, writing, and math. During the summer, AASK provides a four-week ESL Summer Learning Program (day camp) for intensive ESL instruction, as well as experiential learning with classroom, nature, sports, art, and computer activities. Tutoring, combined with day camp and classroom work throughout the year, have helped Vose students gain an average of two grade levels of reading skills each year.

(Continued)

(Continued)

Figure 3.3   AASK

AASK also has partnered sixth-graders from OES with students from Vose to plan and carry out service learning projects that can make their world a better place. Every three weeks, they meet to develop their projects, work on writing skills related to the projects, and have a lot of fun! The OES Spanish III students also read in Spanish to Vose first-graders and help Vose second-graders in their science classes.

Preparing Tutors to Work With Others

"As you can tell from the program description, there could be and are many pitfalls in this kind of adventure, but what makes it all so much fun are the relationships between the young people and how much they have to give each other. It is definitely a two-way street for learning and for feeling rewarded for the effort," says AASK Director Myra Clark. "I have learned tons, but have tons more to learn about facilitating true partnerships in which everyone brings resources and a definite cultural viewpoint to the partnership table."

OES, an independent pre-K–12 school, has a 59-acre campus in the southwestern hills of Portland. It offers an enriched academic experience for college-bound students. OES provides cultural and outdoor experiences to both day students from the Portland area and boarding students from the Northwest and around the world—including students from Asia, Europe, the Middle East, Africa, and representing countries such as Rwanda, Korea, Taiwan, China, and Japan.

Because of their family backgrounds, most of the tutors are working with students from cultures that are very different from their own. Sixty percent of the Vose students are English language learners, and 87 percent are from families with incomes below the poverty line. One OES student said of AASK, "I usually share with people how much I love AASK and tell them it is a great experience. You learn so much about an area of Portland, and a different culture and people in a totally different situation than you are in."

To help build a bridge between these two worlds, Clark has created a six-hour training for the tutors before they are paired with a student to mentor. The tutor training sessions focus on preparing students to work with others from a different cultural background. Training is infused with information and experiences to illustrate the intercultural aspects of the program:

- Opening warm-ups include learning each other's names with activities on the origin and meaning of participants' names and how people identify culturally.
- Paper-folding and tearing exercises demonstrate the uniqueness of each person and different learning styles.
- "Elements of Culture" exercises.
- An introduction to intercultural sensitivity and its stages of development.
- Key reasons intercultural relationships work taking time to get to know others, adapting behavior to acknowledge the viewpoints that are different from one's own.
- Sessions on "what makes a good tutor" emphasizing building a bridge between the tutor and tutee, along with positive regard, respect, and a balance between work and fun.
- "Expectations" includes encouragement to advance intercultural understanding and to adapt behavior.

Making AASK more student centered was also part of Clark's vision. The program formed a six-member student advisory council with previous experience tutoring or staffing the summer day camp. They meet weekly and advise Clark on all aspects of the program that pertain to OES students. The advisory council also recruits and trains new tutors. Because of the group's involvement and input, AASK is more responsive to the needs of the tutors and the students with whom they work.

Benefits of AASK

The partnership with Vose Elementary School allows OES students to discover skills, talents, and interests that might not surface in regular classroom situations. Even when the tutors do not see dramatic improvements in the students they are tutoring, they still learn about themselves and their world. "They learn how to take responsibility and to make a commitment to another person. They learn about being patient, and about seeing things from another person's point of view. They also learn how to have authority—not just to be a friend, but to be somebody who gives a child direction," Clark says. "Another big lesson is how to put somebody else first."

One OES student said, "AASK has reinforced the fact that I really like working with people. I want a career that is focused on helping people be in a better place in their life, which is like what I am doing with AASK . . . trying to help my student academically and emotionally by helping him be more confident."

Another OES student wrote, "For me, AASK isn't about getting credit. I would not be here if it weren't for the kids." One participant said, "AASK is an important opportunity to step outside of OES and work with others. Especially in light of recent events [9/11/2001], I think it is going to be essential for us to feel this connection to our communities."

(Continued)

(Continued)

A tutor described how, through the mentoring process, she got to know her Vose student and how that changed her outlook about people. "This child with little family time, struggling grades, and little money was able to teach me more about my own life than many people ever have. I have become more aware of the fact that people should not be judged by the amount of money in their bank accounts, but by their love for others and their desire to become a better, stronger person in the world. In the end, I know he taught me just as much as I taught him."

For Vose students, the impact of AASK can be seen in their improvements in reading, writing, and math skills. The Vose principal has also reported decreased turnover rates in his student body—parents want to make sure they find housing in the Vose district so their children can continue in the AASK program. For OES students, their involvement in the AASK program has taught them the intrinsic value of doing for others and giving back to their community.

To learn more about the AASK Program, visit www.oes.edu/AASK.

Figure 3.4   An AASK tutor helps a fifth-grader with reading

Photo by Myra Clark.

TOOL 7

SELF-ASSESSMENT ON TRANSFORMATIONAL TEACHING AND LEARNING

Read each of the statements on the self-assessment and rate yourself. Think about the areas where you are very capable and the areas where you need improvement, and set learning goals. Before you begin the assessment, remember that it is not a test and there are no wrong answers: it is merely a tool to help grow in your CRSB practices. Assess yourself periodically to check for growth.

Rating scale: D = Developing, M = Meeting, E = Exceeding

Transformational Teaching and Learning	D	M	E
I understand cognitive, social, physical, and emotional development as it pertains to my students.	☐	☐	☐
I have high academic and social expectations for all my students, regardless of their cultural backgrounds.	☐	☐	☐
I help youth identify their strengths, and I teach from a strengths-based perspective.	☐	☐	☐
I have a good understanding of the history and contemporary issues faced by many cultural groups.	☐	☐	☐
I help my students to understand how they learn best and encourage them to take leadership in their own learning.	☐	☐	☐
I create opportunities for parents to reflect on and give input about their students' learning.	☐	☐	☐
The lessons I teach help my students to develop higher-order thinking skills such as critical thinking, planning, management, problem solving, and independent questioning.	☐	☐	☐
The lessons I teach encourage students to look at an issue or problem from multiple perspectives and connect meaning in those multiple perspectives.	☐	☐	☐
The lessons and activities I teach are culturally relevant and connected to the lives of my students and their home, family, and community culture.	☐	☐	☐
I help my students to take the social and academic lessons learned in the classroom and apply them to the world outside the classroom.	☐	☐	☐

Reflections on my knowledge about transformational teaching and learning:

Snapshot 3.4 "Belief in Action" describes a project initiated by a courageous teacher that resulted in transformational learning among middle school students about two major (challenging and sensitive) issues of our time: religious tolerance and equality.

Snapshot 3.4

BELIEF IN ACTION: A CLASSROOM UNIT ON THE EXPLORATION OF FAITH

Asheville Middle School, Asheville, North Carolina

Grade levels: 7–8 grade

Subject areas: Social studies, language arts

Highlights: Middle school teacher promotes the exploration of faith and culture in a social studies unit starting with his students' lives and ending with discussions on field trips to centers of faith, culminating in the bridging of understanding the role of religion for people of many cultures.

Teaching Tolerance, a project founded in 1991 by the Southern Poverty Law Center, has a wealth of classroom lessons, units, and whole school activities focusing on bridging cultures within the education system. One example, entitled "A Pilgrimage to Atlanta" by language arts and social studies teacher Reid Chapman at Asheville Middle School in Asheville, North Carolina, describes his unit of study on the world's major religions for his seventh-grade social studies students. The goal was to learn about the "influence of religions, beliefs, and values of life" and to be able to compare the major religions of the Eastern Hemisphere, while integrating language arts. The students, who were predominantly of Christian and Jewish faiths, live in Asheville, a community where the Jewish population, the growing Muslim population, and the small Buddhist population are beginning to catch up to the number of Christians. He hoped that his students would come face to face with other cultures, acknowledge various traditions, and recognize these customs as equally meaningful and unique to their own.

Chapman prepared himself by seeking advice from local clergy on potentially challenging issues—both to clarify their beliefs and to help him in selecting stories that fully inform readers about each religious tradition. He attended services at a nondenominational Christian church, meditation meetings at the Zen Center, and the feast at a mosque that marks the end of the Ramadan fast for Muslims. The people he interacted with at these sites became important resources for his unit, opening his eyes to the rich religious tapestry of his city.

Chapman began the unit by examining with students the role of religion in people's lives, asking questions such as, "What purpose does religion serve? What does it do for individuals? What do they get out of it?" Then, after studying the tenets and traditions of Buddhism, Christianity, Hinduism, Islam, and Judaism, students, in groups, chose one religion to study in depth. They also honed their literary analysis skills by identifying devices such as similes and metaphors. He saw this as an excellent opportunity to explore the origin of religious allusions students might encounter in their study of literature, particularly in the literature of Africa and Asia. Understanding religious stories introduces readers to central concepts of the religion and helps them better understand what motivates their members. With this foundation, they continued by examining the various religions one by one. Using texts, encyclopedias, and other resources, they collected a common set of data for each faith tradition.

They also discussed agnosticism and atheism, pointing out that not all people believe in God or participate in a religion. Some people join a secular group or adopt an ideology for many of the same reasons others turn to religion. They also found that in the study of one religion, one continually comes across concepts that seem irrational because religious faith is based on the belief in the unseen—that is, on faith.

In order to see belief in action and gain an understanding of the role of religion in the community, the last part of the project involved a day-long journey to various religious centers in nearby Atlanta, Georgia. The first stops were historical: Ebenezer Baptist Church (Dr. Martin Luther King's home church, now under the care of the National Park Service) and "The Temple" (formally, the Hebrew Benevolent Congregation built in 1931) that was bombed in 1958 because it was a center of civil rights activity. These sites gave them a sample of how religious institutions often have to grapple with worldly issues. They also visited a Hindu temple and the Al-Farooq Masjid (mosque).

Students reported that their visit to the mosque and its Dar-Un-Noor Academy was their most meaningful experience. In one encounter, a Dar-Un-Noor student, a 12-year-old girl wearing the *hijab,* or head scarf, typical of a devout Muslim woman,

asked the pointed question, "If you saw me at the mall, would you think I looked stupid?" Her frank question resonated with the students, as the Asheville girls processed the daring question that seemed to cut to the heart of all the issues they had talked about. Then one girl replied, "Well, no—I would think that that was just how you were, what your culture was like. I would think it was how your parents raised you, to dress like that. I wouldn't think it was bad, and I would respect you for it. Just like I hope you would see that my parents raised me to be like this and that would be OK, too."

The opportunity for open dialogue at the mosque offered his students a means of understanding differences and the importance of not seeing one group's way as right and another's as wrong. It was a safe setting to honestly discuss issues of religious diversity. Chapman observes, "Rather than trip over our own perceptions and suspicions, we got a chance to see face to face how these students addressed their faith and 'otherness.'"

"I didn't just learn about religions and what the people believe," said one student. "I learned something a little more in depth: Nobody likes to be different. Most of the people we met—not *saw* but *met*—would be considered different from the majority of U.S. citizens. The Muslim teenagers were just like me and my friends. I realized that what I used to think of as a strict religion—and horrible rules to abide by—is just a way of life for some people."

Another observed, "I learned to expect different ideas and different ways of doing things for each religion. I observed that no matter what religion, race, or culture you are, everyone has feelings. Lessons such as these cast a whole new light on how we view "others."

For more information on the unit "A Pilgrimage to Atlanta," go to Belief In Action at http://www.tolerance.org/print/magazine/number-20-fall-2001/belief-action

Adapted from *Teaching Tolerance*, http://www.teachingtolerance.org.

REFLECTION QUESTIONS

1. What surprised you while you completed the tools for this chapter? What questions were you not able to answer and why?

2. When you were a student, did you have a strong personal connection with a teacher? What did he or she do? How did he or she teach? What was it about that teacher that made the connection? How did the connection impact your learning?

3. What are some ways that teachers can build relationships with their students—especially teachers who have many students (like those in middle and high school)?

4. When you were a student, was there something about you or your family that you did not want anyone at school to know? Why? What could the school have done to make it safe for you to share this information?

5. If you asked the parents of your students what you should know about their child in order to be a more effective teacher, what might they say?

6. What assumptions have students or their families made about you based on some aspect of your culture (e.g., ethnicity, class, gender, age) that were wrong or limiting? What did you do, or what can you do in the future, to interrupt these assumptions?

7. If you wanted someone to know more about your culture, what would you suggest they do? What questions should they ask? Who should they talk with? What books, music, art, and so forth should they access?

8. Review the reflections in this chapter on cultural pluralism, cultural awareness, and treasuring everyone's culture. Write your own reflection that describes your journey to becoming more culturally aware or culturally responsive.

9. What are some "stories" your students hold about school, schooling, and educational achievement?

10. What more do you need to know about your students' families' past experiences with education in order to be able to teach them more effectively and to build relationships? How can you access the information you need?

11. Sometimes an aspect of a student's home or community culture is viewed negatively in the school setting (e.g., slang, dress, musical tastes, interest in pop culture). How can it be turned into something positive at school? How can it be used as part of a standards-based learning experience?

12. Are there certain groups of students that your school or district is not serving well? How can you use the information in this book to improve the situation?

13. Have you ever had a transformation on teaching or learning experience? What happened and why?

14. Pick one of the snapshots from this chapter (3.1 "Family Story Book," 3.2 "Using Students' Writing to Build Relationships and Community," 3.3 "AASK What You Can Do for Your Community," or 3.4 "Belief in Action"). Describe how you could use one or more of the strategies in this snapshot to get to know your students and their families better.

4

The Environment for Culturally Responsive Standards-Based Teaching

Without clear connection and conversation across differences, we have little hope of building the respectful relationships upon which equitable learning depends.

—Gary R. Howard (2003)

When visitors walk into Cherry Valley School, located on the Flathead Indian Reservation in Polson, Montana, they see a permanent tepee in the lobby adorned with Kootenai words and symbols. They're greeted by photographs of local chiefs of the Salish and Kootenai tribes on the school walls. They may notice signs promoting culturally relevant Family Fun Nights at the school and an annual "Celebration of Families" powwow.

"The message," says Principal Elaine Meeks, "is that this school belongs to *every* child and family." According to Meeks, creating a positive school environment, as seen through the eyes of *each* child, is essential to convey the school's overriding belief: "*Every* child counts." Cherry Valley has even come up with an inventive way to share school events with family members who may not be able to be involved in their child's classroom. Fostering cooperation rather than competition among children and staff creates a climate in which everyone is encouraged to help solve problems, share expertise, listen respectfully, and resolve conflicts openly and honestly. The Cherry Valley faculty considers this emphasis on teamwork and community to be a crucial element in the school's continually evolving understanding and implementation of culturally responsive teaching. (To learn more about Cherry Valley, see Snapshot 4.1 "CVTV: Cherry Valley News.")

This chapter gives tips, ideas, and tools for creating a physical and emotional environment that will encourage CRSB teaching and learning. It discusses the first two points on the Continuum of Options and Opportunities for CRSB Teaching (Figure 1.3, page 21): (1) incorporating culturally relevant materials into the environment and engaging students in conversation and (2) fully engaging students in conversation about their home, family, or community culture.

While these two points are on the "less-complex" side of the continuum, all points are important for CRSB teaching and learning. These two items can pave the way for the development of more-complex CRSB strategies by giving teachers important information about their students and how to reach them.

Snapshot 4.1

CVTV: CHERRY VALLEY NEWS

Cherry Valley Elementary School, Polson, Montana

Grade levels: Participants are 3–4, users are K–4

Subject areas: Public speaking, journalism

Highlights: Originally planned as a literacy project, the videos have become a unique way to communicate with parents and to document school activities.

Creative extension: A high school video production class could edit and produce the monthly video.

As a picture of the school is displayed on the screen, the announcer booms, "This is CVTV, Cherry Valley News, with third-graders Erica and Dante!" The two smiling anchors sit with their hands folded in front of them on the table. They greet their viewers much as any professional news anchor would, and begin reading the school news for the month of March.

But Erica and Dante don't just read the news. Video clips and digital photographs of a wide variety of engaging school activities bring the stories to life: a snowshoe trip to Glacier Park, a pet show, Book Characters' Dress-Up Day, a community powwow, the annual art show, a music concert and talent show, and a celebratory lunch for teachers.

The anchors make announcements, such as the winners of the tribal education teacher, student, and parent of the year (congratulated with a message from Principal Elaine Meeks). The final story highlights student and teacher birthdays for the month, with a background soundtrack of the students singing "Happy Birthday." The anchors do an official sign-off, and then—as the camera pulls away—viewers overhear their "informal chat," complimenting the background display of the school's mascot made by one classroom.

The news reports, complete with scripts and edited soundtrack of popular music, are produced by Cherry Valley teachers. The video footage for the 20-minute newscasts is taped by students, teachers, parents, and other volunteers. Videos show examples of student work and cover school events and family involvement activities. Consistent with the school's philosophy, recognition is given to event organizers and participants in each story.

The project was originally conceived as a literacy project for students. Third- and fourth-grade students take turns as anchors, and, once a month, the video is transmitted into each classroom. Students benefit from the opportunity to practice presentation and public speaking skills, and are engaged by an activity that their families and classmates will see. As students watch their fellow anchors, they learn to make good eye contact and to use expressive voices to describe the "five W's": Who? What? When? Where? and Why? of the events. In addition, the project is student centered—it gives students the opportunity to see themselves and their work at school as worthy of notice, providing evidence of the learning engaged in by a community of students, staff, and families. The videos show a school climate where each student and his individual culture is included, valued, and appreciated.

Teachers realize that the videos are a nice showcase of the school and its family involvement activities. After watching the news together as a class, students can check out a video to take home and share with their families, just like the popular Traveling Books students already bring home daily. The tapes have turned out to be an excellent way to let parents know what is happening in school, especially those who may not be able to attend family events there. Teachers have found that some parents have felt more comfortable coming to the school, getting a better idea of what to expect after seeing pictures and video clips of what happens at school events.

To get a sense of the strong family/community focus at Cherry Valley, see the school's website: www.polson.k12.mt.us/cherry/

INCORPORATING CULTURALLY RESPONSIVE MATERIALS INTO THE ENVIRONMENT

What students see in their school and classroom environment gives them important clues about what is and is not valued by their teachers. A culturally responsive environment can help students feel a sense of belonging and emotional safety, opening the door to learning. What is not seen in the physical environment can be as powerful a statement as what *is* seen. The challenge for educators is to provide materials and ideas that reflect the cultures of the children, youth, and adults in the school community, while eliminating stereotypic and inaccurate materials from daily use (Derman-Sparks & the A.B.C. Task Force, 1989).

Tool 8 "Self-Assessment on Classroom Environment" can help you examine the environment that exists in your classroom.

TOOL 8

SELF-ASSESSMENT ON CLASSROOM ENVIRONMENT

Read each of the statements on the self-assessment and rate yourself, then complete the reflection questions that follow. Think about the areas where you are very capable and the areas where you need improvement, and set learning goals. Before you begin the assessment, remember that it is not a test and there are no wrong answers: it is merely a tool to help you grow in your CRSB practices. Assess yourself periodically to check for growth.

Rating scale: D = Developing, M = Meeting, E = Exceeding

Classroom Environment	D	M	E
My classroom environment reflects the cultures of the young people I work with.	☐	☐	☐
The texts that I use are culturally inclusive.	☐	☐	☐
My classroom incorporates multiple perspectives and materials that provide alternative explanations and worldviews.	☐	☐	☐
I have literature in the classroom that authentically depicts various cultures (race, family structures, gender, religion, socioeconomic background).	☐	☐	☐
I feel comfortable facilitating conversations in my classroom about my students' home, family, and community culture.	☐	☐	☐
I find ample opportunities to bring my students' home, family, and community cultures into the classroom, including the use of cultural traditions, community history, music, art, language, and literature.	☐	☐	☐

Reflections on my knowledge of my classroom environment:

Ideas for Adapting the Environment

Here are some examples of actions that teachers can take to create a more culturally responsive school or classroom environment. These examples have been observed in elementary, middle, and high schools:

- Post pictures of students on a classroom wall. Take pictures of students while they are engaged in class activities or ask students to bring a picture of themselves to post.
- Post pictures of people who are important to the students. One teacher asked her students to bring a picture of a family member or other special adult to class; those pictures were hung on a wall, "watching over" the students as they worked. In the younger grades, pictures of students' families can be posted and used as a tool for discussing the diversity among children and families. Some schools that serve Native American students have placed pictures of local tribal leaders and chairpersons in the hallways. Some teachers have given students disposable cameras to take home to take pictures of their families and things that are important to them. These pictures then become jumping-off points for student essays, presentations, and exhibits.
- Post student work. In the younger grades, it is common to post student artwork and writing. Teachers of higher grades may not see that posting a student essay would have an impact, or they might be concerned about producing a negative impact. One teacher worked around this by putting a discussion question related to the current unit's study on a bulletin board; over the course of a week, students posted short responses to the question.
- Post quotes from the students—words of wisdom or encouragement. Alternatively, post quotes from family and community members, or famous people who represent the cultures of the students.
- Post signs in the multiple languages spoken by students and family members at the school. This includes welcome signs at the school entry and signs in the school office. Using quotes, posters, music, or literature in students' languages in the classroom also recognizes students' culture.
- Include culturally relevant books in the classroom library. Have an abundance of books and other materials on hand for students to read that are written by people from the various cultural groups represented in the classroom or about topics that reflect their culture. (See box on page 115 on selecting culturally responsive literature.)
- Bring family and community members into the classroom. Guests can share information about topics such as their occupation, talents, culture, family, or childhood. (See how teacher Lilia Doni did this in Snapshot 5.5 "Fairy Tales, Folktales, and Family Stories.")

ENGAGING IN CONVERSATION

One of the most important ways that teachers can let students know they are valued and respected is to have conversations with them about their home, family, and community life. These conversations are essential to culturally responsive teaching: they help practitioners understand students' worldviews and build relationships with them. These conversations give teachers important clues about the background knowledge and strengths students bring to the classroom on which the curriculum can capitalize. Teachers should use the information gained from these conversations to adapt the curriculum so it is more relevant and meaningful to students.

When students explore their own and their classmates' lives and share them with each other, classroom communities of respect and personal connection are created (Christensen, 2000; Ginsberg & Wlodkowski, 2000). When these conversations are used by teachers to help students think about the connections between themselves and class content, they contribute to student engagement, understanding, and achievement. Tool 9 "Student Conversation Starters" was created to help educators begin these types of conversations. Some of the questions are more appropriate for different age groups, so adapt them for your students. Have your students help you create additional meaningful conversation starters.

Conversing about culture in your classroom may take practice, both for you and for your students (especially if you have not had much experience). Remember, a conversation is a two-way street, so be willing to share your personal experiences with students as well. There are many ways to use the conversation starters, both one on one and in a group setting.

- Embed relevant questions into an existing lesson. For example, if you are teaching about the Oregon Trail and the migration west, you could ask students, "Over the years, what cultural groups have come to our community?" "What are some of the features of our community that represent these groups (e.g., architecture, place names, types of restaurants, religious organizations)?"
- If you have 10 or 15 minutes of extra time at the end of the day, select one or two questions from the list and lead an open discussion with your students about their home, family, or community culture.
- Use the questions as prompts for student journal entries, essays, or speech topics.

Creating a Caring and Nurturing Environment That Encourages Real Conversation

For these conversations to be authentic, meaningful, and engaging, students need to feel safe to voice their thoughts—the classroom must be a caring and nurturing environment. Activities in the "Building Relationships With Students" section (page 47) can help students feel comfortable with each other and the teacher; the tips in Tool 9 "Student Conversation Starters" can help practitioners facilitate deeper conversations.

Snapshot 4.2 "Celebrating Differences—Achieving Results" (page 80) features a school that is working with its community and finding unique ways to create a safe and culturally responsive environment. In this snapshot the school name is fictitious and the village is not identified (although the events are true) as many of the staff members are no longer at the school and current staff requested anonymity.

TOOL 9

STUDENT CONVERSATION STARTERS

- What is a favorite tradition in your family?
- What object in your home best describes your culture or your family?
- Name a family member or community member whom you admire, and explain why.
- Why do you have the name you have? What is the meaning of your name?
- What type of music do you like? What kinds of dance do you like?
- What kinds of art do you like?
- What kinds of books do you like?
- What do you like to do outside school? What do you do when you get home from school?
- How does it feel to know you are part of a cultural group that shares many ideas and beliefs?
- How would you describe your culture to someone who knows nothing about it?
- What is the definition of culture? Is there one American culture?
- What are some things that you do that you learned from your culture?
- What can you do to learn about and understand other cultures?
- Discuss ways that your culture, gender, or generation needs to be better understood, appreciated, or celebrated.
- Who were the original inhabitants of our area, and what contributions did they make?
- Through the years, what cultural groups have come to our community?
- What are some of the features of our community that represent these groups (e.g., architecture, place names, types of restaurants, religious organizations)?
- Are there different cultural ways for thinking about mathematical concepts (such as measurement, counting, computation, fractions, probability, geometry, money, and calendar time)?
- Are there different cultural ways for thinking about scientific concepts (such as health, medicine, and astronomy)?
- Name a historical figure you admire and explain why you admire that person.
- What does a teacher need to know about your learning style?
- What languages do you speak? What are the benefits of knowing those languages?
- How do other languages compare with English?
- Social mores are the "rights" and "wrongs" in a culture group. Do different culture groups have different social mores? What impact does this have on communication between cultural groups?
- What if you were part of another culture? How might you be different from the way you are now?
- Does culture explain why other people sometimes seem to act differently? Are all of our behaviors related to culture?
- How does culture influence textbook writers and publishers?

Snapshot 4.2

CELEBRATING DIFFERENCES—ACHIEVING RESULTS

"Arnaq School," a school in remote Alaska

Grade levels: K–12

Highlights: In this school of 153 students, all of them Alaska Natives, the staff worked with the community to support an environment that promotes CRSB teaching.

Integrating Local Culture and School Culture

The staff of "Arnaq School" continually worked to bring in the culture of the students in ways that enhance learning and self-identity and promote community—resulting in student test scores that show the effectiveness of this strategy.

The staff strongly believed in creating a safe and caring school in which each child feels respected. They provided an environment conducive to allowing every child to learn. "It has to be a place where the students can learn to see tomorrow," a staff member said. "Many only see to the end of the week, but we strive to help them see beyond today and look to their future."

The staff worked to soften or erase the line between the community and school—making it transparent so community and school are one and the same. Their main goal was to bring the culture of the community into the school, encourage students to be proud of their Native heritage, and get away from a "white is right" philosophy.

Physically, the school infuses students' culture by painting the walls with pictures of fish, bear, moose, and caribou. A first-grade teacher worked with students to paint murals in the cafeteria and classrooms that depict village life. Photographs of elders were taken out of a storage closet and hung in the cafeteria.

Culture in the Curriculum

Since the community is so important to students, many choose to stay in the village after graduation, with only 10 percent going on to college or vocational education. Because of this reality, the staff taught their students how education can be part of their daily lives. They embedded into the curriculum the local economy and the skills required to be successful in the community. Learning was organized around local ways of creating and imparting knowledge with emphasis on the subsistence lifestyle that is the foundation of the community. Hunting and fishing were part of the regular curriculum, as well as other locally relevant courses that were taught by itinerant teachers. The state also offered a hunter safety program in partnership with the village, so they teach safety with respect to Native ways. Students were taught how to use math, language arts, reading, and writing to build Native structures such as a smokehouse and a steam house. Thematic units in Grades 9–12 provided a way for all teachers to work together on incorporating culturally responsive material.

The staff did not want an "Indian Day," but wanted local Native culture to pervade the school at all times. A certified Native Alaskan teacher worked as a full-time culture coordinator to help teachers design curriculum around local ways of knowing to do community outreach, and to coordinate an "Elders in the School" program.

The school made a point of asking what the family and community members want for their children. When community members said it wanted more of its culture in the school, the school responded. One way it seamlessly integrated local culture was to organize classes in units, not grades. Another powerful approach was their commitment to infuse local Native language instruction in the curriculum at all grades and for all students—as well as offering Native language classes for adults, because the use of the local language had been steadily decreasing.

Growing Community

The community was brought into the school in many other ways as well. Parents, elders, and all community members were always welcome in the school. Elders ate lunch with students every day, and the school invited elders to share wisdom, knowledge, and traditional skills with the students, as well as to read with them. Some elders did not speak English, "but their presence made a world of difference in the school," said a staff member. Because they knew the school welcomed their presence, parents were also in the school every day. In the mornings, parents had a coffee klatch in the school. Then they went into classrooms to demonstrate beading and other crafts.

The administration believed that you must surround yourself with a faculty that is willing to become part of the community. Villagers and teachers hunted and fished together, and teachers visited the steam house with villagers—partaking in one of the community's important spiritual traditions.

Prior to these changes (around 2004), test scores at Arnaq were the worst in the district, and the school was labeled a Level Three Crisis school—the most dire designation. This was demoralizing to the community and prompted the state to give additional funds to the school and bring in new administrators. Within two years, the school went from 30 suspensions to four; in addition, state test scores increased to be on a par with the district; scores were even above in 11th- and 12th-grade math and reading.

Community events encouraged more-positive relations as well as student success. For example, the district has held a Book Bash for several years with schools competing to have their students read the most books. In previous years, Arnaq School did not participate. In 2005, they participated, cheered each other on, and won. It was a community effort, encouraged at community meetings and celebrated with a basketball game. Teachers also invited the community to a Thanksgiving celebration. Teachers cooked 12 turkeys and served the community a feast.

Because of all these changes, more community residents volunteered. The school also had developed a strong instructional aides program, with many aides earning college degrees, spurred on by the fact that the district paid for the coursework.

Embodying the heart and soul of CRSB teaching, the staff acted on their vision: "We are more alike than different, so we need to celebrate the differences."

In his article "Recreating Schools for All Children," former Seattle principal John Morefield identifies 12 characteristics of successful schools. One of those characteristics is "a total school environment of pervasive caring and nurturing." Morefield (1996) explains,

Schools have not seen it as important, historically, to be environments of pervasive caring and nurturing. We see a great deal of blame placed upon children. We often hear the argument put forth, even in kindergarten, that life is tough so we must toughen up the children. The truth is, children do better in safe and nurturing environments. Children do not do as well in environments where adults are continually critical, constantly accentuating the negative, and not accepting children for who they are. Since we know this is true, then we are obligated to foster warm and caring environments where children will blossom.

Teacher and author Linda Christensen states that a curriculum that encourages students to empathize with others—through sharing their lives—is key in building community. She explains, "Once they've seen how people can hurt, once they've shared pain and laughter, they can't so easily treat people as objects to be kicked or beaten or called names. When students' lives are taken off the margins and placed in the curriculum, they don't feel the same need to put down someone else" (2000, p. 7).

For all of us, emotions are a crucial source of information for thinking and learning: they help us pay attention and create meaning, and they have their own memory pathways (Greenspan, 1997; Jensen, 1998). In *Teaching With the Brain in Mind*, Eric Jensen (1998) explains why engaging children's emotional response is important for robust learning: "Emotions engage meaning and predict future learning because they involve our goals, beliefs, biases, and expectancies . . . the systems [for thinking and feeling] are so interconnected that chemicals of emotion are released virtually simultaneously with cognition." (p. 93)

Emotions also can inhibit the thinking process. Under conditions of high stress, the brain goes into "survival mode," impeding higher-order thinking abilities. In schools where there are few opportunities to talk about feelings and concerns, children's ability to learn is often jeopardized by the neglect of their emotional well-being. "In the rush to get to the learning, schools often miss the point that students need to feel connected and valued and known before they'll bring their truest and best selves into the room," says Northwest educator Dawn Dzubay (Novick, 2002).

Fostering a caring and nurturing environment is essential to encouraging students' personal and academic development and requires careful attention to the interactions and relationships between teachers and children and among children. In their book *Creating Highly Motivating Classrooms for All Students* (2000), Ginsberg and Wlodkowski advise, "The challenge we all face as facilitators and teachers is to model respectful practices consistently from the beginning to the end of every class session, course, and personal interaction. However, we all have personal challenges and contradictions that can interfere with the perfection we would like to achieve. When necessary, we can demonstrate the importance of being willing to learn from one's own mistakes, and in that way we can still be courageous leaders" (p. 77).

What can teachers do to create a caring and nurturing environment that will encourage real conversation? Here are some tips for facilitating conversations or the sharing of written work about home, family, and community culture (adapted from Fletcher, June 17, 2003):

- Remember that teachers and students put themselves in everything they speak and write. Critical feedback can shut students down if not handled sensitively.
- Ask students to brainstorm a class list of norms (ground rules) for listening and responding to someone's comments or writing. Some common ground rules include these: use "I" statements, allow the "right to pass," respect privacy and confidentiality, be open to changing your mind, ask questions instead of assuming or debating, and search for common ground.

- Interrupt negativity. It only takes one negative comment to change the climate of the entire room.
- Have students share thoughts or writing in pairs and then have students nominate peers to share their thoughts or writing with the whole class.
- Ask everyone to share just one sentence.
- Share often in class. Give students more opportunities to respond as well as to ask questions.
- Ask students to give compliments to each other.
- Have students use a 3 x 5–inch card to respond to each student's writing or oral reporting. They can describe what they loved about the writing or reporting or ask questions about what they want to know more about. Ask them to sign their names on the cards.
- First respond to the content—the meaning—of what someone is saying or has written.
- When demonstrating a point, use students' work as examples.
- Use powerful literature to give students permission to be honest in their comments and writing and show what that might look like.
- Share your own thoughts, writings, and experiences with students. Demonstrate how you have made mistakes and how you have dealt with them.
- When you ask students to write, write with them.
- Ask questions that encourage critical, reflective thinking.

STUDENTS TALK ABOUT CULTURAL DIVERSITY

In an after-school writing workshop, students at Madison High School, Portland, Oregon, wrote about diversity in their school, and what diversity means to them (see Snapshot 4.3 "Gay–Straight Alliance" for a description of the "zine" they created). Here are some of the things they had to say:

"I've found that it works better to focus on all differences in people. Like whether someone is shy/crazy, [has] different interests. . . . It has worked for me."

"Just because there is diversity doesn't mean that everyone is happy with it."

"Diversity is important, unity between diversity & adversity is more so."

"I think it's safe to cross boundaries only when you know a person."

"Safety is being able to be who you are."

"I'm actually used to diversity since I used to live in San Francisco. San Francisco is one of the most diverse areas. I remember in the fifth grade we were doing an activity on the colonial times and the teacher asked all white males to stand up. I was the only one. I never realized until then that I was!"

"I'm probably the most diverse person you'll ever meet. I can't fit into any category. I'm not the usual high school 'prep' or 'jock' or 'punk.' I'm me and because I have many different sides to me I am diverse. I think that being diverse is one of the greatest traits that you will ever know, not just for high school but for life as well."

Talking About Difficult Issues

Sometimes students bring up sensitive issues in the classroom that we would rather not talk about. In her book *Reading, Writing, and Rising Up*, Linda Christensen (2000) shows that while it may bring challenges, it is vital to respond to the needs of students in order to build community in the classroom.

Christensen explains that her high school English students faced violence almost daily in their community. As she read aloud to them from Ruthanne Lum McCunn's novel *Thousand Pieces of Gold* she found students related the violence in the book to their own experiences. Christensen (2000) states, "At first, I worried that inviting students to write about violence might glorify it. It didn't turn out that way. Students were generally adamant that they'd made poor choices when they were involved in violent activities. More often students shared their fears. Violence was erupting around them and they felt out of control. They needed to share that fear" (p. 5). Allowing them to relate their experiences, Christensen captured her students' interest and then used their connections to, in her words, "drive us through the content." For example, students used their personal experiences as well as the story characters to illustrate their points in literary essays.

Talking about difficult issues can bring up concerns about preserving confidentiality and safety. It helps to think first about what you are comfortable with students discussing (for example, concerns about gang activity in the neighborhood), and decide what they may write about but should not share (for example, a parent who is going through Alcoholics Anonymous). Teachers may respond to student needs one on one rather than as a whole class. Look for allies to help you: school counselors or staff from community-based organizations often specialize in these types of issues and can offer advice and assistance.

Resources on Preventing Harassment and Bullying

Preventing and Countering School-Based Harassment: A Resource Guide for K–12 Educators (http://educationnorthwest.org/webfm_send/124)
This guide addresses the more comprehensive issue of school-based harassment by capturing similarities in causes, types, and remedies for all forms of harassment. It also addresses unique aspects of racial and sexual harassment. The material aims at helping teachers, administrators, communities, and students create a safe and bias-free learning environment.

Schoolwide Prevention of Bullying (http://educationnorthwest.org/webfm_ send/465)
It is essential to understand—and take seriously—the dynamics of bullying behavior among school-aged children if we are to succeed in building safe and effective schools. This booklet provides an overview of what is currently known about bullying behavior and successful efforts to address it. The "Northwest Sampler" section at the end of the booklet profiles a number of antibullying programs and offers resources for further research and program development.

Delving Deeper: From Conversation and a Supportive Environment to Dialogue

Dialogue is a process in which students and teachers talk deeply and personally about issues and realities that affect them, such as racism, violence, privilege, prejudice, and discrimination. The goals of dialogue are to improve intergroup understanding, foster collaboration, transform conflicts, promote active citizenship, and build peace—offering an alternative to continuing the same destructive ways of handling conflict (Adams, Edwards, & Dirks, 2003).

Dialogue has several basic stages. Participants usually begin by discussing their individual experiences, focus on community issues and possibilities for community change, and conclude with planning an action to respond to the issue.

"In the classroom, dialogue can be a powerful tool to help build self-awareness, educate students about diverse perspectives and experiences, improve communication skills, resolve conflicts, strengthen community in the classroom, and foster active citizenship and community change," explain Adams and colleagues (2003). While it can be difficult at first, dialogue feels more comfortable as students develop experience with it and trust with each other. It is important for the teacher to gauge students' readiness to engage in dialogue, and to continually work on creating a safe and nurturing environment.

Resource on Dialogue

Study Circles Resource Center (www.everyday-democracy.org)

Many tough public issues—from crime to racial tension to substance abuse—directly involve and affect young people. But, too often youth are absent from discussions on these issues. Study circles provide a process to help build the trusting relationships necessary for long-term change. They bring people from diverse backgrounds and experiences together so they can develop trust, understand each other's experiences, and find ways to work together. (To find Study Circle Resources, use the search feature on this website.)

Topics for Dialogue: Student Voice in Decisionmaking

Once meaningful conversations start to take place in the classroom, students may want to take action with regard to the issues that concern them. Giving students a say in school and classroom decisionmaking is one way to make real the power of these conversations. Including student voice in school and classroom decisionmaking encourages relationships between and among teachers and students, develops student leadership skills, helps students feel valued, and increases students' buy-in in their education.

Christensen found a simple way to connect with a class of uninterested students: she asked them to write about their history as English students, and to describe what they liked, hated, and wanted to learn. She found that the assignment excited her students, and that they were eager to share their feelings about their school experience. The assignment helped her learn what they were looking for in class and what would turn them off.

Some examples of ways that students can take action in their community, increase their sense of empowerment, and improve their relationships with classmates are discussed in Snapshot 4.3 "Gay–Straight Alliance."

Immediately following Snapshot 4.3 is Snapshot 4.4 "Students' Voices" (page 87), which describes a collaboration with "outside" organizations, in this case a university and an advocacy group, that sponsor workshops attended by students from multiple schools.

Snapshot 4.3

GAY–STRAIGHT ALLIANCE

Madison High School, Portland, Oregon

Grade level: 9–12

Subject areas: English, history, sociology, and psychology

Highlights: This student-formed and student-led school club made connections with teachers to promote and support CRSB teaching.

Matt is a large young man with a cleanly shorn head, grunge-style clothes, and heavy black boots. He is a thespian and a Dungeons and Dragons master, and he proudly claims affiliation with the "Park Rats," an alternative group of youth at his school. Sonja has multiple piercings and wears baggy cargo jeans cinched at the waist with a chrome-studded belt and an oversized canvas jacket festooned with brightly painted symbols of her favorite band. A cap sits twisted backward on her dark spiked hair. "Sonny" (Sonja's preferred name) challenges gender every day. "She" more strongly identifies as "he," although she says she isn't considering a sex change operation due to the pain involved. Jordan is a tall, lanky, mixed-race youth with an Afro that stands a foot high. He has shared that sometimes he doesn't know quite where he fits in between his two cultural worlds. But he is a quiet boy who prefers to listen, and he expresses his feelings best through his intricate pencil drawings of political subjects.

On any given day that Madison High School's Gay–Straight Alliance (GSA) meets, 20 or so students from all walks of life sit in a circle and discuss whatever is on their minds. These students consider themselves just regular high school students—but students with a purpose. They aim to create safe spaces on their campus for everyone, regardless of the clique they are in, the color of their skin, or their sexual orientation. David Colton, the counselor at

Madison High School, has been advising the GSA for the past year. He initially envisioned the group as a place where students could come together to support one another about sexual orientation issues—whether they were gay, bisexual, or transgendered, or had parents or family members dealing with those matters. Today, the group is a safe space for students to talk about all sorts of issues, and membership has grown to 32 students. The success of the GSA lies in Colton's ability to center the group's activities in the lives of its members. The issues they tackle come directly from concerns they face: from family relations to personal identity and fitting in.

Throughout the school year, the GSA works on activities that promote understanding and celebrate diversity. Even though they are officially a student club, they often ask classroom teachers to get involved in GSA-sponsored activities. For example, the GSA wanted to build awareness in their school about the powerful force of hate and discrimination. They organized a "field of flags" to remember and honor all who had died in the Holocaust. To prepare the larger student body for the event, several teachers taught a segment on the Holocaust. The following week, GSA students erected around 600 color-coded flags on the front lawn of the school, each flag representing 10,000 members of a particular ethnic or cultural group (including Jews, gays, gypsies, Jehovah's Witnesses, intellectuals, and others) massacred during the Holocaust. In a solemn open-mike tribute, students, staff, and community members came together to reflect on the tragic events and denounce hate of all kinds. Teachers from a variety of disciplines brought their students to view the flags. Back in the classroom, teachers used the event to initiate conversation about the challenges of diversity and the consequences of hate. Many students also created essays or written reflections about the event.

During the last few meetings of the school year, GSA members created a "zine," a self-published magazine that documented their experiences at school with diversity, safety, student-teacher relationships, and family support. This zine is a part of Portland Public Schools' Stories Project (see Snapshot 7.5, page 186). Their final printed magazine will accompany a series of photographs of the group and individual GSA members, and will be used in professional development activities to stimulate conversations about the dynamics of difference.

Dozens of students helped write, type, and cut and paste the 53 pages of wisdom that emerged in the zine's artwork, stories, and poems. The finished publication—which impressed young people and adults alike—is titled "Walking in Someone Else's Shoes." The introduction, written by a GSA youth, invites readers to peer into "the true psyches of the students at Madison High School." We are reminded that Madison students are "not a collection of scores and figures, of grades and attendance records, but a complicated potpourri of passion, ideas, hormones, and opinions." Teachers, administrators, parents, and other caring adults are challenged to think about how they "influence the students whom they mentor, can best guide them based on the 'truths' presented in their zine, and be the artists who shape the clay of things to come."

Snapshot 4.4

STUDENTS' VOICES

The Detroit Youth Writers Project

Multiple high schools in Detroit, Michigan: Collaboration between the University of Michigan and "What Kids Can Do"

Grade levels: 9–12

Subject areas: Language arts, race relations

Highlights: This interschool writing and interracial dialogue project brings together high school students from downtown Detroit, Michigan, to explore and write about culture, racism, prejudice, and to promote visions of social justice recorded in an anthology to reach across racial and ethnic boundaries and to build bridges amongst youth.

An effective example of bringing together students from many cultures and many schools to participate in interracial dialogue has been developed by the University of Michigan's Program for Youth and Community with support from two foundations and in

(Continued)

(Continued)

collaboration with What Kids Can Do (www.whatkidscando.org).

For several years now, young people in Detroit—the nation's most segregated metropolitan area—have been coming together to confront the stereotypes that color their lives. "People in my neighborhood don't like to leave it," explains one youth, "and most parents don't want you to hang out with other races." Schools and organizations across greater Detroit have sent them to join an interracial dialogue and produce a small book of reflective writing about their own personal experience with race, a task that requires the courage to explore the feelings created by exclusion, isolation, and prejudice.

"These writers are young people of African, Asian, European, Middle Eastern, and Latin American descent. In these pages, they write about their own cultures, racism, sexism, freedom, learning, the past and the future. They explore growing up in segregated social worlds and living on the borders of change. In particular, they examine how their lives and visions of social justice form a bridge. The mission of this anthology is to reach across the racial and ethnic boundaries and build bridges with other youth," writes Barry Checkoway, the program's organizer from the University of Michigan. In the introduction to the collaborative poem "My Dreams Are Not Secret," What Kids Can Do writer Abe Louise Young—who led the writing project and its kick-off writing workshop—explains:

> Writing together has a strange magic. It is ceremony and solitude at once. Wounds we never knew we had can heal. Wisdom we did not know we had can surface. People we saw in simple stereotypes will reveal their inner conflicts, and we will empathize.

In a city like Detroit, opportunities for direct, honest communication about racial identity are so rare as to be outrageous, precious. It was a great honor to be with these young people as they spent the weekend formalizing their courage as truth-tellers. May you be inspired by their words, and even more inspired by their commitments to action.

Each of the writers also participates in Youth Dialogues on Race and Ethnicity in Metropolitan Detroit. In this program, they discuss their own identities, their similarities and differences, and policy issues about which they are passionate. They take a metropolitan tour, live and work together in a residential retreat, and plan action projects to create change. The program enables them to break their silence, use their voices in a new community, and discuss ideas they usually keep to themselves. In so doing, they grow into leaders.

Excerpts from the book . . .

"[When I was] a young child, my mother would repeatedly refer to me as an endangered species. What did she mean by this? . . . She called me an endangered species because there are not that many intelligent, successful, and respectful Black men left in our community."

From "Endangered Species" by Mychael Fields, Southfield Lathrup High School '07

"You may see her as the quiet Asian, but don't see her too quickly, she might surprise you."

From "She Is Indeed Asian, But Who Is She?" by Nou Lee, Osborn High School '07

A secret in my life is that I love to go up on the roof
(even though my mother thinks it's dangerous)
and look up at the heavens and write.
My dreams are making something of myself, helping young black men,
and making a change in the city of Detroit. . . .

From "My Dreams Are Not a Secret," a collaborative poem by the Detroit Youth Writers: For the full text, go to the What Kids Can Do website, My Dreams Are Not a Secret—Teenagers in Metropolitan Detroit Speak Out, at www.whatkidscando.org/featurestories/2008/02_my_dreams/index.html. On that page you can access the complete book, My Dreams Are Not A Secret: Teenagers in Metropolitan Detroit Speak Out, as a PDF file.

Learn more about Youth Dialogues on Race and Ethnicity by writing to Youth Dialogues on Race and Ethnicity, Barry Checkoway, UM School of Social Work, 1080 S. University Ave., Ann Arbor, Michigan 48109–1103.

Resources on Student Voice

Student Voice in Transforming Education (www.newhorizons.org/voices/front_voices.html)

Many students have valuable ideas about what would make their learning more meaningful and engaging, yet they often are taught without having a voice or choice in the process. This site includes articles by educators about how to encourage student involvement and how to create more open and participatory environments for learning.

Listening to Student Voices (http://educationnorthwest.org/service/729)

Listening to Student Voices provides a process for school leaders and school-based teams to include students in continuous school improvement. This product includes a set of tools to set up unique avenues for student leadership in gathering and analyzing data to be used for school improvement efforts. The tools are flexible and can be adapted or combined to engage students in leading focus groups, conduct classroom observations, design and administer surveys, and examine student work samples. School groups learn to build a more collaborative school culture among students and between students and adults.

From Talking to Working Together: Cooperative Learning

As teachers engage students in conversation and use more CRSB teaching practices, they may find that these activities lend themselves to small-group work or cooperative learning. Cooperative learning has been found to promote relationships among diverse students, improve students' ability to see other perspectives, and promote self-esteem (Johnson & Johnson, 1994). Cooperative learning is another way to help students feel supported. It gives students a sense of belonging—and lets them see themselves as part of the class team, part of a collective effort.

"Culturally relevant teaching advocates the kind of cooperation that leads students to believe they cannot be successful without getting help from others or without being helpful to others," writes Gloria Ladson-Billings (1994, p. 70). In this way, it encourages students to work together to make their community in and out of school what they want it to be rather than to compete against each other in destructive ways.

Studies show that cooperative learning has a powerful effect on learning, resulting in higher individual achievement than competitive or individualistic efforts (Marzano, Pickering, & Pollock, 2001; Johnson, Johnson, & Stanne, 2000). Cooperative learning encourages higher-level reasoning, problem solving, and critical thinking (Johnson & Johnson, 1994). Working together in cooperative learning groups, students reinforce their own learning as they help their classmates learn. This structure also allows teachers to provide a learning style that is more culturally relevant to many students, including Native Americans. Cooperative learning strategies have been found to have positive effects on children in early childhood and elementary grades as well as in middle and high school (Lyman & Foyle, 1988).

Teachers can foster children's emotional and academic competency through the use of cooperative learning—but for cooperative learning to be effective, it needs to be implemented well. Marzano and colleagues (2001) offer the following suggestions for implementing cooperative learning in the classroom:

- Keep student groups small, usually around three or four students.
- Make sure students clearly understand the task they are being asked to do.
- Make sure students understand how they will be assessed, and what good work will look like. Many teachers find ways to give individual grades as well as team grades.
- Ask students to choose a leader or organizer, recorder of group discussions, and other roles as necessary.
- Ask each group to decide how they will break up the work.
- Encourage groups to take time every couple of days to evaluate each individual's progress as well as the group's progress.
- Meet with each group periodically to monitor progress, help solve problems, and assist students in working together effectively.
- Group students randomly or use a variety of criteria, such as common interests or shared characteristics. Use ability grouping sparingly, if at all.
- Use different types of groups depending on your purpose. Informal groups are ad hoc groups that may work together for a few minutes or up to an entire class period. Formal groups may work together on a thorough assignment spanning a few days to several weeks. Base groups are used to provide students with support throughout the semester or year, helping with homework or other classroom chores.
- Use groups consistently and systematically, but make sure students still have time to work individually and independently.

Resources on Cooperative Learning

The Essential Elements of Cooperative Learning in the Classroom ([ERIC Digest] http://www.eric.ed.gov/PDFS/ED370881.pdf)

During the past decade, cooperative learning has emerged as the leading new approach to classroom instruction. One important reason is that numerous research studies in K–12 classrooms, in very diverse school settings and across a wide range of content areas, have revealed that students completing cooperative learning group tasks tend to have higher academic test scores, higher self-esteem, a greater number of positive social skills, fewer stereotypes of individuals of other races or ethnic groups, and greater comprehension of the content and skills they are studying.

REFLECTION QUESTIONS

1. In what ways does your classroom or school environment reflect the students you teach? In what ways does it reflect you and your fellow teachers?

2. What changes can you make to your environment to make it more culturally responsive? What small things can be done immediately? What can you do by the end of the school year?

3. If you are finding that the current environment is a major challenge for you, what are the main barriers that you feel are keeping you from adapting your classroom environment to include CRSB teaching practices? How might you overcome these barriers? Who are some allies that can assist you in overcoming these barriers?

4. How can you create or maintain a "space" that encourages honest, open conversations and dialogue with the students in your classroom? What resources do you need, and how can you tell if this space is helpful?

5. Review and reflect on the snapshots in this chapter (4.1 "CVTV: Cherry Valley News," 4.2. "Celebrating Differences—Achieving Results," 4.3 "Gay–Straight Alliance," or 4.4 "Students' Voices"). What examples of cooperative learning did you notice in these snapshots?

6. How could you incorporate a student conversation starter in your classroom? What would you hope to accomplish?

7. How could you help your students take action in the school and encourage them to become decision-makers? How could this improve their learning and your classroom community?

5

Culturally Responsive Standards-Based Curriculum

In culturally relevant classrooms, instruction is foremost.

—Gloria Ladson-Billings (1995)

The Continuum of Options and Opportunities for CRSB Teaching (Figure 1.3, page 21) illustrates multiple possibilities for modifying the curriculum—ranging from less to more complex—so that the lessons are culturally responsive and standards based. On the continuum, distinctions were made among lesson, unit, project, and interdisciplinary activity to show that CRSB approaches can be integrated into the curriculum at any or all of these levels. Practitioners may choose to operate at any point on the continuum, gradually trying out and moving toward points that are more complex. While there may be some overlap, more time, involvement, and planning generally are involved as one moves from left to right on the continuum. As a guide, here are some definitions of the levels:

- A *lesson* is usually something that can be done in one or two class periods, generally focusing on one or two specific learning goals.
- A *unit* is usually a series of lessons linked by a common topic or set of learning goals, and is generally planned by the teacher.
- A *project* is a more in-depth experience involving hands-on learning where students make connections between academic skills and "real-world" applications. Students are usually involved in several phases of a project, including planning, doing, assessing, and evaluating.

- *Interdisciplinary activity* refers to an activity that bridges at least two subject areas. It may be team-taught by two or more teachers.

There are various entry points to begin the process. Curriculum ideas can be generated from any of the following:

- *Standards* (and the texts and curriculum guides that reflect those standards): If ideas come from standards, look to the home culture to guide their implementation.
- *Home and community culture*: If curriculum ideas are generated from the home or community culture, then look to the standards for learning goals and targeted student outcomes.
- *Other sources*: Ideas may spring from any number of places or situations. Compelling local, national, or international current events and topics can be a good source. Examples are elections, terrorism, and climate change. Local history and culture are also a good source for ideas. Examples are the study of nearby Indian tribes, the history of the school's neighborhood, or past and present racial relations, politics, and policy in the town, city, or state. If ideas come from these sources, look to both the standards and to the home and community culture for guidance.

This chapter describes and gives examples of the five points along the middle of the continuum: Adapting existing lessons and creating single lessons, units, projects, and interdisciplinary activities. This chapter also gives tips for building from standards and involving community members in developing curriculum. At the end of the chapter, the Tool 10 "Culturally Responsive Standards-Based Teaching Curriculum Planner and Curriculum Wheel" helps teachers plan a lesson, unit, project, or interdisciplinary activity that integrates state academic standards and other learning goals with culturally responsive strategies. Tool 11 "Culturally Responsive Standards-Based Teaching Project Checklist" helps practitioners think through the stages of a successful project, including planning, doing and documenting, reflecting and assessing, and evaluating.

First we look at how to identify the critical components of standards—what the students will learn—to recognize how these components are both intrinsic to and support culturally responsive curricula, then we look at ways to incorporate these components into a dynamic, engaging curriculum relevant to students' lives. As we look at these components, which include critical thinking, we are reminded that enabling students to master a rigorous curriculum—the standards—requires that they be engaged in and recognize themselves in that curriculum. Projects and project-based learning are excellent ways to convey critical concepts in a culturally responsive way.

USING STANDARDS IN CURRICULUM PLANNING

State and district standards have become critical measures of success for students, teachers, schools, and districts. Most sets of standards establish high expectations for students and are excellent guidelines for what students should know in a particular subject area along a continuum. When there is a mismatch between the curriculum and a set of standards, often the curriculum is lacking and the standards are more comprehensive and demanding. The challenge for teachers is to create the link between what students should know and what each student learns—bearing in mind that each student has a unique learning style, cultural self, motivation to learn, educational history, set of emotional needs, and knowledge base. If standards come with the unrealistic expectation that all students of the same age will be at the same place at the same time in their learning then they are counterproductive. But if they are used as an aid to the teacher in moving students along the continuum and facilitating learning at a high level, standards are helpful.

In effective classrooms, existing lessons on important topics, including lessons developed to promote cultural connections, are adapted to better meet one or more standards. New, culturally responsive lessons are developed to meet standards. In most classrooms, both approaches are used so that the curriculum is driven by standards, by vital content (including emerging issues such as current events and students' needs), and by cultural responsiveness, with no single approach dominating. Ideally, all lessons are connected directly to a standard and are clearly culturally responsive.

Optimal Teaching and Learning: When Standards-Driven Curriculum Is Culturally Responsive

Janet Hurt, in *Taming the Standards: A Commonsense Approach to Higher Student Achievement, K–12* (2003), wisely advises teachers to use standards to teach higher-level skills and knowledge, rather than to teach the standards directly. She provides an approach that mitigates the potential negative impact on teaching (and therefore on students) of poorly developed or poorly articulated standards. She states, "Teachers not only have the right to improve their standards, they have a responsibility to find a deeper meaning in standards by using their common sense and professional judgment to sprinkle the standards with connectors, purpose, and relevance" (p. 3). Hurt recommends analyzing standards to determine what is behind the standard that makes it important, what is within each standard that students need to know, how the standard can be used to teach something more durable than the standard itself, and how the standard can be used to transfer learning to other aspects of students' lives and the world around them. In short, Hurt contends that standards cannot stand alone to guide teaching and learning, but must be "unpacked," analyzed, interpreted, "owned," and then embedded into a meaningful and engaging context for students. These are all attributes of culturally responsive curriculum; it is important to always keep the alignment of these two elements—cultural responsiveness and standards based—in view.

Hurt's (2003) main strategy for using standards effectively is to bundle similar standards across content areas under broad "umbrella concepts" such as "change, relationships, or movement" (p. 20). If done collaboratively across the entire school, this strategy helps ensure that all standards are covered while minimizing unnecessary duplication of effort. Connections are made across the curriculum, and higher-order thinking is promoted. The major impediments to this approach are textbooks (and similar prescribed curriculum guides) and teachers working in isolation within their content areas, which particularly happens in secondary schools.

One concern with this approach is that umbrella concepts can be as devoid of meaning and relevance to students as are content-specific concepts. If umbrella concepts remain abstract and nebulous, and are not connected to the cultural selves of students, they will not necessarily lead to increased engagement and motivation. However, these concepts can easily be connected to students' cultural selves when teachers ask students to identify how they have experienced the concepts in their own lives, both positively and negatively. A teacher can then draw connections to a variety of academic examples.

A student who hated frequent moves with her migrant worker parents when she was a young child can learn from life science that all living things thrive on an optimal amount of change—too little or too much hinders healthy development. Planting the same crops in the same soil year after year leads to depletion, but careful crop rotation can bring healthier and bigger yields. Too much change to the ecosystem of a forest from overlogging, pollution, or dramatic climate change can lead to the extinction of species of plants or animals that live in that forest. Later in the school year, after lessons have been conducted on change in science, art, math, or history, teachers can refer back to students' personal examples to make the concepts more relevant.

The following vignette shows how one teacher made a standards-based writing lesson culturally responsive, resulting in greater student learning:

Aaron Anderson, a third-grade teacher, has been teaching at the elementary level for eight years. One of the writing standards taught in third grade at his school is to use correct punctuation, grammar, and sentence structure to write dialogue. Each year, he has given his students worksheets copied from a curriculum guide of a short, unformatted dialogue, in which they are to add the quotation marks, commas, new paragraphs, and other points of grammar so that it is correctly formatted. While a few students pick up the proper grammar very quickly, Anderson has seen that many of his students do sloppy work on the worksheets and still make mistakes when trying to write dialogue into their own stories.

After thinking about how he could teach the dialogue standard in a way that follows the elements of CRSB teaching, Anderson came up with a different approach. He first asked students to work in pairs and interview each other. Students worked together to brainstorm questions such as, "What is your favorite sport or game, and why?" or "What music do you like, and why?" After the interviews, students helped each other write out the interviews using full sentences and proper grammar and formatting. Anderson walked around the room during this time to observe how each pair was doing and offered assistance and additional instruction when needed. For homework, he asked students to interview an adult friend or family member about that adult's childhood, and then write the interview in dialogue form. Students again brainstormed interview questions. As practice, the students asked Anderson some of their questions and he wrote the dialogue on the chalkboard, purposefully making a few mistakes for the children to catch as a challenge.

Requiring that students interview someone meant that Anderson had to give the students a few extra days to complete the homework. However, he was pleased to find that students were invested in the assignment, working very hard to write the dialogue correctly. When given a real-life context, he found that the lesson became an opportunity to teach other concepts as well, such as creating interview questions and expanding dialogue vocabulary—beyond "she said," to include words like commented, exclaimed, whispered, remarked, explained, questioned, queried, and so on.

This vignette shows that CRSB teaching generally requires a movement away from a textbook-driven curriculum and instruction (where the goal is to cover the book) to a curriculum based on the best thinking about what students should know and do (embodied in the standards) and student-centered instructional strategies. The goal of Anderson's lesson remained connected to a writing standard for third grade: to use correct punctuation, grammar, and sentence structure to write dialogue. While keeping the focus on the standards, he was able to alter the teaching strategy so that it

- became student centered and was about the lives of the students and their families, and included their ideas for interview questions;
- built relationships by providing opportunities for the students and teacher to learn about each other and their families;
- was integrated with other important concepts in the language arts such as interviewing and writing and with an activity that involved families in children's learning; and
- involved critical thinking by encouraging students to develop their own questions and by looking for errors in the teacher's example.

Even in the current climate of accountability and high-stakes testing, CRSB practitioners try to make family and community partnership activities central to meeting standards. They value cultural, community, and family considerations, attributes, goals, and strengths. They also value the students themselves—resulting in relationships based on trust, mutual support, and a commitment to partnership for the benefit of the students and everyone involved in their growth.

Resources on Academic Standards

Below are websites where you can access national and state standards. Check your specific state or district website first because there might be more up-to-date standards there.

National standards are usually developed by professional associations, such as the National Council for Teachers of Mathematics. In general, content standards are broad descriptions of what students should know and be able to do. Performance standards or benchmarks are more specific, describing how students at different grade levels can meet the content standards.

Academic Benchmarks (www.academicbenchmarks.com/search/)

Education World State Standards (www.educationworld.com/standards/state/index.shtml)

Education World National Standards (www.educationworld.com/standards/ national/)

Mid-Continent Research for Education and Learning (McREL), Content Knowledge-4th edition (www.mcrel.org/standards-benchmarks/index.asp)

Teacher Tap. Links to both state and national standards (eduscapes.com/tap/topic28.htm)

Demonstrating Knowledge: Standards Assess True Learning

In *Learning in Overdrive: Designing Curriculum, Instruction, and Assessment from Standards: A Manual for Teachers*, authors Mitchell, Willis, and the Chicago Teachers Union Quest Center (1995) advise teachers who are developing a curriculum to start with the end in mind. They suggest that teachers ask themselves these questions:

- What do I want my students to know at the end of the year, semester, or unit? This should be some iteration of the academic standard students are expected to reach.
- What culminating task can students do that requires them to know and perform the selected standard(s)?
- What is the best way to ensure that my students learn these things?

The authors' approach encourages teachers to develop a culminating project that will ask students to perform the standard. This project can be an event, presentation, debate, performance, exhibit, piece of writing, or the creation and implementation of a solution to a real problem. It is designed to measure students' performance on the standard rather than to be a showcase or sample of what students have been doing. Culminating projects are guided by driving questions that students attempt to answer: for example, "Is the quality of our community's water affected by individual uses of the land?"

After brainstorming and developing a culminating project, teachers build a plan of instruction, including the lessons and intermediary tasks that will lead students to the culminating activity. Teachers also assess whether the culminating project meets the CRSB essential elements.

Other Standards to Guide Curriculum Development

In addition to standards for students, there are sets of standards or guidelines designed to promote culturally responsive high-level instruction. These are standards for teachers, schools, and school systems. Below are examples of guidelines from three organizations that can be used to develop and enrich CRSB curriculum. (Note: While these organizations have used the term "standards" to describe their work, the term "standards" is used elsewhere in this guide to refer to state academic content or performance standards for students.)

Alaska Standards for Culturally Responsive Schools

The Alaska Native Knowledge Network was created to provide support for the integration of Alaska Native culture in the educational system. In addition to publishing the Alaska Standards for Culturally Responsive Schools, the network has published a number of guidelines, including guidelines for respecting cultural knowledge and for nurturing culturally healthy youth. Native educators from across the state contributed to the development of these standards and guidelines.

Although written specifically for Alaska schools with Alaska Native cultures in mind, these standards can be useful in other cultures and regions as well. Below is an excerpt from the Cultural Standards for Students taken from the website where the standards are described in detail (www.ankn.uaf.edu). These standards have been endorsed by the Alaska Department of Education and Early Development.

1. Culturally knowledgeable students are well grounded in the cultural heritage and traditions of their community.

2. Culturally knowledgeable students are able to build on the knowledge and skills of the local cultural community as a foundation from which to achieve personal and academic success throughout life.

3. Culturally knowledgeable students are able to actively participate in various cultural environments.

4. Culturally knowledgeable students are able to engage effectively in learning activities that are based on traditional ways of knowing and learning.

5. Culturally knowledgeable students demonstrate an awareness and appreciation of the relationships and processes of interaction of all elements in the world around them.

Criteria for Evaluating State Curriculum Standards

The National Association for Multicultural Education has established curriculum guidelines to help educators teach the knowledge, skills, and dispositions necessary for living in a multicultural society. More details on the curriculum guidelines can be found on the Association's website: www.nameorg.org/resolutions/state-curr.doc.

1. Inclusiveness: Represents a broad range of experiences, people, and understandings, and the interdependence of groups

2. Diverse perspectives: Recognizes multiple constituencies and competing constructions of understanding

3. Accommodating alternative epistemologies or social construction of knowledge: Provides students with the means to understand the ways knowledge is socially constructed

4. Self-knowledge: Fosters a sense in students of how their own identities have been constructed by the complex interplay of historical, social, political, economic, and even geographic factors

5. Social justice: Emphasizes constitutional rights, the development of critical understanding of actions and decisions, and the promotion of social action

Five Standards for Effective Pedagogy

The Center for Research on Education, Diversity, and Excellence (CREDE) in California has researched and established principles for best teaching practices. They have found these practices are effective with all students in K–16 classrooms across subjects, curricula, cultures, and language groups. Indicators for each of the principles are on the Center's website (http://crede.berkeley.edu/research/crede/standards.html).

1. Teachers and students producing together: Facilitate learning through joint productive activity among teachers and students.

2. Developing language and literacy across the curriculum: Develop students' competence in the language and literacy of instruction throughout all instructional activities.

3. Making lessons meaningful: Connect curriculum to experience and skills of students' home and community.

4. Teaching complex thinking: Challenge students toward cognitive complexity.

5. Teaching through conversation: Engage students through dialogue, especially through instructional conversation.

An Essential Component of Successful Standards-Based Education: Promoting Critical Thinking

As discussed in Chapter 1, an essential element of CRSB teaching is that it includes opportunities for students to develop critical thinking skills by providing an environment that promotes the use of these skills in real-life situations and by fostering the understanding of how to apply these concepts in other contexts.

Critical thinking skills are reflected in a person who

- raises questions and problems, formulating them clearly and precisely;
- gathers and assesses relevant information, using abstract ideas to interpret it effectively;
- comes to well-reasoned conclusions and solutions, testing them against relevant criteria and standards;
- thinks with an open mind, recognizing and assessing assumptions, implications, and practical consequences as necessary; and
- communicates effectively with others in figuring out solutions to complex problems.

Students need critical thinking skills to make sense of what they are studying, solve problems, reason, create, and explore. With critical thinking, students can generalize specific concepts and apply general concepts to specific situations. They see and consider various points of view and understand ways that concepts apply in other contexts. The critical thinker also uses metacognitive skills—the skills that help students become aware of their own thinking. The ultimate goal is for students to acquire the disposition to think critically when it counts in their school experiences and in meaningful contexts in their personal lives (Perkins & Tishman, 2000).

The following is a list of some types of critical thinking along with sample questions that illustrate each type:

- Clarity: "Could you elaborate on that point?"
- Accuracy: "Is that really true?" "How could we check that to find out if it is true?"
- Precision: "Could you give me more details or be more specific?"
- Relevance: "How is that connected to the question?" "How does that bear on the issue?"
- Depth: "How does your answer address the complexities of the question?"
- Breadth: "Do we need to consider another point of view?" "Is there another way to look at it?"

- Logic: "Does this really make sense?" "Does that follow from what you said?"
- Significance: "Is this the most important problem to consider?"
- Fairness: "Do I have any vested interest in this issue?"

Teachers can create an environment where there are activities and interactions that not only build students' critical thinking skills but also encourage their motivation and ability to think critically in their everyday lives (Paul & Elder, 2001). For example, students might learn to analyze a persuasive letter to understand the perspective of the writer, but not be sensitive to other situations that call for this skill, such as examining commercial advertisements or considering the impact of diversity on fellow students' learning. Teachers, through discussion and activities, can help students make these connections. By integrating the goals of culturally responsive teaching with the goals of standards-based education, students master important concepts and thus are able to apply their learning to all their academic work.

By focusing on the key concepts in culturally responsive teaching—drawing from the experiences of students and their families and communities—educators can build a curriculum that is as engaging as it is challenging. With the tools of inclusion and responsiveness, teachers and students can achieve the goal of the standards: an effective curriculum and successful students.

SOCIAL NETWORKING CLASSROOM ACTIVITIES THAT EMPLOY CRITICAL THINKING

David R. Wetzel

From http://www.suite101.com/teachingtechnology (In the search box enter "12 expert twitter tips.")

A dozen activities are presented for using an online education technology tool to engage students in classroom activities to develop a better understanding of concepts.

Using Twitter in the classroom is becoming mainstream in many schools around the country and the world. The challenge with any use of an online education technology tool is the appropriate engagement of students in a meaningful manner. To this end, the successful use of Twitter is about making connections with other teachers and students around the world to support significant learning events.

The use of Twitter for improving student learning also requires movement beyond just collaborating with other teachers, pedagogical self-reflection, and professional development activities. It is essential to involve students in social network activities focused on research, data gathering, communicating with experts, examining other points of view, and dialogue within all curriculum areas using online resources.

Online Education Technology Uses of Tweets

The tips provided below are based on expert teacher experiences using the social networking tool Twitter. These activities are designed to encourage students in making

(Continued)

(Continued)

connections beyond a basic understanding of concepts using this online education technology.

1. *Gathering data*: Use a class Twitter network to support student collection of scientific data, historical facts, geographical information, and poll data. Examples include collecting rainfall pH data around the world and identifying geographic locations of specific places around the world.

2. *Creative story theme*: Select any genre and begin a story opener that is Tweeted around the class network of participating schools for contribution to the storyline. Once all Twitter network participants have contributed, have students develop a coherent story. This involves editing, story structure, creative writing, and proper use of grammar.

3. *Polls*: Students develop polls regarding controversial issues using current events, historical events, or scientific events using *Twitter Poll*. Once the poll data are collected, students can make data tables, draw graphs, investigate mathematic probability, analyze data, and use logical reasoning skills to explain poll findings.

4. *Word literacy*: Have students select a word of the week and Tweet it around the network requesting synonyms, homonyms, and antonyms of the word. Once all responses are received, have students check for accuracy and develop a Wordle of the word for strengthening literacy skills. (Wordle is a way to generate "word clouds" from text that you provide. The clouds give greater prominence to words that appear more frequently in the source text. You can tweak your clouds with different fonts, layouts, and color schemes. The images you create with Wordle are yours to use however you like. You can print them out, or save them to the Wordle gallery to share with your friends.)

5. *Communicating with experts*: When burning questions develop during classroom discussions, have students' develop a 140-character question to ask a class Twitter network expert. This causes students to create clear and concise questions and to develop research skills.

6. *Online scavenger hunts*: Task students with finding appropriate online resources that support a specific concept or topic being studied and post them on the network. Part of the challenge is that once a resource has been posted it cannot be used again.

7. *Facts 140 characters at a time*: Have students in the class share facts about math, science, English, or history topics on the network for others to learn. For example, task groups of students with sharing 10 key facts about geometric shapes. Once a fact has been used, it cannot be used by other groups.

8. *Online research*: Have students share, inquire, and engage in using the network to conduct research. Examples include investigating the cause of the disappearance of honeybees around the country, global warming, and disappearing water resources.

9. *Informal assessment*: As students work on projects or other assignments, have them use Twitter for periodic updates to provide tips, resources, interesting information, and difficulties. These updates allow for periodic progress checks, along with an assessment of student project activity.

10. *Online debates*: Arrange for a real-time debate with another classroom on the class Twitter network. Examples of topics include, "Do zoos do more harm than good?" "Is fast food bad for your health?" "Should the United States ratify the Kyoto Protocol?"

11. *Geo hunt*: Arrange with Twitter network participants to provide clues to find their location using Google Earth. Students piece together clues using different layers of Google Earth to locate the exact location of the person providing clues. Students make concrete connections regarding time zones and geographic locations around the world in social studies.

12. *Current events*: Have students use Twitter to receive updates of current events in science, math, history, and literature. This removes the classroom walls and allows timely discussions of what is happening in the world outside the classroom. Selected current events are then used for debates and research connected to the concepts being studied.

More of Dr. Wetzel's helpful writings can be found at Suite 101 (www.suite101.com/profile.cfm/drwetzel), where David is a feature writer. His blog on continuing education at Suite 101 can be found at www.suite101.com/blog/drwetzel. His website, *Wetzel's Word Solutions*, is at www.wetzelswordsolutions .com. His Science/Math Blog, *Teach Science and Math*, is at www.teachscienceandmath.com.

Involving the Community in Standards-Based Curriculum Development

A student-centered curriculum that is culturally responsive builds on students' personal and cultural strengths. Students see themselves and their families reflected in the curriculum in ways that are not trivial; they see that the curriculum does not treat them as tokens or stereotypes. Their culture is included in the daily activities of the classroom, and is not observed merely through the "tourist approach to diversity" that emphasizes the exotic differences among cultures by focusing on holidays, foods, and customs.

Whether you are planning minor or major changes to your curriculum, it is important to involve the community that is going to be the focus of the curriculum. Julie Cajune, Indian Education Coordinator of the Ronan School District in Montana, suggests that one of the simplest things educators can do is seek out people who can be resources to them as they develop culturally relevant curricula.

Cajune meets regularly with community members and repeatedly asks two questions: "What are the most important things for students to know?" and "What should be taught in school?" While the goal is to identify culturally responsive curriculum topics, Cajune has found that these discussions also build understanding and relationships between the community and the school.

Larry Erickson and Libi Susag, teachers from Poplar, Montana, took such suggestions to heart when they worked with the International Traditional Games Society to create a physical education unit for teaching traditional Native American games to their middle school students. Snapshot 5.1 "Rediscovering a Lost Heritage" describes the program. Also see page 41 in Chapter 3 for Susag's story of how she began a journey toward understanding her own culture and that of her students.

ACTIVITY: IDENTIFYING RESOURCES

Brainstorm a list of people in the community who can be used as resources to guide you in the development of new curriculum that is culturally based. Exchange your list with a colleague's, and see what new resources (and ideas for action) you can think of to add to your own list.

Once you have identified people, you can go to for information, it is important to think about culturally appropriate ways to work with community members. In general, community members want educators to be explicit about the kind of information they are looking for, specifically what information they seek, why they are seeking it, and how it will be used. Community members often appreciate the chance to come to the school to share their knowledge with students, but they may need specific guidelines or, alternatively, to be allowed to make their own way. Some Native American tribes have developed protocols to guide teachers in the local appropriate ways of contacting tribal members and bringing them into the classroom.

As David Cort, a teacher at Tulalip Elementary School in Washington State, explained in Chapter 3, "If I go into a community with a different culture and a different heritage, I need to go very humbly as a learner, and seek out guidance from elders who can help me learn from their community." Cort also encourages students to talk with family and community members and seek guidance from them on how they should bring their culture into the classroom. Activities that involve students in interviewing family members about their knowledge and experiences can lend themselves to this kind of approach; Snapshot 5.1 "Rediscovering a Lost Heritage" gives an example. (Also see Snapshot 5.5 "Fairy Tales, Folktales, and Family Stories.")

Snapshot 5.1

REDISCOVERING A LOST HERITAGE

Poplar Middle School, Poplar, Montana

Grade levels: 7–8

Subject areas: Physical education and health enhancement classes

Highlights: Traditional Native American games of strength, skill, stamina, and intuition were taught to middle school students from the Fort Peck Indian Reservation.

Creative extension: The school could host a campus Olympics on the last day of school with tournament-style play in three main games. Parents, elders, students, teachers, and tribal leaders would be needed to accomplish this undertaking. The school also could host a feed for all participants, for which the tribe perhaps could donate a buffalo. The goal would be to make this an annual event run by the tribal leaders.

"Looking into the gym on the beginning of the first day, you could see that the students were tentative. Some were quite shy and hesitant to jump in, but as the day progressed attitudes changed dramatically," says Susag as she describes her students reactions as they were introduced to the unit on Native American games. "The first-period students went a little slower than the rest," continues Larry Erickson. "The simple explanation is that once they found out how much fun the games were they told every-one. Then the other students could not wait to get to class."

Susag and Erickson, physical education teachers at Poplar Middle School, decided to partner with the International Traditional Games Society to teach traditional Native American games to their 400 middle school students (97 percent of whom are Native American, enrolled in the Sioux and Assiniboin tribes). They invited the Society to spend two days teaching games such as doubleball, lacrosse, shinny, ring and hoop, and the stone game.

The unit began with an introduction by the members of the Society. "To watch the expressions on the students' faces as they sat mesmerized by the introductory video was entrancing. Students eagerly raised their hands to ask questions. Many students seemed to accept and form an instant connection with these new teachers once they learned they were from other reservations in Montana. They warmed up even more when they realized that some Society members knew many students' relatives," exclaims Susag.

Once the students knew the purpose of the unit and the rules of the games, they quickly joined in and followed the rotation throughout the class period. The gym was filled with the exuberant sounds of pounding feet, clattering sticks, and encouraging and eager voices cheering and laughing as they learned each game. The sound of the rotation whistle would bring a brief whine of disappointment when the students realized they had to quit a game that was just beginning to get intense. This was quickly followed by whispers of excitement about what new game was waiting for them at the next station. Word spread though the school during the day, so each successive class came to the gym eager to see what games awaited them.

On the second day, the students were familiar with the games. They came to class already split into teams, eager to dive into the activity. First, the elders took time to explain to the students about their culture and the significance of the games. They also talked to the students about the importance of their heritage and taking the games seriously. The majority of students listened compliantly and embraced the message that they were responsible for keeping their heritage alive through these games. Once the students realized they could take these games farther than just a PE class, some became very competitive and a mixture of smiles and serious looks appeared on their faces.

"Looking around, I realized the best part was that not a single student was left out. Even students who have refused to be involved in any activity to date were participating. Every student was participating with 100 percent effort!" Susag exclaimed. "Furthermore, there were zero behavior problems during the two days. Students set new personal bests for respectful behavior."

"In this particular unit, sportsmanship was easier to evaluate than in any unit I have ever done," Susag continued. "The dynamics with the Native games were different. The only reason I can attribute to the high sportsmanlike behavior was a cultural connection between the students and the elders teaching the games. The students seemed eager to please. They cheered and encouraged each other during the games. One of the biggest bonuses I noticed was how willingly the students were to accept constructive correction on skills and game rules—which is often an area where many middle school students struggle."

Importance of Bringing Back the Old-Time Games

"Two hundred years ago, Native American life was rich in relationships, teamwork, art, music, dance, and gaming," Susag explains.

(Continued)

(Continued)

"In talking with elders, I found it was the general consensus among most Native tribes that, due to the loss of the thousands of Native games that teach important skills, many children and adults are losing their abilities of keen observation and natural intuition. Many feel these skills are just as important today as they were 200 years ago."

Within the tribal community, there was an obligation to share the economic gain of superior abilities with others. Competitions taught social responsibility and gave personal strength to their spiritual way of life. Cooperation was the essence of all sports. The best players held a traditional place of honor in their communities.

Even though humor is still very evident in Native culture, the idea of games or play was almost wiped out after the introduction of the Christian work ethic. Most Native Americans agree that work is a highly important value, but feel that the games are able to teach these values much better than they are being taught in modern-day reservation life. Traditional Native games were not merely for play, but were meant to teach cultural values and survival skills. It was through the games that much education occurred. The social values of the traditional games were—and still are—highly important:

- Honoring the person who challenged you the most
- Respecting the rules of the competition
- Respecting your competitors
- Honoring the wager you made before the event
- Having courage, intuition, or skill
- Being humble even when winning

Carrying on the Tradition

In the days when these games were very common, an elder usually helped young people learn and practice the games. The elders advised them how to be good at the skills they were trying to learn. Everything they needed to play the games, including equipment, was provided by nature or could be easily made, and the games could be played anywhere. After the equipment was made and the games learned, the youth played on their own with little adult supervision.

The old-time Native American games of strength, skill, stamina, and intuition were played by tribal members of all ages. Everyone was encouraged to participate in the spirit of the games. Young people played the most rigorous games of strength and endurance, while the elders played their own games of intuition and chance. The players of these games always got better with age.

The most important aspect of all games was the development of the natural physical and mental skills of the people. This was highly integrated into the spiritual beliefs as well, combining the efforts of mind, body, and spirit. Sometimes the clans and tribes would gather for days, fasting, praying, and playing the most exciting games. Prayers by all members helped the players to give their best to the competitions. Prayers in which players asked for power and reward for their efforts were an important part of the gaming ways.

Native American Curriculum in Physical Education Classrooms

For more than a decade, the International Traditional Games Society has collaborated with urban and reservation Indian experts to research and revive the tribal games in central and western Montana. Indians from the Blackfeet, Salish–Kootenai, and Little Shell Tribe of the Chippewa Cree have partnered with the University of Great Falls and Montana State University College of Technology to demonstrate and teach the traditional tribal games to Indian children and adults, and to public school teachers.

Upon deciding to bring the Games Society to Poplar, Erickson and Susag settled on four goals for the Native Games Unit:

- To bring awareness of Native games to middle school students
- To find activities that could help bridge the gap between students and their home cultures and involve parents in school activities
- To increase students' interest in physical activities
- To increase cultural understanding while incorporating it into classroom curricula

"We believed the back-to-basics feel and values of the Native games seemed like a useful tool to create unity among our students, while giving them an opportunity to once again reconnect with their families and their culture," Susag explains. Erickson adds, "With this project I too hope to initiate some cooperation between my students, my community, and myself."

Before the International Traditional Games Society came, teachers seized every opportunity to increase the students' awareness about culture, family background, and how these factors influence skill development. "Culture is defined as the ideas, skills, arts, tools, and way of life of a certain time," Erickson writes. "So knowing that I would bring the students a lesson that was based on their culture, I had to find out what they knew. It is actually scary to discover how many students know nothing at all about their culture. Some students knew they were Native American, but could not even tell me to what tribe they belonged."

To prepare the students, Erickson and Susag talked to them about how the traditional games used to prepare the participants to be warriors, survivors, and important members of the tribe.

"I pointed out the skills the games developed and how those same skills have grown and changed over the past generations. I explained how the throwing and striking skills once used for hunting and surviving are now used in athletic sports—emphasizing that the skills that once put food in people's mouths now could help folks earn hundreds of thousands of dollars at the professional levels of basketball, baseball, hockey, and football—as well as provide lucrative college scholarships," says Susag. "Slowly the students seemed to see connections, and I knew game day would be a well-accepted activity, thanks to the advance awareness of the students." Erickson added, "The students were even more excited to play and you could tell that the attitude of 'this is just a dumb old game' was gone."

"This unit was successful. The students enjoyed themselves, and I truly feel every one of them learned at least one new thing," says Susag. "The students increased their own awareness of culture, even if it took some digging to get them to realize that connection. I believe that a unit such as the Native games can help students begin to understand and value their culture. Because it has such a student focus, it gives them a power and a connection to something larger that they may never have known existed."

"Giving kids the chance to explore their own culture, and having a lesson geared totally to them is a great teaching strategy," concludes Erickson. "I hope that this unit shows the students and their families that I have a commitment to this community and that I care about preserving traditional Native American culture."

For information about the International Traditional Games Society, visit http://www.traditionalnativegames.org/

Linking Learning With the Community

In addition to going into the community to find a cultural liaison to help guide your curriculum development, you can choose from many student-driven CRSB projects that bring the community into the classroom. CRSB practices can build on community-based learning techniques, which are designed to enable youth to learn what they want to from any segment of the community (Owens & Wang, 1996).

These community-based learning practices provide students with strong community connections, raise their awareness of local issues, and build support within the school community for CRSB practices. By engaging students in activities derived from local issues that concern them, teachers can merge students' idealistic desires for positive change and social justice with academic content that is connected to standards. Such projects are responsive to both youth and the community, and provide great vehicles for bringing meaningful learning into the community context. Snapshot 5.2 "Collaborative Action Research Projects" and the "What Kids Can Do" resource on p. 109 show how CRSB practices can link learning with the community.

Snapshot 5.2

COLLABORATIVE ACTION RESEARCH PROJECTS

Aberdeen High School, Aberdeen, Washington

Grade level: 12

Subject areas: English and service learning

Highlights: Students engage in projects based on their interests, while they benefit many in the community. Students report on their work to school board members and district administrators, informing them of what they have learned.

In much of their work during the year, students in David McKay's English classes gather information from the community for various projects. Students take the information and use it to enhance the lives of those who live in the community. Each senior creates a Collaborative Action Research Project that will be, in McKay's enthusiastic words, "their crowning achievement."

In teams of four or fewer, the students identify and research a need in the community. Next, they come up with an action plan to address the need and then work to realize the plan. There have been more than 40 senior projects completed that have benefited many people directly and indirectly, positively changing the community in which the students live. A few of these projects are below:

- Students found unfair athletic practices in the high school and helped change existing school policy.
- Students found poor food quality in the school cafeteria and helped improve the quality of food served.

- Students worked with the city park manager to renovate overrun and hazardous parks: weeding, reseeding, and putting in park benches and trails.
- Students worked with adults from the community and the elementary school principal to address a lack of arts education at the elementary school. They created a drama program that culminated in a play put on by the elementary school students.
- Students found that some teachers in the district were not shown adequate appreciation, so they sought people who valued teachers. They created certificates (and a website) honoring the teachers, using quotes from students about what was special about individual teachers and how the teachers had made a difference in students' lives.

It makes sense that many student projects relate to the school: students view the school as their community, they spend a great deal of time there, and they know it well. Improvements to the quality of the school community have the most direct impact on the students themselves. However, many projects also have great benefits to others in the broader community—as seen by the titles of some projects:

- A Handbook for Improving the City of Aberdeen
- Computer Integration at Aberdeen High School (AHS)
- Creating Harmony in Teenage Relationships
- Solutions Regarding Parking at AHS
- Foreign Language Instruction at the Elementary Level
- Wirta Hotel Renovation for Low-Income Housing
- Creating a Junior High Pregnancy Prevention Program
- Video Documentary to Promote Local Food Banks
- Memorial Erected for Bobcat Soldiers

The Collaborative Action Research Project does not end with students' research and implementation of their plan. It culminates in a 20-minute professional presentation to a panel of judges that includes the president of the school board, district superintendent, principal of the high school, director of technology, and the curriculum/instruction/assessment (CIA) director. The judges use a score sheet containing the state standards for oral presentations to grade the team participants. The presenters are instructed to dress professionally, present at least one visual, and speak in standard English. The presentation can be stressful, but the students and judges all realize it is a chance to celebrate the good work that was done on the project and to honor the changes the students have made in their community.

Resource: What Kids Can Do

The organization What Kids Can Do features many stories on its website (www.whatkidscando.org) about youth learning new skills and making positive contributions through community projects. One such story features the remarkable work of students to rebuild their small, rural town. Working with the Rural School and Community Trust, a national nonprofit organization that involves youth in learning linked to their communities, students in a Texas border town developed a community action organization based in the school. A major thrust of their activities is to reclaim the heritage of their own community, which is largely missing from traditional history textbooks. To do so, students seek out the stories of local elders, publish them in their bilingual Llano Grande Journal, and record them on videotape. For more information, see Small Towns, Big Dreams (http://www.whatkidscando.org/archives/smalltowns.html).

Another story from the What Kids Can Do website documents the youth from a small school in New York City known for its progressive, hands-on curriculum. These students helped organize a relief effort for Hurricane Katrina victims while studying the cultural, economic, and racial aspects of the disaster and documenting its impact on their lives. Students interviewed scores of activists, contacted their legislators, and read policy papers. After raising money, they traveled to New Orleans and participated in eight days of gutting houses in the Ninth Ward, and went door to door for the People's Hurricane Relief Fund, encouraging residents to come to

(Continued)

(Continued)

Survivors' Council meetings. Back in New York, students created a series of documentary photographs and a short DVD about their experiences. This transformational experience gave students a sense of empowerment that they could bring back to their own communities. Bringing a disaster of such great scale and magnitude down to a personal and concrete level was an invaluable learning experience for the students—and hard work. For more information, see Katrina as a Classroom (http://www.whatkidscando.org/featurestories/a.html?/archives/SEPTEMBER06/urbanarcade/index.html).

ADDING CULTURALLY RESPONSIVE STANDARDS-BASED PRACTICES TO THE EXISTING CURRICULUM

Sometimes CRSB teaching emerges out of minor modifications or new visualizations of existing activities. (To see an example of this, read Snapshot 2.1 "Molecules—With a Twist of Culture.") Culturally responsive curriculum connects the cultures of the students to academic subjects. This differs from multicultural education, which might tell students about the diverse peoples who have populated history, literature, or the media. Units on Native Americans or African Americans in U.S. history are important to all children's education; but to engage your students, they have to see and know themselves in the curriculum, too.

When teachers are asked to make standards-based curricula more culturally responsive, they often state that there are prescribed units that must be covered. They wonder how a "canned curriculum" mandated by a district can become culturally responsive. One example is Oregon's requirement that students study the Oregon Trail curriculum. Every fourth-grader learns how white settlers migrated, often on foot, from St. Louis to the Columbia River. However, teachers may supplement this curriculum with diaries and reports of women, Native peoples, Asians, and African Americans on the Oregon Trail. This is a laudable way of turning a narrow, prescribed curriculum into a multicultural lesson by adding historical documents that reveal the diversity usually hidden in explanations of the Trail.

To go farther and make the lessons culturally responsive, ask your students about their own migration stories. Where did their parents, grandparents, or great-grandparents set out from? When did they leave their homes? Why did they leave? How did they travel? You can compare their experiences with those recorded on the Oregon Trail. Students can talk about what their families found when they arrived at their destination, how hard the first years were—and again, compare them with the experiences of the early Oregon settlers. Look at the Oregon pioneers' experiences with the Native inhabitants of the land they colonized and contrast that with your students' and their ancestors' encounters with their new neighbors. This will reveal both the violence of history and the dramatic changes that have occurred during the past 150 years. Your students can see themselves as actors on the historical stage.

Snapshot 5.3 "Family Maps" shares a kindergarten teacher's process of enhancing her Lewis and Clark curriculum by exploring and comparing her students' family stories of immigration and travel.

Snapshot 5.3

FAMILY MAPS

Parkdale Elementary School, Parkdale, Oregon

Grade level: K

Subject areas: History, social studies, language, and art, as well as the concepts of story sharing and sense of place

Highlights: Students and parents share stories of coming to the little town of Parkdale, Oregon. They compare and contrast their cultures and experiences with each other and with the historical figures of the Lewis and Clark Corps of Discovery.

"Overall, I think this is one of the best projects we did in our class this year. It showed students and parents that their own histories are fascinating and worth sharing!" exclaims Jill Spaulding. "Implementing a culturally responsive project in our classroom opened doors for all of us (my teaching partner, Joeinne; our students; other teachers; other students; and me)," reports Spaulding, a kindergarten teacher at Parkdale Elementary School in Parkdale, Oregon.

"It provided a link between our six-week study of Lewis and Clark and our own family histories. Our project was called Family Maps and it impacted many people. By sharing our Family Maps stories, we learned more about everyone in our class. We discovered how diverse and interesting our own stories are. And we shared what we learned with the rest of our school."

Twenty lively kindergarten students make up Spaulding's class: twelve girls and eight boys. Twelve of those students come from homes where Spanish is the first language. Of the 242 students that attend the K–5 Parkdale Elementary, 60 percent are English language learners. The community of Parkdale is located in the Hood River Valley, which is dominated by the towering slopes of Mt. Hood immediately to the south. Major local industries are fruit growing and timber production. Many residents are farm workers from Mexico. Parkdale has a significantly higher number of Spanish-speaking and foreign-born community members than the state average.

About 17 miles to the north of town flows the mighty Columbia River, the main waterway used by explorers Lewis and Clark while pursuing the Northwest Passage from the Rocky Mountains to the Pacific Ocean. Learning about the history of people who came to the area was the focus of a CRSB project developed by Spaulding, and two of her colleagues. During this history unit (centered on the content standard "to understand the importance and lasting influence of individuals, issues, events, people and developments in U.S. history"), her class examined why the Lewis and Clark Corps of Discovery came to the Pacific Northwest. Her class also learned the personal stories of Corps members. After looking at these stories, Spaulding steered the class to the stories of people in their own families—parents, grandparents, and great-grandparents. For their Family Maps project, students and families worked together to tell where their immediate and extended families came from and why they picked Parkdale, Oregon, as their home.

(Continued)

(Continued)

Family Maps Process

Originally planned as a three-week project, the Family Maps project extended to seven weeks. To begin, Spaulding wrote letters to her students' parents (in English and Spanish) asking them to share their family stories with their children and to write a brief family history. In the letter, she included her own family story, accompanied by a marked world map of her family's origins. "For kindergartners, modeling is one of the most effective teaching strategies, building understanding through seeing, hearing, and then acting on the information," Spaulding shares. "Because of this modeling, students were more engaged in the stories—asking questions and making connections to what they already knew about their teachers."

Earlier in the year, Spaulding had told students about visiting her family in England over the summer. Using the Family Maps process, she extended her story—tracing her family's emigration to Canada and later to the United States on the map, using Parkdale as a point of reference. She discussed leaving behind close relatives—grandparents, aunts, uncles, and cousins—and talked about how much she missed them. She then told her students how she had reconnected with her relatives during the summer visit, sharing old times and the influences she had while growing up. Because of Spaulding's story, her students asked more questions and felt safe discussing their own connections and feelings about family members they had left behind.

Students took home Spaulding's letter a few days before spring break. Initially, only five students and their parents completed the assignment. As students brought in their stories, they shared them with the class in English and Spanish. Each student took a turn sitting in a chair with his or her classmates seated on the floor. Although Spaulding had modeled the telling of her family story, students were only able to tell a little bit of their stories because of their reading abilities and memory, so she read the stories in Spanish and translated them into English; or read them in English and then translated them into Spanish (depending on the home language of the family that prepared the story).

Spaulding recalls, "These were exciting times for all of us. I observed how much all of our kindergartners enjoyed sharing their stories. Students asked questions of each other and discussed how our stories were similar and different. This was a great way to reflect on the stories. Students were thrilled when they made connections between where different families came from and why they came to Parkdale."

A Family Maps bulletin board slowly developed, including a world map surrounded by family photos with a brief caption telling where each family came from. Students, parents, and classroom visitors were drawn to this display. It turned into another reflection tool for Spaulding and her students, as well as a conversation starter for visitors to the classroom. During student-led conferences in April, students and parents spent a good deal of time looking at the pictures and talking about where different families were from. Four families learned that they came from the same cities in Mexico, but hadn't known each other prior to moving to Parkdale. The bulletin board also prompted some parents to tell Spaulding that they knew nothing about the project and had not seen the assignment letter. Fortunately, she expected this to happen and had letters available for parents to take home.

In the following days, all the students brought in their family stories to share. At this point, every student was eager to share, but she had to limit the stories to two a day.

After all had shared their stories, students used oil pastels and watercolors to draw pictures of their families, like the one on this page (Figure 5.1). Giving students the opportunities to talk about their families within the context of a family "story" helps provide students with rich details from which to draw their own pictures. The artwork was mounted on construction paper and shared with the class. Spaulding recalls, "Through this sharing of artwork, I learned how powerful student art can be. I observed how students notice details—colors, shapes, and patterns—in the artwork, as well as how much they like to share what they have created."

During the project, Spaulding observed student and parent reactions and interactions as her primary tool to assess the impact of the activities. "Originally, I had planned to assess students by having them reflect on the project by drawing another student's family. Although they had learned about each other's families, they wouldn't

have been able to create someone else's family with all of the details that they showed in their own family portraits. Their portraits are truly amazing. One teacher told me, 'I would frame these pictures for permanent display in my home. They are just so great!'"

Spaulding's students displayed their family histories and artwork on the main hallway bulletin board. The display included family photos taken during home visits Spaulding and her teaching partner conducted the previous August, student-created family portraits, brief family biographical sketches, and a world map. It also included a picture of Meriwether Lewis and a brief biographical sketch of his family. According to Spaulding, "the display drew so much attention and admiration of other teachers and students that I will not be surprised if I see some similar projects next year."

Figure 5.1 Watercolor Portrait of One Student's Family

(Continued)

(Continued)

Lessons Learned

One of the biggest lessons Spaulding learned was about timing communications with parents. Sending the initial assignment letter at spring break wasn't effective, and many of the letters never made it home. This can be remedied by introducing the project to parents at the school's well-attended, student-led conferences—personally inviting families to share their stories and having them leave with assignment letters in hand.

One idea Spaulding is considering to scale up this project is to stage a schoolwide art show—to be called Family Album—featuring art based on the family. By the time the current kindergartners are in the fifth grade, they would have six pieces of art based on this theme. The springtime exhibit would feature different media—clay, collage, photography—with artwork lining the hallways at students' eye level.

"I am excited to think about changes that could improve the Family Maps project. Bringing more parents into the classroom is something I would like to see," says Spaulding. This year three parents helped on a regular basis in her classroom. Spaulding understands how difficult it is for many parents to volunteer because of their work schedules and the school's location. "Our school is not conveniently located so that parents can easily volunteer during their lunch breaks. With a special project, perhaps parents would be willing to make a commitment to come and share their time and story with their child's class," she believes.

The Family Maps project led to cooperation and more understanding among parents, students, and teachers, which is a better outcome than Spaulding expected. "The topic also let families know how much school values their stories. I think this was the biggest impact of this project for families."

To add CRSB practices to existing curriculum, educators can think about

- ways to incorporate families and communities, such as inviting family and community members to make presentations to students, attend community exhibits or events, or become involved in activities at home that help students learn;
- ways to incorporate students' culture, such as building from students' stories and prior knowledge, using culturally responsive literature (see resource box on page 115), or studying all genders, racial and ethnic backgrounds, and socioeconomic groups in different subject areas, especially those who have been underrepresented in the curriculum; and
- use of the Curriculum Planner and Wheel (page 127), which can help educators think of additional ways to modify the existing curriculum.

Resources for Math and Science Curricula

Culturally Responsive Science Curriculum (www.ankn.uaf.edu/publications/handbook/front.html)

Washington Mathematics Engineering Science Achievement (www.washingtonmesa.org)

Eisenhower National Clearinghouse for Mathematics and Science Education (www.goenc.org)

Selecting Culturally Responsive Literature

For most children and youth, reading a book that they can relate to is a powerful experience. Unfortunately, it can also be difficult for students to find books in school that accurately and respectfully reflect their culture. There are many resources available online that review multicultural children's and young adult literature, and that provide tips for selecting materials. Here are just a few:

Cynthia Leitich Smith: Children's Literature Resources (www.cynthialeitichsmith .com)

Oyate, a website of Native American Resources (http://www.oyate.org/index .php?option=com_virtuemart&Itemid=97)

Barahona Center for the Study of Books in Spanish for Children and Adolescents (www.csusm.edu/csb/english/)

New York Public Library: Includes links to annotated book lists related to Asian-Pacific American History Month, Latino Heritage Month, African-American History Month, Women's History Month, and more. (http:// kids.nypl.org/ holidays/)

African American Bibliography: Books for Children (http://www.lib.usm .edu/~degrum/html/collectionhl/ch-afroamericanbib.shtml)

Russian Children's Books in English (www.natashascafe.com/html/book.html)

The World of Arab and Muslim Children in Children's Books (http://www .auburn.edu/academic/education/eflt/lechner/arabbooks.pdf)

Beyond Female Protagonists—Female Voices in Picture Books (www.scils .rutgers.edu/~kvander/Feminist/fempic.html)

Examining Multicultural Picture Books for the Early Childhood Classroom: Possibilities and Pitfalls (http://ecrp.uiuc.edu/v3n2/mendoza.html)

10 Quick Ways to Analyze Children's Books for Racism and Sexism (http:// teachingforchange.org/files/033-A.pdf)

CREATING CULTURALLY RESPONSIVE STANDARDS-BASED LESSONS AND UNITS

Educators who make their classroom curriculum relevant to the needs of their students frequently become "proactive curriculum makers" (Powell, Zehm, & Garcia, 1996). The Curriculum Planner and Wheel (page 127) is designed to help educators plan a lesson or unit that integrates state academic standards with culturally responsive strategies. On the following pages are examples of a CRSB lesson (Snapshot 5.4 "Family Stories Books") and a CRSB unit (Snapshot 5.5 "Fairy Tales, Folktales, and Family Stories").

Snapshot 5.4

FAMILY STORIES BOOKS

Tubman Middle School, Portland, Oregon

Grade levels: 6–8, in an after-school program

Subject area: Literacy activity that focuses on family diversity

Highlights: This project helped students begin thinking about the interactions between their families and the school.

Creative extension: Give students disposable cameras to take home so they can photograph their families and share the pictures with teachers and classmates or use them as writing prompts.

The Tubman Middle School library has been transformed into a gallery, with 40 black-and-white and color portraits elegantly perched on the tops of bookcases and tables. As far as you can see, large photographs of kids with their families and teachers invite you to take a closer look into their diverse worlds.

The 30 students in the Tubman SUN Community School after-school program carefully view each photograph and read the simple narrative that accompanies it. A photograph of a grandmother and five youth who are playfully "asleep" in a queen-size bed captures a lot of attention, as does the portrait of a shyly smiling elementary school girl surrounded by her two moms and her dad. As they walk through the exhibit, the students have been given the assignment of jotting down "similarities or differences to their own families, or something in the photos they want to know more about."

The students return to their tables in groups of five or six and the conversation begins. The family involvement facilitator for the school district has come to lead a discussion about the value of all families. The students have lots of questions about the stories of the families in the photographs. One young man asks why all those children live with their grandmother. Another student wonders why a little girl in one of the pictures has no dad. Several students comment on how some of the families are like their own, but some they do not understand, like the girl with two moms. A lively, honest, and sometimes awkward discussion follows about how families may look different, that "one size doesn't really fit all" when it comes to family structure, and how all families still need to be acknowledged and respected.

The students are then asked to use words, pictures, or symbols to describe and reflect on their own family experience. They write in booklets made of letter paper that is folded in half, each page headed with a question such as, "What does your family look like?" "How does your family support you to be the best you can be in school?" "What happens when home and family come together?" "What does your teacher need to know about your family to teach you better?" The booklet format is easier to share with teachers and family members than a loose compilation of individual pieces would be.

The hour-long discussion in the library is just the beginning of honoring all families at Tubman. The after-school teachers who brought their students to participate in this lesson are encouraged to continue the conversation about family diversity and to create activities that infuse the information from the students' discussion back into their classrooms.

Snapshot 5.5

FAIRY TALES, FOLKTALES, AND FAMILY STORIES

Whitman Elementary School, Portland, Oregon

Grade level: 1

Subject areas: Reading, writing, language arts, and social studies

Highlights: This project used parents' knowledge at home and in the classroom. It emphasized that English language learners possess extra knowledge and skills worth valuing.

Amy Le and her mother are taking turns reading to the class "A Bunch of Chopsticks" from their homemade books. Mrs. Le reads a few lines in Vietnamese and then Amy, a precocious first-grader, reads her English translation. Behind them are maps and handwritten posters listing titles of stories, main characters, plots, and more—all in the various languages of the students. The rest of the English as a Second Language (ESL) students are lying on their stomachs, taking notes on clipboards. They sketch quick drawings or jot down words in the six boxes on their papers, listening hard to follow the storyline. The story concludes with a moral about the importance of the family sticking together like a "bunch of chopsticks": separately they are not as strong. It is a familiar story that Mrs. Le heard when she was a little girl in Vietnam. Amy's father is nearby, beaming with pride and keeping an eye on Amy's two little sisters who are playing in the corner of the room.

Almost every day for two and a half weeks, different families repeat the storytelling. During this time, the children hear parents' favorite childhood stories from Russia, Ukraine, Mexico, and the Philippines. Home language, culture, family history, and values become central elements of the literacy curriculum.

Lilia Doni, an ESL teacher, developed this activity as a culminating unit for the year. In addition to sharing the stories themselves, Doni incorporated short lessons in geography as parents and children showed the location of their countries of origin and told a bit about the climate and terrain. Each family taught the class how to say "hello" in their language and then, after finishing the story, how to say "thank you." These terms were written on chart paper and posted. During the course of the unit, Doni and the children read many other folktales and fairy tales, including several versions of the same story told in different cultures. They discussed the elements of fairy tales and folktales that make them a unique form of literature. New vocabulary words were listed and discussed.

On the last Friday of the school year, all the students' parents and siblings were invited to the school to see the children perform a reader's theater version of one of the stories. All the homemade books were exhibited, as were some of the notes. The completed charts and posters were also on display. Each child showed and talked about his or her "heritage doll"—a paper doll clothed by the parents in traditional dress from their countries of origin (Doni got the idea from Woodmere teacher Diana Larson, whose work is explained in Snapshot 6.2 "Heritage Dolls"). A few visiting dignitaries came including the principal and a district ESL coordinator. Refreshments were served, and there was much celebration and appreciation for the hard work and commitment of parents. Doni concluded with a short speech thanking the parents for teaching all

(Continued)

(Continued)

the children so much and for helping to show that speaking more than one language is not a problem but a strength. She gave each family a small photo album book with one or two photos from the project and plenty of blank pages for future pictures from school. One could feel a great sense of pride from both parents and children.

The achievement of Doni's students was readily measured by districtwide tests. During the school year, 3 of Doni's 12 first-grade ESL students made two years of progress in reading, entering the year just below grade level and leaving nearly two years above. This is truly remarkable, considering that little or no English is spoken in their homes. All the children made adequate progress. In addition, parents who had previously voiced concerns to the principal about a lack of rigor at the school became very engaged in the project and were happy with the results.

Doni closely aligned the project with key literacy standards for first grade, such as identifying the plot, main characters, and setting; understanding story genres; and learning new vocabulary. Additional standards were taught and practiced in areas such as speaking, engaging in discussion, and critical thinking. Assessment happened in various ways: Levels of writing skill and the ability to recall and retell a story were assessed through the notes children took. Teacher-led discussions of the stories and literacy concepts gave Doni information about children's understanding. Moreover,

the children directly experienced the similarities and differences that exist among diverse cultures. They learned that fairy tales and folktales are told in all cultures, but that they might reflect different values; and they learned that all languages have words for "hello" and "thank you," but that different languages have different sounds and tones for those words.

It took much effort to get some of the parents to participate, requiring letters, phone calls, and personal contacts (several of them, in some cases). However, Doni feels the pay-off was well worth the effort, and plans to continue with the project. She understands this effort is required to overcome a number of barriers, including the many other priorities in the lives of low-income, immigrant parents, and any previous negative experiences parents may have had at school. For parents who were uncomfortable reading in front of a group, Doni made available alternative ways for involvement, such as working on the heritage doll, recruiting other parents, and helping make decorations and other preparations for the reader's theater presentation. Doni also took advantage of one very engaged bilingual (Spanish/English) parent who was willing to serve as the link to the other Spanish-speaking families, acting as a parent coordinator and cultural liaison. In the end, because of their positive experience with this project, Doni has no doubt that more parents will be willing and eager to be involved in the school in various ways in the future.

DEVELOPING CULTURALLY RESPONSIVE STANDARDS-BASED PROJECTS

A good project connects academic, work, and life skills. It demands critical thinking and problem solving. It has a beginning, middle, and end and is worked on for an extended period—often a week or more. Young people, adult facilitators, and community partners design the project in concert, and it results in a final product or presentation.

Using projects as the basis for learning (also called project-based learning) results in hands-on, contextual learning that integrates young people's interests with the "real world" and gives young people a voice in what they learn. Project-based learning increases student motivation and engagement in learning (Bottoms & Webb, 1998; Moursund 2002). Many teachers have found that students who struggle in most academic settings find meaning and justification for learning by working on projects (Nadelson, 2000).

Tool 11 "Culturally Responsive Standards-Based Project Checklist" is designed to help practitioners think through the stages of a successful project, including planning, doing and documenting, reflecting and assessing, and evaluating.

Resources on Project-Based Learning

Project Approach in Early Childhood and Elementary Education (www .projectapproach.org)

Project-Based Instruction: Creating Excitement for Learning (educationnorth west.org/webfm_send/460)

Snapshot 5.6 "Know Our Roots" and Snapshot 5.7 "Project of the Year Books" are two examples of oral history projects. Know Our Roots took place at the elementary level and Project of the Year Books took place at the high school level.

Snapshot 5.6

KNOW OUR ROOTS

Glenoma Elementary School, Glenoma, Washington

Grade levels: 3 and 5

Subject areas: History, writing, and language arts

Highlights: A project about community history that built relationships between elementary school students and senior citizens, high school students, and business representatives.

The unincorporated town of Glenoma, with fewer than 1,000 residents, is located in the Cowlitz River valley in central Washington about 40 miles east of the Interstate-5 corridor. The community has been deeply affected by an economic downturn sparked by the closing of several lumber mills and a decline in tourism. More than half the students are eligible for free or reduced-price lunches. In light of this, "It became important to implement a program that was connected to the students' future," says District Superintendent Rick Anthony. During the last decade, the school has gradually built a focus on promoting youth entrepreneurship, contextual teaching and learning, and service learning.

A Mini-REAL (Rural Entrepreneurship to Action Learning) program was the foundation of this change. The program, which ran

(Continued)

(Continued)

for eight weeks each year, engaged students in building their own community within the school. Each of the roughly 100 students at the school had a job and worked within the community, which included a court system, bank, revenue department, and mall with student entrepreneurs running various shops, the post office, and recycling department. From this experience, service learning came to the forefront for students, along with an interest in their local community—a village without a real government—and the history of that community.

Elementary school teachers Linda Mettler and Janet Collier built on this interest. For several years, Collier's fifth-grade classes created "life maps," where students documented their personal history from birth to the present. The year of this project, the teacher expanded on this theme to include family history. They also introduced a new project in which students learned about the history of the local community through reading books, visiting local historical museums, and interviewing local long-term residents. They aligned the project with state writing, communication, and social studies standards, and used it as an opportunity to put into practice what they were learning through professional development opportunities in both technology integration and contextual teaching and learning.

To prepare for their interviews with community members, students were trained in interviewing techniques. A reporter from the local East Lewis County Journal visited the classes to give students pointers on nonverbal communication, questioning, and note taking. In the words of one student, "We learned to shake hands, make eye contact, and try to look interested in the person." Students from the nearby high school then came to talk about their interviewing experiences and participate in mock interviews with the grade school students.

Students were given additional preparation through a field trip to the Lewis County Historical Museum, where they learned about the county's history, giving them a context for the information they would gain through the interviews.

Once they had sufficient practice, the students scheduled interviews with the senior citizens. They mailed between 30 and 40 invitations out to people who had lived in the community for most of their lives. About 16 people agreed to come to the school for an interview. On the interview day, most of the subjects arrived early for their interview.

Though not entirely unexpected, it did catch the school off-guard, and the teachers hastily put a few chairs in the library where people could gather. The visitors ended up staying after their interviews to socialize in the library. Most of the visitors had not been in the school since they were students, and they appreciated the opportunity to come to the school and reconnect with others. Later, students also interviewed additional residents at the Morton Senior Center.

After the interviews, students used scanners and PowerPoint to create presentations bringing together the students' writings and observations, and the pictures the interviewees had brought. The project expanded into an after-school program when teachers were given an opportunity to create a writing class, freeing up time for the students to write more-developed stories based on their interviews. A community business owner who also was a skilled writer volunteered to assist with the project, helping the students find the most interesting aspects of their interviews and expand on them. They called the senior citizens with further questions when necessary. Students worked through the writing process, and used a rubric to assess each other's work. The stories were compiled into a student-published book featuring the 16 senior citizens. The stories covered a range of topics, including early May Day celebrations, Christmas celebrations, a women's basketball championship, and school experiences. One of the stories was published in the local newspaper.

As they did their research, students were intrigued to learn that there used to be a Community Day in Glenoma and decided they wanted to revive the event. Mettler and Collier never intended to carry out such an event, but agreed to do so because of the students' excitement. Students chose to use the day to celebrate the 70th birthday of the school building—another fact they had discovered in their research. Again, students wrote personal invitations to those who had been involved in their local history research. More than 100 parents, students, and senior citizens came to the school on a Saturday to participate in square dancing, May Pole dancing, and building tours. Students were in charge of taking pictures and running the camcorder, documenting the event.

Students used journals to reflect on their field trips, interviews, and the Community Day. The project gave students an opportunity to write in real contexts, practice interviewing skills, and use technology, all while meeting state academic standards in writing, communication,

and social studies. The teachers report that previously unmotivated students became motivated because they saw relevance for their schoolwork. They were eager to learn about history and felt pride in their rural community. In addition, many of the students do not have grandparents who live in the area, and they benefited from the opportunity to learn about the lives of the elderly and to appreciate generational differences.

The senior citizens had an opportunity to meet the students and get to know them better in a positive light—countering the negative stereotypes of youth often portrayed in the media. They felt valued by the teachers and students for their knowledge and experience, and the school improved its relationship with the major voters in the area.

Unfortunately, due to declining enrollment, the Glenoma Elementary School was forced to close at the end of the 2003–2004 school year. The loss is surely felt by everyone in this small community. As Collier explains, "This makes it even more significant, I feel, that we were able to document some of the school's history with our Know Our Roots project."

Snapshot 5.7

PROJECT OF THE YEAR BOOKS

Aberdeen High School, Aberdeen, Washington

Grade levels: 9–12

Subject area: English

Highlights: This teacher built on student and community interests—high school sports—to do an oral history and book publishing project.

Ask anybody from Hoquiam or Aberdeen, Washington, the score of the ball game the year they graduated from high school and they will immediately be able to tell you. They know "the ball game" is the annual

Thanksgiving Day football game played between these two high school rivals from 1906 to 1973. It was extremely important to this community and has become legend. So in 2000 when Aberdeen High School

(Continued)

(Continued)

English teacher David McKay was looking for an engaging assignment for his students, he decided to have them research, write, publish, and sell a book about the Thanksgiving Day football games.

McKay recalls feeling that it was difficult to motivate all his students to write high-quality papers. While some students did excellent work, he was frustrated that many were doing just enough to get by. He had had his classes write papers before, but the assignments didn't seem to have an authentic enough feel for the students. He wanted to find a project that would inspire them to do their best work, creating a formal document that adhered to demanding publishing parameters. He thought having an authentic audience and a professional publication might create the needed inspiration.

It turned out that the enthusiasm of the community motivated the students. Most of the roughly 20,000 people in the two cities, located about 100 miles southwest of Seattle along the Washington coast, knew of the high school rivalry. Many recalled fond memories of their participation in the many school events and community rituals associated with the game. The students first interviewed parents, family, and members of the community who graduated from either of the two high schools between 1906 and 1973. When they found that they did not have enough information from the very early days of the Thanksgiving Day games, they visited an assisted-living facility and a local restaurant to collect stories from some of the long-time residents of the community. People were excited to tell the students about their days as a player on the field, a cheerleader on the sidelines, or a fan in the stands. In the end, the students recorded and transcribed 120 oral histories.

The students then did library research. They double-checked facts and figures on coaches, game scores, and team rosters by reviewing old annuals, programs, and newspapers. These newspapers, which printed special sections the Wednesday before each game, inspired the students to create scrapbook pages of team photos, headlines, and articles for each year to include in the book.

All of McKay's students participated in collecting the stories and research, with one junior English class working as the editing team that compiled all the documents into a book worthy of publication. When the writing and compiling were completed, McKay found a short-run publishing company 50 miles away that created a professional cover (see Figure 5.2) and soft-cover binding, and then printed 1,000 copies of the book. He secured a loan to pay for the book's printing costs. While waiting for the invoice from the publishing company to be paid by the district, the books were sold at the school, drugstore, a restaurant, museums, and gift shops. Within three months, the community had bought all 1,000 books and McKay did not even have to take out the loan.

Because of the enormous demand, a second printing of 500 books was made, which again sold out. All in all, book sales equaled twice the printing costs. The additional money was put in the general associated student body fund and was used to pay for subsequent publications. In 2002, students asked community members to pass down bits of wisdom through stories, poems, essays, and one-liners; these were edited into "The Grays Harbor County Book of Wisdom." Students also wrote four editions of "Lutefisk for the Bobcat Soul: Personal Essays Written by Students of Aberdeen High School," including a 2002 edition about overcoming adversity, a 2003 edition honoring mothers and other "mother-types" titled "Your Mama's Edition," and a 2004 edition honoring fathers and other male role models, titled "Who's Your Daddy?"

Figure 5.2 The Students' First Published Book

McKay was amazed by the dedication of the students and the hours they spent writing, editing, and revising. Students built relationships with community members through their repeated interviews, sharing drafts and making corrections. They also gained an appreciation for their school and community history and enjoyed reading newspapers and annuals from nearly 100 years ago. The community support, interest, and enthusiasm in the books have been rewarding for the students and the school.

Sadly, David McKay passed away in 2004, so the Who's Your Daddy edition of Lutefisk for the Bobcat Soul will be the last edition in the series.

In Snapshot 5.8 "Learning From Aundre'a," the term "culture" is broadly defined. But for people with disabilities or chronic health issues, there is little doubt that they inhabit a culture apart from and poorly understood by people who live without disabilities. This exciting project brought the two cultures together in a way that changed the lives of everyone involved. It's a great example of transformational teaching and learning.

Snapshot 5.8

LEARNING FROM AUNDRE'A: A CURRICULUM OF CARING AND CONCERN

Newsome Park Elementary School, Newport News, Virginia

Grade level: 3

Subject area: A project that integrated curriculum content (science, health, math, and writing standards) with technology

Highlights: Cystic fibrosis, and its impact on a fellow student, became the focus of a six-month project. The student's classmates were highly engaged in learning and, with their support and empathy, she thrived.

Ms. Billie Hetrick, a third-grade teacher at Newsome Park, a diverse inner-city magnet school, was always looking for ways to infuse meaningful topics into her projects. So when children asked "What's the matter with Aundre'a?"—showing concern about her many trips to the nurse's office for medication and frequent absences—Hetrick realized the potential for a terrific project built around Aundre'a and her illness. Rather than an abstract idea, the students would learn first-hand about cystic fibrosis, and understand and empathize with a classmate who had this type of challenge.

The project began with students using a computer program that provides graphic organizers to plan projects. They first used a "circle map" to describe what Aundre'a was going through, and then used a "tree map" to explore what they wanted to know: How did cystic fibrosis affect Aundre'a?

Among the first questions they asked, which was undoubtedly the hardest, was "Is there a cure?" After learning that there is no cure, the students wanted to raise money to help scientists find one. They decided to participate in the Walk-a-Thon for Cystic Fibrosis. The Walk-a-Thon provided many real-world opportunities to apply the math skills they were learning. Since this activity entailed taking pledges from families,

friends, and fellow students during lunch breaks, the students needed to count and track the money donated. Paper cutouts of shoes plastered the walls, each representing a donation. Hetrick also had students graph the donations to determine which lunch period gave the most money. Participating in the Walk-A-Thon was logistically complicated because it took place on a weekend; nonetheless, many of the families of Hetrick's students were engaged.

Other activities incorporated science, health, and writing standards. Students brainstormed things they could do to help Aundre'a stay healthy, such as washing their hands frequently and covering their mouths when they coughed. In small groups, they researched the disease and other related topics. Then the groups created posters and PowerPoint presentations to share what they had learned. Guest speakers included experts from the local Cystic Fibrosis Foundation and Aundre'a's mother. With Aundre'a's help, the speakers demonstrated the machine that cleared her lungs, after which they responded to questions. At a culminating event—Project Day—parents, school administrators, and guests strolled the halls of the school, reading the students' displays and stopping to learn more.

That year, Hetrick's students gained more than knowledge. They had the experience of improving the life of a classmate. Looking back on the six-month period of the project, Aundre'a's mother realized that it was one of the healthiest periods of her life. As of the winter of 2010, Aundre'a is in high school and doing well—academically and physically.

Video on project-based learning at Newsome Park Elementary School can be found on the Edutopia website: http://www.edutopia.org/newsome-park

DEVELOPING CULTURALLY RESPONSIVE STANDARDS-BASED INTERDISCIPLINARY ACTIVITIES

Interdisciplinary activities make learning more relevant for students because they emphasize the connections among subject areas, demonstrate the purpose for studying different subjects, and more closely resemble how things are done in the "real world." After all, in the real world most people don't start out their day by doing 50 minutes of math! McBrien and Brandt (1997) state that interdisciplinary studies include the following elements:

- A topic that lends itself to study from several points of view
- Two to five themes or essential questions the teacher wants students to explore
- An approach and activities that further students' understanding more than is possible in a traditional, single-discipline unit

One way to begin planning for interdisciplinary activities is to look for the natural connections among standards. Mitchell and colleagues (1995) explain:

It is usually a natural match to hook standards focused on content (such as broad concepts and knowledge from different subjects) to standards focused on processing information (such as reading, writing, listening, talking, critical thinking, speaking, manipulating mathematically). Hooking ideas from science, social studies, and the arts to the processing skills necessary to gain new information, to manipulate that information, and to explain to others what has been learned is a natural way to learn. . . . Process and content are fundamentally intertwined and therefore make natural connections. (page 39)

The preceding oral history projects illustrate Mitchell and colleagues' point through integrating history with reading, writing, and communicating. See Snapshot 7.1 "Tulalip-Based Curriculum and Lushootseed Classes" for examples of interdisciplinary work in science, math, art, and technology. For a project that uses youth culture and students' interest in roller coasters to integrate science, math, and language arts, see Snapshot 7.2 "It's a Wild Ride."

Snapshot 5.9 "Students Express Themselves Through Theater" uses the medium of drama as the mechanism for interdisciplinary CRSB teaching, and deals with issues that are topical and intensely important to almost all high schoolers.

Snapshot 5.9

STUDENTS EXPRESS THEMSELVES THROUGH THEATER

Providence High School, Charlotte, North Carolina

Grade levels: 9–12

Subject areas: Theater, language arts, social studies

Highlights: Students in a high school theater group perform a play based on the tragic shootings at Colombine High School in Littleton, Colorado.

The arts in schools can provide an excellent media for bridging students' cultures. The Chaos Ensemble, a group of teen actors formed from Providence High School's drama department, decided to use their theatrical skills to focus on teen socialization and school culture, and to shine a spotlight on the underlying prejudice in school that can lead to desperate teen actions. The production, "Columbinus," a drama by Stephen Karam and P. J. Paparelli, depicts the incidents that happened 10 years before at Columbine High School, including a reproduction of the infamous 911 call and footage of the shootings on a video screen at center stage. The focus is on the type of bullying and stereotyping that goes often unnoticed by adults, but builds to long-term destruction in kids.

"We did a survey of ninth-graders, and they said that most bullying happens where adults don't see it: in the halls, in the lunchroom," says guidance counselor Sharon Walker. "The demographics of Columbine are similar to our school. We don't have a lot of violence or fighting, but technology now makes cyber-bullying possible and often keeps it under our radar. This isn't a problem adults can really solve, but we can create an awareness of it in kids."

While James Yost, the high school's drama teacher, supervised rehearsals, he brought Jillian Claire in as student director to make sure the play was reflective of the students' perspective. "With Mr. Yost, it's more than just taking notes for him," she says. "I'm the same age as the characters in the play, so he wanted my viewpoint about the ways they might behave. People around the school come to shows all the time, but I'm not sure they realize how unusual this is."

Yost hopes "Columbinus" will cause students and adults to be less willing to pre-judge and condemn. He hopes Chaos Ensemble will stay strong at Providence but grow to embrace any high-schooler drawn to unusual drama: "Maybe we'll do 'The Laramie Project' (about the murder of a gay student in Wyoming) or 'The Wrestling Season' (in which eight young people struggle with the destructive power of rumors)."

While "Columbinus" is about the worst that can happen when troubled teens snap, it reminds us of the conditions that can lead to turmoil for a school setting.

For the full story go to the *Charlotte Observer*, December 20, 2009 (www.charlotteobserver.com/local/story/1115963.html).

To learn more about the Chaos Ensemble, visit their website at www.chaosensemble.webs.com.

Reprinted with the permission of the *Charlotte Observer*.

TOOL 10

<table>
<tr><td colspan="2" style="text-align:center">CULTURALLY RESPONSIVE STANDARDS-BASED CURRICULUM PLANNER AND CURRICULUM WHEEL</td></tr>
</table>

The Curriculum Planner helps you plan a lesson, unit, or project that integrates state academic standards and other learning goals with culturally responsive strategies. It can be used to develop a new activity or to bring breadth and depth to an existing activity. The Curriculum Wheel (page 130) is a visual layout of the Curriculum Planner. It can be used to give you the big picture of how your planned activity meets state academic standards and the essential elements of CRSB teaching.

As you modify an existing activity or develop a new activity, consider each of the planning questions on the Curriculum Planner. Write down your ideas in the right-hand column. Questions are provided for each of the six CRSB essential elements. While not all activities will fully address each essential element, expanding your activity to address these elements more fully will improve its cultural responsiveness. Detailed descriptions of the essential elements are on pages 11–15.

The Curriculum Planner helps you expand an activity so that it is culturally responsive and standards based. After you write down your ideas, you might want to write down sequential lesson plans to help guide you through the activity with your students—or you might want to use the Curriculum Wheel as a one-page reference. An example of a completed Curriculum Wheel is included on page 131.

Multiple learning goals and elements of CRSB teaching can be met with one activity; try to see how many emerge along with new activities, themes, and interests.

Creative Extensions

- The Curriculum Wheel can be photocopied at 200 percent to fit onto 11 x 17–inch paper to allow more space for writing. It can also be laminated to make a poster-size planner for group planning or training.
- One of the most effective means of professional development is to have a fellow teacher observe you while you are teaching a class. The Curriculum Wheel can be filled in by the observing teacher writing down evidence he sees of the standards, goals, and essential elements that are taught. The teacher being observed might ask the observer to look for evidence of a single element or for all six elements.

CRSB Curriculum Planner

Use these planning questions to help you develop an activity that integrates state academic standards and the essential elements of culturally responsive teaching. (See pages 11–15 for a review of the CRSB essential elements.)

Planning Questions	Curriculum Plan
Starting Points At what point on the Continuum of Options and Opportunities (Figure 1.3, page 21) is this activity?	
What is a working title for this activity?	

(Continued)

(Continued)

Planning Questions	Curriculum Plan
Standards and Goals	
List the state academic standards that will be addressed.	
List any alternative learning goals that could be addressed.	
Describe what the skill or learning looks like when it is done well, or when it meets the standard. What are its characteristics? Are any prior skills needed? Are standards and goals written clearly enough for students to understand? If not, how should they be restated?	
Student Centered	
Describe interests and personal experiences your students have that could be used in this activity.	
Describe connections to students' families or communities that could be used in this activity.	
Describe how connections can be made to students' cultures in this activity.	
How could students' different learning styles be accommodated in this activity?	
What strengths and skills do students possess that they can use to build on this activity?	
How could students have input into planning this activity?	
Transformational	
How could this activity help students examine the strengths and significance of their culture, family, or community?	
How could this activity help students critically examine and challenge the knowledge and content that is presented to them?	
How might this activity transform the thinking of students, teachers, family, or community members?	

Planning Questions	Curriculum Plan
Connected and Integrated How could this activity be related to students' lives outside the classroom? How could this activity involve students in a real-world endeavor?	
How could this activity enhance or build on other activities students have done in school (in or outside this classroom and grade)?	
Critical Thinking What critical thinking skills could be taught and used in this activity?	
How can this activity promote and enhance students' thinking dispositions and metacognitive skills?	
Reflection and Assessment What information will be used to see if this activity helps students meet the standard or learning goal?	
In what ways could student learning be documented?	
How will student engagement in the activity be demonstrated?	
How could students be involved in the assessment process?	
In what ways will students reflect on their learning?	
Relationship and Community Building How can this activity help teachers know and better understand their students, students' families, and students' communities?	
How can this activity help students to better know each other, their families, and their communities?	
What community resources or connections can be leveraged to provide more support to this activity?	
Teacher Knowledge What new knowledge do I need about the subject, the students, or their families and communities to teach this activity well?	

(Continued)

(Continued)

CRSB Curriculum Wheel

This wheel is a visual demonstration of how the CRSB essential elements, state standards, and other learning goals can come together in a lesson, unit, or project.

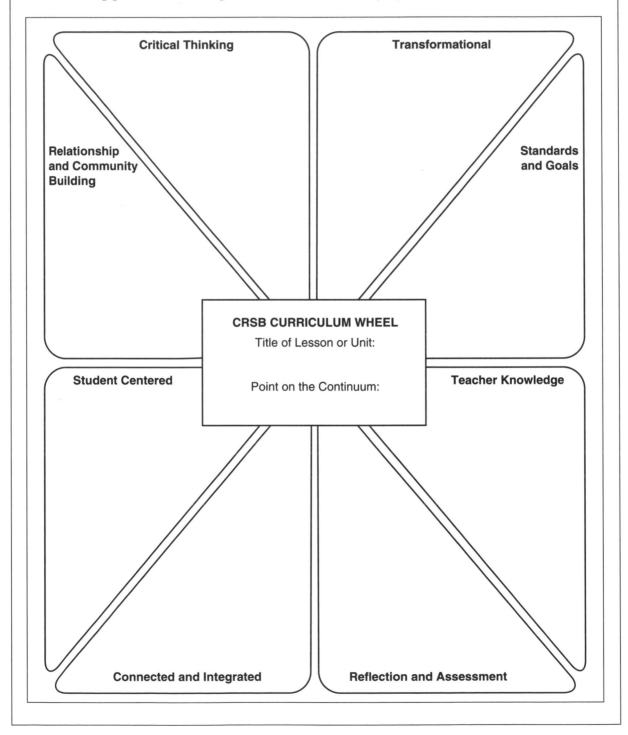

Critical Thinking

Transformational

Relationship and Community Building

Standards and Goals

CRSB CURRICULUM WHEEL

Title of Lesson or Unit:

Point on the Continuum:

Student Centered

Teacher Knowledge

Connected and Integrated

Reflection and Assessment

Example of a Completed Curriculum Wheel

This completed wheel is a plan for Snapshot 5.7, "Project of the Year Books," on page 121.

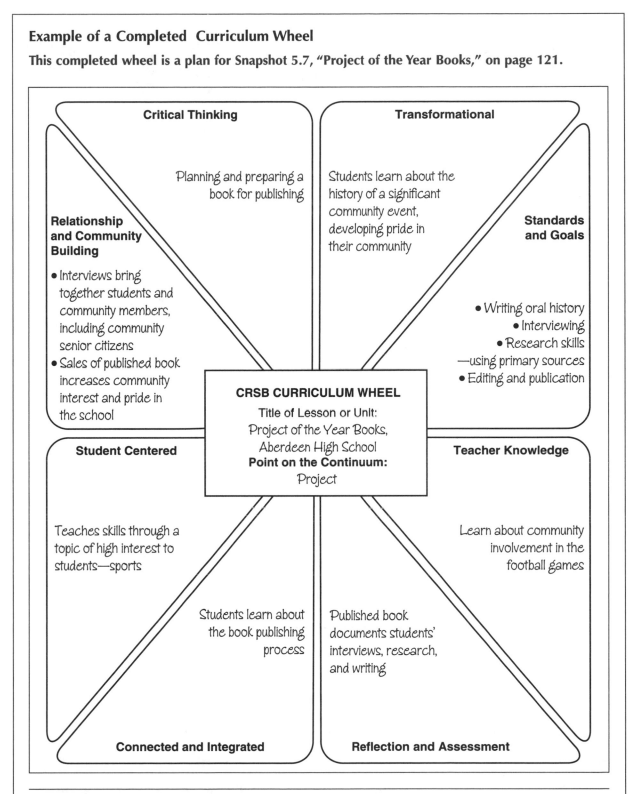

Critical Thinking

Planning and preparing a book for publishing

Transformational

Students learn about the history of a significant community event, developing pride in their community

Relationship and Community Building

- Interviews bring together students and community members, including community senior citizens
- Sales of published book increases community interest and pride in the school

Standards and Goals

- Writing oral history
- Interviewing
- Research skills —using primary sources
- Editing and publication

CRSB CURRICULUM WHEEL
Title of Lesson or Unit:
Project of the Year Books,
Aberdeen High School
Point on the Continuum:
Project

Student Centered

Teaches skills through a topic of high interest to students—sports

Students learn about the book publishing process

Teacher Knowledge

Learn about community involvement in the football games

Published book documents students' interviews, research, and writing

Connected and Integrated

Reflection and Assessment

TOOL 11

CULTURALLY RESPONSIVE STANDARDS-BASED PROJECT CHECKLIST

Facilitating a great classroom project requires careful planning. The CRSB Project Checklist helps practitioners think through the stages of a successful CRSB project, including planning, doing and documenting, reflecting and assessing, and evaluating.

Creative Extensions

This tool can be used in conjunction with the CRSB Curriculum Planner. Instead of recording your project plans and ideas on a blank piece of paper, use the CRSB Curriculum Wheel to record your thoughts.

The more students are involved in the preliminary planning of a project, the greater connection they feel to the project, and the more successful the project will be. Moreover, all the elements of project planning (such as creative and critical thinking, teamwork, and problem solving) are invaluable skills to teach your students. Which parts of the planning can you do with your students? Use questions from the Project Checklist to help your students carefully think through their work on the project.

Use this checklist as a brainstorming and planning tool. Review the questions and think about the meaning each question has for your project. Use a blank piece of paper to record any ideas, plans, or additional questions.

Plan

❑ Is the project mindfully linked to one or two state academic standards (or other rigorous learning goals)?

❑ Are there clear outcomes for students that connect to standards?

❑ Do all participants involved (students, parents, community members, other staff) understand the project goals and desired outcomes?

❑ Does the project have an identifiable structure with a beginning (planning and community building), middle (doing, documenting, and reflecting), and end (reflecting, assessing, recognizing, celebrating, and evaluating)?

❑ How is (or how can) the project be connected to larger school, district, and community initiatives?

❑ How can students, families, and community members be involved with planning the project and its goals?

❑ What are the possible challenges in doing this project? What are possible ways to address these challenges?

❑ As a facilitator of the project, how do your own beliefs and experiences intersect with and relate to the project? What skills, talents, and experiences do you bring to the project?

❑ What new learning or growth might you need to do to facilitate the project well?

Do and Document

❑ Does the project emphasize the development of skills and competencies that are valued by the home, school, and community?

❑ Is the project relevant to the lives of students? Is it authentically rooted in the cultures of their families and communities?

- ❏ Does the project challenge young people to understand and use the style of learning that works best for them as well as use higher-level thinking skills, creative thought, and problem solving?
- ❏ Does the project encourage all sorts of new and meaningful connections for students and the staff involved (i.e., among and between peers, families, teachers, community members, and their various cultures)?
- ❏ Are there ways to work in collaboration with community members or other practitioners? (Consider what other teachers in your building are doing, what other schools and community-based organizations are doing, and community or district initiatives.)
- ❏ Are the young people encouraged to look at an issue from multiple perspectives throughout the project?
- ❏ Does the project incorporate social justice values, diversity training, and equal opportunity for everyone involved?
- ❏ Do the young people document competencies gained throughout the project?

Reflect and Assess

- ❏ Is reflection built in throughout the project? Are several types of reflection used throughout the project (writing, discussing, drawing)?
- ❏ Is assessment built in throughout the project? Are several types of assessment used throughout the project (self-assessment, peer assessment, community assessment)?
- ❏ Are the results of the built-in assessment used to make project improvements?
- ❏ Does the project help young people to connect and integrate their academic learning with their lives outside school?
- ❏ Are there opportunities and encouragement for the young people to make connections among themselves and all the cultures they must learn to negotiate to become caring and productive citizens (connections among themselves, their home and community culture, and the "dominant" culture)?
- ❏ Does the project encourage students and staff to value their own cultures and the unfamiliar?
- ❏ Are there opportunities and encouragement for parents to reflect on and to make connections about their students' learning?
- ❏ After the project is completed, are young people offered opportunities to reflect back on the work and connect it to new learning?

Evaluate

- ❏ Is evaluation addressed during the preliminary thinking and planning of the project? Is it a central, ongoing part? Do you have effective evaluation tools?
- ❏ Is the evaluation of the project aimed at strengthening positive outcomes for the young people?
- ❏ Are the young people (and others involved, such as parents and community members) an active part of the evaluation process from beginning to end?
- ❏ Are the results of the evaluation shared in meaningful ways with students, parents, and community members?

Snapshot 5.10 "Making Social Studies Meaningful for Young Children" shows how Marcy Prager, the 2009 Elementary Social Studies Teacher of the Year, uses her knowledge of the geography and cultures of the many places she has visited around the world to help her students understand people who are different than themselves. She also employs the child-centered artifacts, photos, and videos she has obtained in her travels to help her young students understand and appreciate their own cultures and the cultures of their classmates.

Snapshot 5.10

MAKING SOCIAL STUDIES MEANINGFUL FOR YOUNG CHILDREN

Michael Driscoll School, Brookline, Massachusetts

Grade level: 1 and 2

Subject areas: Social studies and literacy

Highlights: One teacher integrates the content standards for social studies, literature, and other subjects into culturally responsive and engaging lessons.

Marcy Prager understands young children. Her ability to connect her first- and second-grade students at Driscoll School (close to Boston) with their own cultures, their classmates' cultures, and the cultures of diverse peoples beyond their borders, earned her the honor of Elementary Social Studies Teacher of the Year in 2009 from the National Council for Social Studies.

The first half of the year in Prager's first grade is spent focusing on the cultures of the children in the class. Although nearly all the students come from middle- and upper-income homes, typically a third of the students' families emigrated from such countries as Korea, Russia, or Nigeria. And, although they may appear to be homogenous, there is great diversity among the students.

The first step toward students understanding and appreciating other cultures is to understand their own culture and the cultures of their classmates. To be responsive to the learning needs of young children, it is best to start with direct, concrete experiences, so Prager. first explores tangible things—the neighborhoods and houses they live in and the foods they eat—and more emotionally meaningful topics such as what happens when they misbehave, how their family celebrated their birth or adoption,

and why they were given their particular name. Students interview their family members and then discuss what they learned. They write short essays through which first- and second-grade writing standards are taught. Their stories are diverse— in some families a rabbi officially named them when they were eight days old, and in others grandparents came to help for several weeks after their birth. In some families, children were named after a beloved relative and in others, a big meal was served to an extended group of friends and family members to celebrate their birth.

Then, during social studies, she ties these to practices in other cultures. Among the Hopi, cornmeal of a certain color is ground and spread on babies' cheeks. Later, on the 20th day of life, the child is named by the paternal grandmother. In Ghana, children are named based on the day of the week on which they were born. After learning about the diversity of birth celebrations and naming traditions among classmates, the practices they learn about in social studies do not seem so "odd" or "foreign" to Prager's students, but part of the wonderful, interesting diversity of the world.

It's no surprise that Prager's goals for her students are grand. "Global awareness is a responsibility I hold dear," she states. "Children have a better chance to create world peace as adults if they gain an understanding of people's differences and similarities in their classrooms, in their neighborhoods, and in neighborhoods throughout the world."

Prager does not shy away from dealing with more controversial differences among her students, such as values and beliefs. For suburban first-graders, there may be no belief more salient than the existence of Santa Claus. At this age, some children firmly believe in the "big guy," others firmly do not, and more than a few are unsure. She facilitates discussions among the children in which they develop skills to clearly state their views, make cogent arguments, and, more importantly, learn to listen to and respect the strongly held beliefs of others.

For Prager, social studies provides the opportunity to empathize with others by learning how geography shapes their lives. The children develop a keen sense of the where they live through an extensive project that results, with the help of parents, in a three-dimensional model of their concept of an ideal neighborhood—from a kid's perspective. It combines elements of various neighborhoods they have experienced or read about. Parks, ponds, playgrounds, toy stores, movie theaters, video stores, a diversity of restaurants, and a fire station are some of the places that are always present in this "neighborhood." Then in the second-grade unit on the Hopi (a people she has studied and visited extensively), students learn that much of the Hopi culture stems from living in the desert. The Hopi pray to Katsina spirits in order to help bring rain so the corn will grow. Complex dance ceremonies throughout the Hopi calendar year serve the same purpose.

Prager focuses on aspects of geography and culture that are meaningful for young children. She collects artifacts and stories, and takes videos and photos from a child's perspective during her extensive world travels. (Some of her travel has been funded by the local Brookline Education Foundation and assisted by Primary Source [www.primarysource.org], which promotes history and humanities education by connecting educators with people.) Her students learn that if a child acts like a good Hopi and prays, he or she will be rewarded. However, if children misbehave, the Ogre Katsina will "get" them. She asks, "What does good behavior look like in your house? What happens when you misbehave?" All parents in all societies expect kids to act "right," but exactly what constitutes behaving and misbehaving—and the consequences for misbehaving—varies greatly.

To expand their understanding of this issue, which is very compelling to first- and second-graders, they read folktales from around the world. Nearly all describe a setting, which the class investigates (integrating geography standards) and reflect beliefs about what it means to be "good." Anansi stories from West Africa—Ghana is another country Prager has visited and knows well—are often about the importance of not being selfish. Many Japanese folktales promote the value of self-control. (Yes, Prager has been to Japan, too, and has a deep understanding and appreciation for their culture.) While making text-to-text, text-to-self, and text-to-world connections among these folktales, a literacy standard for this grade, the children also learn that different cultures value different behaviors.

Prager has even journeyed with her students to actively promote intercultural connections beyond the classroom. One year, after reading *Sadako and the Thousand Paper Cranes* (Coerr, 2004), they made cranes and sent them to the Hiroshima Children's Peace Park. They soon discovered that Seattle also has a peace park modeled after the one in Japan, which led them to the idea that there should be one in Boston. They wrote letters to the mayor making this request, which provided great motivation to write clearly worded, well-constructed arguments. Students even designed Sadako statues and plaques for the mayor to place in their proposed peace park.

(Continued)

(Continued)

Many educators want to know how they can promote cultural competence and be culturally response when they teach. Prager's approach provides one powerful model. She helps her students understand that they do indeed have a culture, know the key aspects of their own cultures including how they are shaped by geography, identify the similarities and differences among cultures, and respect and appreciate all cultures. Prager embraces Nigerian writer Chimamanda Adichie's idea that there is "no single story" about a person or any group of people and that thinking so is dangerous. (See her speech on this topic on the TED: Ideas Worth Spreading website: go to http://www.ted.com and type "Adichie" in the search box.) Human beings and societies are always complex and multifaceted. The more we know about ourselves and each other, the less likely we are to stereotype, or be afraid, or feel superior to others, and the more likely we are to understand and care and to want to know more.

REFLECTION QUESTIONS

1. Choose a particular standard that your students must meet this year. What are some ways that you could adapt your lesson plan in order to connect this standard to your students' lives in a concrete and personal way?

2. "Unpack" a particular standard that you are familiar with, as explained on page 95. What is the intent of the standard? What are its umbrella concepts and implications? Can you "own" it? If not, what would you need to know or do in order to "own" it?

3. What are some of the challenges that you would expect to arise (or have experienced) when connecting standards to students' family and community cultures? How can you overcome these challenges?

4. What are some compelling local issues or unique aspects of the community that could be used to develop a curriculum that would engage your students? How could you include your students in the planning process for developing this curriculum?

5. From a quick review of the standards section of this chapter, are there important standards missing from your list of state standards? Are they standards that may be necessary for the students in your district, school, or classroom to be successful?

6. Read the snapshots in this chapter (5.1 "Rediscovering a Lost Heritage," 5.2 "Collaborative Action Research Projects," 5.3 "Family Maps," 5.4 "Family Stories Books," 5.5 "Fairy Tales, Folktales, and Family Stories," 5.6 "Know Our Roots," 5.7 "Project of the Year Books," 5.8 "Learning from Aundre'a," 5.9 "Students Express Themselves Through Theater," or 5.10 "Making Social Studies Meaningful for Young Children"). Have you participated in or used culminating projects as a curriculum strategy? How could your projects be made culturally responsive and standards-based? What are some of the challenges involved in using culminating projects?

7. What is your own family's migration story? How has it impacted your life? Did it help shape your sense of identity, your beliefs, and what you do for a living?

8. What are your own interests and passions that could be used as the basis for standards-based curriculum? How do think your students will respond to the change in the curriculum?

6

Assessment and Reflection

You learn as much—if not more—from your mistakes as you do from your successes.

—Ruth Mitchell, Marilyn Willis, &
the Chicago Teachers Union Quest Center (1995)

Assessment and reflection—for both teachers and students—is an essential element of culturally responsive standards-based (CRSB) teaching. Assessment and reflection activities should be thoughtful and promote critical thinking; should be about and for the user; and should be ongoing and infused throughout the curriculum. As students and teachers assess and reflect on their work, both groups understand their own teaching and learning styles better; make academic, personal, and cultural connections; and become more skillful in evaluating and improving their own performance and thinking.

In these days of high-stakes accountability and increasing curricular mandates, teachers need to be able to show that what they are doing in the classroom will lead to improved student achievement. It is also critical that teachers are able to articulate why their teaching practices are effective. It is our belief that keeping a focus on CRSB teaching will increase student motivation and engagement, improve school–family–community partnerships, and create challenging curricula, resulting in improved performance on mandated standardized tests. However, standardized tests are usually only given once a year, and often the results are not received until after students are gone for the summer. By integrating assessment and reflection into the classroom on a regular basis, teachers are able to monitor students' learning throughout the year, make midcourse adjustments to their teaching, and gather evidence to show parents and administrators that their practices are working.

This chapter gives tips, ideas, and tools for using assessment and reflection in the CRSB classroom. Before beginning, use Tool 12 "Self-Assessment on Assessment and Reflection" to help you examine your assessment and reflection practices.

TOOL 12

SELF-ASSESSMENT ON ASSESSMENT AND REFLECTION

Read each of the statements and rate yourself. This exercise will help you think about the areas where you are very capable and the areas where you need improvement, and will help you set learning goals. Before you begin the assessment, remember that it is not a test and there are no wrong answers; it is merely a tool to help you grow in CRSB teaching practices. Assess yourself periodically to check for growth.

Rating scale: D = Developing, M = Meeting, E = Exceeding

Assessment and Reflection	D	M	E
I accept constructive criticism and feedback from colleagues, students, parents, and supervisors.	☐	☐	☐
I use my students' achievement data to assess my own classroom practice and performance.	☐	☐	☐
Throughout my lessons and activities there are many opportunities for my students and me to be reflective and assess the learning that occurs (content and process).	☐	☐	☐
I use several different types of reflection in my classroom (written, verbal, artistic, and others).	☐	☐	☐
I use several different types of assessment in my classroom (teacher, self, peer, community, and others).	☐	☐	☐
I use the results from any reflection or assessment to make curricular improvements.	☐	☐	☐
In my classroom, assessment is a central and ongoing piece of any lesson, unit, or project that I teach.	☐	☐	☐
I have effective assessment tools and processes.	☐	☐	☐
Assessment in my classroom recognizes and accommodates varying backgrounds, language differences, cultural differences, and expression in multiple intelligences.	☐	☐	☐
I share evaluation results in ways that are meaningful for students, parents, and other stakeholders.	☐	☐	☐
I can reflect on my own effectiveness.	☐	☐	☐

Reflections on my knowledge of assessment and reflection:

STUDENT ASSESSMENT

Assessment is generally thought of as the process of measuring students' skills or knowledge in a subject area. Teachers use assessment to guide instruction, monitor student progress, make grouping decisions, diagnose strengths and weaknesses, evaluate curriculum, give feedback, and determine grades. There are many ways to assess students, including the use of quizzes and tests. This section will focus on some other types of assessment that align well with a CRSB curriculum.

Rather than thinking of assessment as something done at the end—once teaching is completed—Wiggins and McTighe (1998) suggest that teachers reverse the process. In their book *Understanding by Design*, they describe a three-stage curriculum planning sequence. First, guided by standards, teachers identify what they want students to know, understand, and be able to do. Next, they determine the assessment evidence that will tell them if students have achieved the desired results or met the standards. With these assessments in mind, teachers plan instructional activities that will lead to the desired results. Thus, the assessments serve as teaching targets that help focus instruction.

Authentic Assessment

Authentic assessment is a term used to describe assessments that focus on whether students can use skills and apply them appropriately, rather than simply regurgitating information. Authentic assessment, also referred to as alternative assessment or performance-based assessment, asks students to perform tasks that reflect the kind of mastery demonstrated by experts. Authentic assessment of a student's knowledge of air pollution, for example, might assess whether a student can propose an effective solution to the city's air pollution problem. Authentic assessment goes beyond standardized testing and is grounded in the following principles:

- The assessment has instructional value to students, beyond evaluation purposes.
- Students perform meaningful, worthwhile, significant tasks.
- The criteria for excellence are clear to students.
- Students exhibit quality products and performances.
- The assessment emphasizes higher-level thinking and self-assessment.
- The assessment centers on learning that transfers to real-life problems.
- There is a positive interaction between assessor and student.

Burke (1994) describes several methods of authentic assessment:

- Portfolios: Portfolios are a deliberate collection of student work designed to give a complete picture of a student's progress and skills. These may include homework, tests, learning logs, projects, rough drafts, written work, or recordings of presentations.
- Performances and exhibitions: Performances and exhibitions include speeches, science experiments, debates, artistic performances, mock trials, or publications.

- Projects: Projects allow students to investigate in depth a subject of interest to them. (More on projects can be found on page 118.)
- Learning logs and journals: Learning logs consist of brief, factual entries that can include mathematical problem solving, science experiment observations, or questions about lectures or readings. Journals can include literature responses, descriptions and reactions to events, reflections on personal experiences, and connections to what is being studied in class.
- Observation checklists: Teachers, small groups, and individual students can use observation checklists to monitor specific skills or behaviors in students. A checklist may include students' names, space for four to five targeted areas, a code or rating to determine to what degree the student has or has not demonstrated the skill (e.g., "frequently," "sometimes," or "not yet"), and a space for comments.
- Graphic organizers: Venn diagrams, webs, and concept maps can be used to monitor students' thinking in the early stages of an assignment or unit.
- Interviews and conferences: Direct personal communication with students can elicit students' thoughts, opinions, and feelings about their work.

Because authentic assessments are geared to measure the academic content standards or other learning goals being taught, there is no one-size-fits-all measure. When designing assessments, it is helpful to remember the following:

- Be clear about what you want to assess.
- Assess only one or two specific outcomes per activity, lesson, or project.
- Build assessment into your activity, lesson, or unit up front. (To hit a target, it helps to know ahead of time what and where the target is.)
- Let all parties (teachers, parents, and especially students) know the assessment criteria. Whenever possible, involve students in the design of the assessment.
- Frame and use assessment as a personal improvement tool, not as a punishment.
- Keep rigorous learning and high expectations intact, but modify assessment tools if necessary.
- And finally, remember that assessment does not have to be scary. In fact, it can be a wonderful learning tool for all involved.

The following characteristics of effective assessment can be used to examine an assessment's quality and can tell you where modifications may be necessary:

- Effective assessments measure what is being learned and tell how effective the teaching strategy was. They focus on an individual's progress and growth rather than on comparisons to other youth.
- Effective assessments are fair and flexible to accommodate different learning styles and allow for different ways to express knowledge. All youth have had

adequate time to acquire the skills and ample time to complete the assessment, so results reflect performance rather than test-taking ability.

- Effective assessments accommodate for cultural differences like language, environment, and community and cultural norms. They fairly test youth who have different experiences, backgrounds, and motivations. They allow for variation in language, cognitive and communicative styles, and beliefs and values.

- Effective assessments provide opportunities to learn that are meaningful and that ask youth to apply knowledge in real-world situations. They allow youth to demonstrate their knowledge or show concrete examples of how well they are learning.

- Effective assessments focus on reasoning, understanding, creativity, and problem solving rather than on rote memorization. They ask youth to integrate different types of skills or knowledge. They call on the use of multiple intelligences (i.e., verbal/linguistic, logical/mathematical, visual/spatial, bodily/kinesthetic, musical, interpersonal, intrapersonal, naturalistic). They encourage youth to reflect on their own learning and to take responsibility for it.

Developing Scoring Guidelines

Rubrics are scoring tools that help determine grades or ratings for student performance. They describe a continuum of performance levels and can be simple or complex, depending on the grade level.

Rubrics can be useful for instruction, especially when students are involved in their creation, because they help students understand in concrete terms what is expected. When students are involved in determining assessment criteria, they develop an understanding of the components of a high-quality assignment, use the criteria to guide them, and gain greater ownership of the task.

To develop a rubric,

1. Determine what criteria should be used to judge the performance of a skill. Criteria may include aspects of content, organization, presentation, or relevance. Four to eight criteria are usually sufficient without being overwhelming.

2. Describe what the range in quality of performance looks like for each of the criteria. What is novice, proficient, and excellent? Determine how the different levels of quality should be described and distinguished from one another.

On page 142 is an example of a rubric for a high school oral presentation; the rubric has been provided by Judy Kirkham (see Kirkham's reflection in Snapshot 6.1 "Gathering Student Reflections" on page 148). A three-point descriptive scale was used in this example, but scales may have four or five points. Rather than descriptions, points may be assigned numbers, with the sum representing the student's score.

ORAL PRESENTATION RUBRIC

Criterion: Evidence of research		
Not yet	*OK*	*Aha!*
Only one source cited	Two or three sources cited	Four or more sources cited
No one interviewed	Interview that did not add key information	Interview that added perspective
Criterion: Content		
Not yet	*OK*	*Aha!*
Perspective unclear	One perspective given	Differing perspectives given
Not all key ideas addressed	Key ideas minimally covered	Key ideas fully covered
No supportive stats given	Statistics not explained	Supportive stats explained
Criterion: Visual Aids		
Not yet	*OK*	*Aha!*
Not helpful for understanding	Assists understanding	Improves understanding
Unclear organization or illegible	Well organized	Well organized and easy to read
Criterion: Presentation		
Not yet	*OK*	*Aha!*
No eye contact	Minimal eye contact, mostly reading notes	Good eye contact
Organization disjointed	Good organization	Clear introduction, middle, end
Speech that cannot be heard	Speech volume varies	Volume loud, voice clear

Student Self-Assessment

Involving students in their own assessment can be a powerful learning experience. When teachers ask students to think about their learning, teachers develop a deeper understanding of their learners. Students benefit from improved instruction as teachers adjust their approach based on the feedback from students' self-assessments and reflections. Motivation increases when students find out their teachers care about what they think. When students actively reflect on what they know and what is confusing, they activate cognitive strategies helpful for mastering immediate course content and for learning other content.

Students can use rubrics to rate themselves or to provide feedback to a peer. More-informal methods can also be used, such as asking students to grade themselves on a particular aspect of their assignment and to write down a few sentences explaining their grade. Teachers can ask students to describe what they did well, what they would do differently, and whether or not they need help. When these types of assessments come in the middle of an assignment, they can guide students in thinking about what further improvements are needed.

Informal Assessment

Teachers who continually observe students—"kid watchers"—find that this sort of informal assessment helps them monitor student progress and guide instruction. Teacher Lilia Doni exhibits this in Snapshot 5.5 "Fairy Tales, Folktales, and Family Stories." From students' answers during class discussions, she assessed students' understanding of plot, character, and setting. Through students' notes, she was able to see their ability to recall and retell a story, and monitor their vocabulary and writing skills. This information helped her plan subsequent lessons, letting her know what students were learning and what information needed further teaching.

Resources on Assessment

Assessment Alternatives (www.newhorizons.org/strategies/assess/front_assess.htm)

Balancing Local Assessment With Statewide Testing: Building a Program That Meets Student Needs (www.wested.org/online_pubs/kn-01–01.pdf)

Rubrics for WebQuests (http://webquest.sdsu.edu/webquestrubric.html

Critical Issue: Ensuring Equity With Alternative Assessments (www.ncrel.org/sdrs/areas/issues/methods/assment/as800.htm)

REFLECTION

Because CRSB teaching is drawn from the lives of students and their families and communities, it tends to be very fluid, changing from one year to the next to meet the strengths and needs of the students. Being a culturally responsive educator is a continual, growing process. Consequently, expert CRSB teachers are constantly reflecting on what they did—asking what worked, what was challenging, and why.

Closely examining our practices gives us knowledge and insight that can inform decisions on how to improve teaching and learning for all students.

Reflection is defined as activities and assignments that are designed to encourage teachers and other learners to analyze their learning experiences in the context of their interests, abilities, and values; to connect learning in school with real-world experiences; and to set meaningful personal goals. When designing reflection activities, it is helpful to remember that effective reflection is about developing and posing rich questions that help you and your students think critically about individual lessons learned, lessons learned about each other, and lessons learned about the larger world. In this way, reflection can promote higher-order thinking skills such as analysis, synthesis, and evaluation.

Reflection can be organized as group discussion, writing, movement, visual art, and role-playing, as well as any other activities that help learners apply what they have learned to their own lives and future.

Reflection by Educators

Educators can begin reflecting on their teaching practice individually or in groups by asking questions such as

- What happened?
- Why did it happen?
- What might it mean?
- What are the implications for practice?

Tool 13 "Staff Reflection" is designed to help teachers individually reflect on any CRSB lesson, unit, or activity. If you have your students complete Tool 14 "Student Reflection" on page 150, you can compare their responses with your own. To use this tool for staff development, have practitioners complete the reflection as individuals, and then lead a discussion with the group about their responses. For a more focused reflection, select the most pertinent questions from the reflection and have staff members write about and discuss only those questions.

TOOL 13

STAFF REFLECTION

Review each statement and circle the answer that best describes how you feel about the statement. Next, write a sentence or two that describes why you feel that way. If you do not have enough time to complete the entire reflection in one sitting, break it into smaller, more manageable sections. You might find that the questions that seem the hardest to you—or that you "dislike"—will often reveal important information about your teaching practices.

Name: _____ Date: _____

Project title: _____

Description of lesson, unit, or project: _____

1. Through this activity, each student learned new things about her family, culture, or community.　　Not really　Somewhat　Most definitely!

_____

_____

2. Through this activity, each student learned new things about someone else's family, culture, or community.　　Not really　Somewhat　Most definitely!

_____

_____

3. Through this activity I learned new things about my students, their families, culture, or community.　　Not really　Somewhat　Most definitely!

_____

_____

4. Through this activity I learned new things about myself and my teaching.　　Not really　Somewhat　Most definitely!

_____

_____

5. This activity encouraged my students to develop important relationships with their families, peers, and me.　　Not really　Somewhat　Most definitely!

_____

_____

6. During this activity, my students had many opportunities to ask questions, plan their work, solve problems, and be creative.　　Not really　Somewhat　Most definitely!

_____

_____

(Continued)

(Continued)

7. By participating in this activity, my students gained new skills.

    Not really Somewhat Most definitely!

_____

_____

8. My students know how this activity connects to academic (book) learning.

    Not really Somewhat Most definitely!

_____

_____

9. My students were able to bring their learning into their homes, other classrooms, or the community.

    Not really Somewhat Most definitely!

_____

_____

10. My students can explain to someone how this activity connects to or is important to their life outside school.

    Not really Somewhat Most definitely!

_____

_____

11. During this activity, my students had many opportunities to reflect on, write about, or discuss their learning.

    Not really Somewhat Most definitely!

_____

_____

12. During this activity, my students had opportunities to show what they learned and assess their products or performances.

    Not really Somewhat Most definitely!

_____

_____

13. During this activity, my students had many opportunities to give feedback to their peers and me about how the work was going.

    Not really Somewhat Most definitely!

_____

_____

14. During this activity, my students completed commendable individual work.

    Not really Somewhat Most definitely!

_____

_____

15. During this activity, my students were effective team players.   Not really Somewhat Most definitely!

_____

_____

16. My students would say this activity was successful.   Not really Somewhat Most definitely!

_____

_____

17. My students enjoyed working on this activity.   Not really Somewhat Most definitely!

_____

_____

18. If my students were to do this activity again, there are things they would do to improve their work.

_____

_____

19. I am satisfied with the work my students did on this activity and feel they met important learning goals and outcomes.   Not really Somewhat Most definitely!

_____

_____

20. My students are satisfied with the work they did on this activity.   Not really Somewhat Most definitely!

_____

_____

21. My students would say that I am a good facilitator.   Not really Somewhat Most definitely!

_____

_____

Other reflections on this lesson, unit, or project:

Snapshot 6.1 "Gathering Student Reflections" gives insight into one teacher's discoveries as she contemplated her own assessment and reflection practices, and how she incorporated student reflection into those practices.

GATHERING STUDENT REFLECTIONS

Sheridan High School, Sheridan, Oregon

Grade level: 10

Subject area: Language arts

Highlights: Student and teacher reflections were used to improve practice and results.

After completing the teacher assessment, I can sure see that I need to do more work on connecting school, students, families, and communities," teacher Judy Kirkham states. "But I do feel that in other areas I am ahead of the game. I am able to accept constructive criticism from others. I use a variety of assessment tools and try to give students many different ways to show whether they have mastered concepts. I think that I used to do more reflection and ask for student input in my early teaching days and wonder why I don't do that now."

Kirkham, a high school language arts teacher in Sheridan, Oregon, reflects on her current assessment practices after completing Tool 12 "Self-Assessment on Assessment and Reflection" (page 138). She concludes that she does assess student achievement and modify her classroom practices to reflect inadequacies in student understanding. For example, she created a reflection tool to get students' input on a writing unit that was designed to prepare them for an upcoming performance test.

Prior to the Oregon Certificate of Initial Mastery (CIM) writing test at the 10th-grade level, Kirkham teaches a unit that emphasizes the different writing modes that students may see on the test.

In the past, when students were doing the CIM writing assessment, Kirkham found that most of them had trouble writing to specific modes or limiting themselves to two pages. "Most high school students want to write more than two pages, particularly when writing in narrative or imaginative modes," Kirkham explains.

For the practice unit, students are engaged in several "writes" that mimic the writing process used in the test—from gathering ideas to editing. For three days, students practice writing concisely, within a two-page limit; they also work on their penmanship. She has her students score each other's papers using a scoring guide to get an understanding of the process their own papers will go through. She's found that her students are actually tougher on each other than the state readers are.

Since I have been doing this review prior to testing, my perception (borne out by test results) is that students have done better and are more comfortable with the testing format following the unit. This year I decided to see if students also felt this way after the test by using a variation of the student reflection tool (Tool 14 "Student Reflection"). I used many of the same questions, rephrasing them to deal with writing, and added one question on students' perceptions about improved comfort level during the testing situation.

The statements Kirkham used on her student reflection included:

- Through this activity, I learned new things about my own writing.
- During this activity, I had many opportunities to ask questions, plan my work, solve problems, and be creative.
- I was able to bring my new learning into my home, other classrooms, or the community.
- I can explain to someone how this activity connects to or is important to my life outside school.
- During this activity, I had many opportunities to reflect on, write about, or discuss my learning.
- During this activity, I had opportunities to show what I learned and to assess my products or performances.

- During this activity, I worked well on my own.
- During this activity, I was an effective team player.
- This activity was successful. It helped me feel more comfortable when I took the writing CIM.

When the students did the reflection, the state test results weren't back, so Kirkham focused on whether students felt more comfortably prepared for the test after doing the writing review unit. Most students thought that it "somewhat" or "most definitely" helped them.

"After doing this reflection activity, I remembered why I used to do these. It is enlightening, and sometimes fun, to read student commentary. I do think I will try to get back to doing more of these," Kirkham concludes.

Reflection by Students

Students can begin reflecting on their learning individually or in groups by asking questions such as:

- What did I learn?
- What am I still concerned about?
- What would I like to try?
- What do I need help with?
- What surprised me?

Tool 14 "Student Reflection" is designed to help students reflect on their experiences after completing any CRSB lesson, unit, or project. The students first are asked to write a brief description of their project, then to rate how they feel about the various aspects of their project, and finally to write a sentence that describes why they feel that way.

Students can complete the surveys individually, or use the reflection statements as group discussion prompts. For younger students who have yet to master writing, teachers may choose just one or two questions and have students discuss their answers, or draw a response.

In Snapshot 6.2 on page 152, "Heritage Dolls," a fifth-grade teacher shows another way to elicit students' reflections. She asked her students to answer certain reflection questions on a 3 x 5–inch card.

TOOL 14

STUDENT REFLECTION

By thinking about the work you did on your activity, what went well, and the things you might do differently next time, you can learn many things. First, write a brief description of your activity. Next, review each statement and circle the answer that best describes how you feel about the statement. After you circle your response, write a sentence that describes why you feel that way.

Name: _____ Date: _____

Project title: _____

Description of lesson, unit, or project: _____

1. Through this activity, I learned new things about my family, culture, or community.

   Not really   Somewhat   Most definitely!

   _____
   _____

2. Through this activity, I learned new things about someone else's family, culture, or community.

   Not really   Somewhat   Most definitely!

   _____
   _____

3. This activity encouraged me to develop important relationships with my teacher(s), peers, and family members.

   Not really   Somewhat   Most definitely!

   _____
   _____

4. During this activity, I had many opportunities to ask questions, plan my work, solve problems, and be creative.

   Not really   Somewhat   Most definitely!

   _____
   _____

5. By participating in this activity, I gained new skills.

   Not really   Somewhat   Most definitely!

   _____
   _____

6. I know how this activity connects to academic (book) learning.

   Not really   Somewhat   Most definitely!

   _____
   _____

7. I was able to bring my new learning into my home, other classrooms, or the community.

   Not really   Somewhat   Most definitely!

   _____
   _____

8. I can explain to someone how this activity connects to or is important to my life outside school.

   Not really   Somewhat   Most definitely!

   _____
   _____

9. During this activity, I had many opportunities to reflect on, write about, or discuss my learning.

Not really   Somewhat   Most definitely!

10. During this activity, I had opportunities to show what I learned and assess my products or performances.

Not really   Somewhat   Most definitely!

11. During this activity, I had many opportunities to give feedback to my teacher and peers about how the work was going.

Not really   Somewhat   Most definitely!

12. During this activity, I worked well on my own.

Not really   Somewhat   Most definitely!

13. During this activity, I was an effective team player.

Not really   Somewhat   Most definitely!

14. This activity was successful.

Not really   Somewhat   Most definitely!

15. I enjoyed working on this activity.

Not really   Somewhat   Most definitely!

16. If I were to do this activity again, there are things I would do to improve the activity.

Not really   Somewhat   Most definitely!

17. I am satisfied with the work I did on this activity.

Not really   Somewhat   Most definitely!

18. My peers are satisfied with the work I did on this activity.

Not really   Somewhat   Most definitely!

19. My teacher is satisfied with the work I did on this activity.

Not really   Somewhat   Most definitely!

20. Other reflections on this activity:

Not really   Somewhat   Most definitely!

HERITAGE DOLLS

Woodmere Elementary School, Portland, Oregon

Grade level: 5

Subject areas: Social studies, writing, and public speaking

Highlights: This lesson involves family members at home in their child's education. Note how students write a reflection on their learning.

Creative extension: This lesson can be a jumping-off point for other social studies lessons. The information also can be shared with others through presentations or displays at school exhibits, assemblies, or family fun nights.

The teacher's goal was to learn more about the world and where her students come from while fulfilling a public speaking standard, but at the end of the Heritage Dolls activity fifth-grade teacher Diana Larson discovered her students had been transformed, becoming more connected to each other and more interested in learning.

Nearly half the students at Woodmere Elementary School in Portland come from families who are recent immigrants to the United States. Families from Eastern Europe, Southeast Asia, and other countries, including Russia and Mexico, have joined the mostly lower-income white residents who have lived in the neighborhood for decades. One of the greatest challenges of the school is accommodating the diverse backgrounds and languages brought to the school by the students and their families. Providing opportunities—like the Heritage Dolls activity—for students to explore and share an understanding of differences helps everyone to appreciate the diversity.

What is a heritage doll? The activity asks each student to dress a cardstock cutout doll in the native costume of the country their ancestors are from. They draw, paint, sew, and glue on materials such as cloth, ribbon, yarn, and buttons. Students also create faces, skin, and hair. (Figure 6.1 shows an example of a few of the students' Heritage Dolls.) Larson

heard about the activity and started it in another school before coming to Woodmere. Since beginning the project, she has seen high school graduates keep their dolls and noted that they still talk about them.

Larson sends home a letter explaining the activity to parents, translated into several languages, so that parents can assist their children with the creation of their Heritage Doll. Students research the authenticity of their doll's dress, as well as background on the culture, language, food, geography, climate, housing styles, transportation, games, special products, industries, and jobs found in the countries represented by the dolls. All this information is placed on 3 x 5–inch cards that are attached to the back of the dolls in preparation for the student's oral report to the class.

Larson builds student reflection into the activity by having students answer questions regarding which country they chose, how they researched it, how they made the doll, and what they learned about the culture. In addition, she asks students whether they enjoyed the project and to explain why they did or did not.

"Kids become fascinated with other kids' cultures," observes Larson. "It teaches them to be respectful of each other and their differences." Not only do they share their cultural heritage stories with each other but

(Continued)

(Continued)

Figure 6.1 Three Heritage Dolls

also with parents, other teachers, and students at school assemblies. Because the Heritage Dolls project is about the students themselves and their families, students display a high level of interest and motivation to do the work.

Larson recalls how one particular student, who had been using negative behaviors to gain attention and was doing very poorly in school, became engrossed in the project. In the process of learning details of her Cuban culture, she became excited about learning and sharing. She took the assignment very seriously and spent a half-hour on her oral report to the class, describing in great detail what she had learned about her heritage, her doll's dress and hair, and family customs. Gone were the negative behaviors. After this activity, she opened up to other learning experiences, became more positive and engaged in school, and seemed to feel like she fit into the classroom.

Parents have the opportunity to really get into the project and provide information for their child's research. Parents who do not speak English can still participate by working with their child. As a result, Larson has seen more school connections made with the parents. "They feel more comfortable communicating with teachers at the school. They see the school as open to them," she says. For example, one family volunteered to bring dumplings to the class to share one of their traditional foods. Due to school policy, they were not allowed to prepare the food at home so they brought store-bought dumplings, but they passed along recipes for other families to try. In another instance, as a result of the Heritage Dolls lesson, one parent asked if her cultural dance group could practice in the school's larger classrooms, and they have been doing so ever since.

Perhaps parents see that the school promotes cultural diversity and doesn't expect families to become Americanized and lose their cultural identities, Larson surmises. Whatever the reason, parents are responding, building bridges of communication with the school and between generations within their families.

GATHERING FEEDBACK FROM FAMILIES

In CRSB teaching, it is important to work with family members, gathering their input in all stages of curriculum development. While some family members will feel comfortable sharing their opinions with teachers, others may need to be asked several times before they give input. Gathering feedback from families at the conclusion of CRSB activities can be one of several ways to encourage family involvement, while also providing the teacher with valuable information.

The Survey for Parents and Guardians (below) can be sent home to families asking for their feedback. Feel free to modify the survey and letter to better serve your needs and the needs of the families. Refer to the information about home visiting (Chapter 3, page 161) for additional ideas and questions that you can ask parents during the home visit or when they are at school.

SURVEY FOR PARENTS AND GUARDIANS

Name of assignment: _____

Were you aware that this assignment was going on in class?	Yes	Somewhat	No
Overall, do you think this was a valuable assignment?	Yes	Somewhat	No
Was the assignment relevant to your child's life?	Yes	Somewhat	No
Was the assignment sensitive to your child's needs?	Yes	Somewhat	No
Did the assignment provide ways for you to be involved in your child's education?	Yes	Somewhat	No

What do you believe your child learned from this activity?

_____

_____

What are some of the things the teacher or school does well to bring your child's home, family, and community culture into learning?

_____

_____

What are some of the things the teacher or school can do better when bringing your child's home, family, and community culture into learning?

_____

_____

Optional

Name of parent/guardian _____

Phone number or email address to reach you _____

Name of student _____

Thank you for your feedback!

SAMPLE LETTER TO ATTACH TO THE SURVEY

Dear Parents and Guardians,

I'd like to invite you to provide your opinions about our recent Family Stories Book assignment on the attached survey. During the past two months, the children have been working hard on the Family Stories Book, interviewing and writing stories about their family members. Your opinions can help me to improve the project and better teach your child.

 I look forward to hearing from you. You can reach me by phone at (000) 000-0000 or by email at Chris_Doe@City_Elementary.edu.

Chris Doe
City Elementary School

REFLECTION QUESTIONS

1. How do you currently use assessment and reflection in your classroom activities?

2. What forms of authentic assessment do you currently use? What could you easily and (almost) effortlessly incorporate into your activities?

3. Thinking of a current project or activity, how can you include students in the design and implementation of the assessment for this activity?

4. How could you modify your current assessment tools into a "personal improvement learning tool" so that both teachers and learners could evaluate their own growth and progress?

5. What would you need to do to modify your current assessment tools in order to allow students to demonstrate their knowledge? What kind of assessment tools would allow students to show concrete examples of how well they are learning or how well they can apply their learning to real-world situations?

6. How could you use Tool 13 "Staff Reflection" or Tool 14 "Student Reflection" to improve on a current project or activity?

7. Having read information on rubrics, peer assessments and reflections, and family feedback forms, which could you use to help evaluate a current project activity? How could you use that assessment tool to gain more information about the success of the project and how to do it better in the future?

7

Scaling Up

From Schoolwide to State-Level Efforts

We don't need to convince large numbers of people to change; instead, we need to connect with kindred spirits. Through these relationships, we will develop the new knowledge, practices, courage, and commitment that lead to broad-based change.

—Margaret Wheatley & Deborah Frieze (2006)

WHOLE-SCHOOL FOCUS ON CULTURALLY RESPONSIVE STANDARDS-BASED TEACHING AND LEARNING

Are you ready to scale up your efforts with CRSB teaching? When thinking about taking CRSB beyond one or two classrooms, it's important to take stock of the people and structures that can support a schoolwide scale-up. For some teachers and school communities, CRSB teaching may be part of their regular practice and so almost be second nature; for others, it may be an entirely new way of engaging with and teaching students. The experiences, receptivity, and skill of those in your community will help determine the action steps necessary for wider implementation.

Imagine if the students in your school or district were given multiple opportunities in their day to

- have the culture and diversity they bring embraced as an asset and viewed as integral to the learning environment;
- see the history and accomplishments of "their" people regularly and accurately represented;
- be "seen" by their teachers and peers as valuable, smart, and highly capable of doing good work;

- use a variety of learning modalities, particularly those that suit them best; and
- experience stimulating and challenging curricula—tied to high academic standards—that keep them in their "zone of proximal learning."

If your learning environment consistently offered those kinds of opportunities to all students, what do you think the outcomes might be for both students and staff? Ask any mathematician, scientist, or marketing executive, and she will tell you that frequency + duration + intensity is the formula to increase the probability of any desired outcome. It seems reasonable that the more staff members, students, and families are involved in CRSB teaching, the more likely the outcome of increased achievement at the personal, school, and community level.

A whole-school focus aligns the concepts and essential elements of CRSB teaching with whole-school efforts, initiatives, and goals. You might consider the following questions when exploring these changes:

- How can we integrate CRSB practices with what we're already doing so that this is not simply one more add-on?
- How can we maximize professional development time to support teachers in the implementation of CRSB practices?
- Who in our school or district is using CRSB practices? How can we learn from their experiences?
- Are there any structural aspects of our school (e.g., scheduling, staffing, school policies, use of space) that need to be modified to support CRSB teaching?

A Few Thoughts About School-Level Change

According to school change expert Michael Fullan (2007), how individuals in a school community perceive a new policy, educational theory, or practice is deeply influenced by their background, knowledge, experience, expertise, and sense of authority. Many school reform efforts fail because they are focused on structural elements (e.g., scheduling, textbooks, curriculum models) rather than on relationships, the emotional climate, and the hearts and minds of the particular staff, students, and families.

Another way to view the difficulty of school change is to understand what researchers have defined as the two general levels of change: first-order and second-order (Argyris, Putnam, & Smith, 1985; Bateson, 1979; Cuban, 1988). First-order change is superficial and is designed to address needs relating to the quality of teaching, learning, and the organization through changes that improve existing practices and structures. For example, these changes might include selecting new textbooks, increasing salaries, or adopting a new master schedule. First-order change makes adjustments to the system in ways that leave one's tacit beliefs and values secure. In this sense, first-order change reinforces the status quo.

Second-order change, conversely, creates disequilibrium with past practices and creates dissonance in the values and beliefs of individuals, often through system changes that "introduce new goals, structure, and roles that transform familiar ways of doing things into new ways of solving persistent problems" (Cuban, 1988, p. 342). Second-order change challenges teachers, administrators, and community members to examine their most deeply held beliefs and values about teaching, learning, and how the school community works together.

How People Perceive Change: First-Order or Second-Order Change

First-order change . . .	Second-order change . . .
. . . is superficial and designed to address needs relating to the quality of teaching, learning, and the organization through changes that improve existing practices and structures. First-order change makes adjustments to the system in ways that leave one's tacit beliefs and values secure.	. . . introduces new goals, structure, and roles that transform familiar ways of doing things into new ways of solving persistent problems. This change might challenge deeply held beliefs and values about teaching, learning, and how the school community works together.
. . . is an extension of the past.	. . . is a break with the past.
. . . happens within existing paradigms.	. . . happens by "stretching" or moving outside existing paradigms.
. . . is consistent with prevailing values and norms.	. . . conflicts with prevailing values and norms.
. . . is implemented with existing knowledge and skills.	. . . requires new knowledge and skills to implement.
. . . is implemented by single leaders or experts.	. . . is implemented by diverse stakeholders in the community.
. . . focuses on symptoms.	. . . focuses on root causes.
. . . transfers information.	. . . creates knowledge.
. . . reproduces what has already been done.	. . . transforms into something new.

CRSB teaching is about second-order change for teachers, classrooms, and schools. No matter your role in the school, district, or community, you can be the primary catalyst for positive change. Encouraging buy-in from other teachers, administrators, students, families, and community members requires a shift in attitude about the role of schooling. You can help move things along by being articulate about your philosophy and approach. In addition, you can help by being assertive about sharing your results with administrators, staff members, families, and community members. Record any evidence of the impact of your work through assessments and student testimonies. Document your students' work and activities through photos, artifacts, portfolios, videos, letters, and so forth. Display standardized assessment data, attendance rates, community members' feedback, parents' appreciations, and students' statements and actions that show learning. It takes time to develop the philosophy and schoolwide practices that support using students' culture to promote student achievement and family involvement. However, it is time well spent.

Start by Assessing Current Schoolwide Practices

There are many ways to begin the process of reflecting on current practices, which is the important first step in scaling up. One excellent resource for reflecting on how racial issues affect student achievement is the process outlined in Singleton and Linton's *Courageous Conversations About Race* (2006). These authors provide exercises and tools to help the school staff articulate the beliefs and attitudes that may be creating barriers to closing the achievement gap. The process supports and empowers educators to create a shared understanding and language in order to move forward toward the goal of academic equity.

Assessing School Preparation for New and Diverse Students (Nave & Ko, 2004) is another resource to consider when gathering information about current practices. This resource offers a step-by-step guide to implementing the School-PASS (School Practices for All Students' Success) survey and planning process. This guide details how to obtain schoolwide buy-in, collect and analyze student data; complete the Student-PASS survey, discuss and analyze survey results, and develop action items that achieve schoolwide consensus. The survey—with 87 items that address key areas of student development and influence—also includes research, sample results from field-test sites, and resources that focus on student developmental needs. (You can learn more about this guide at http://educationnorthwest.org/catalog/assessing-school-preparation-new-and-diverse-students)

As you expand your efforts, it's important for you to examine how CRSB teaching aligns with building- or district-level policies and practices. Connecting your efforts to existing structures and activities creates a solid foundation for change, provides motivation, and helps identify the most "natural" and fertile places for CRSB teaching to take root. CRSB teaching is a powerful way for your school or district to put its mission statement, values, and plans into action. Tool 15 "School- and District-Level Policies and Practices Checklist" can help you scan the existing activities, resources, and policies that affect all stakeholders by encouraging collaborative discussion regarding CRSB practices.

The Teacher as Change Leader

Teaching can sometimes be a solitary profession. There never seems to be enough time to talk with your peers, compare notes, or pitch ideas. You might think you're the only one in the school trying anything like CRSB practices, so might not feel like your efforts are making a difference.

CRSB teaching can make a difference, even if used in small ways by a single teacher. But, by connecting with peers, family members, community organizations, school boards, school and district administrators, and state initiatives, teachers are more fully supported to develop, expand, and improve their CRSB teaching. Since CRSB teaching can be transformational, the small changes made by individual teachers can have huge impacts on schoolwide practices. If you are a teacher implementing CRSB strategies in your classroom and would like to be a change agent within your school and/or district, ask yourself the following questions:

- Why do I want to move CRSB teaching forward?
- What is my commitment to implementing CRSB teaching schoolwide?

(Text resumes on page 164)

— TOOL 15 —

SCHOOL- AND DISTRICT-LEVEL POLICIES AND PRACTICES CHECKLIST

This is a brainstorming tool, so with your coworkers reflect on the statements below. Discuss the policies and practices that seem to be a natural fit for CRSB teaching.

In the spaces provided, make "resource" notes and include details such as the actual policy or mission statement, the contact information for definite or potential allies, and times and locations for specific meetings. (Note: Your school or district may have different names for the items on the checklist.)

School-Level Policies and Practices

☐ Mission and vision statements

_____

_____

☐ School strategic plan

_____

_____

☐ Schoolwide professional development plans

_____

_____

☐ Individual professional development plans

_____

_____

☐ Building-level plans to address federal elementary and secondary education legislation, especially
  - Title I—Improving the Academic Achievement of the Disadvantaged
  - Title III—Language Instruction for Limited English Proficient and Immigrant Students
  - Title VII—Indian, Native Hawaiian, and Alaska Native Education

_____

_____

☐ Staff meetings

_____

_____

(Continued)

(Continued)

☐ Equity teams

_____

_____

☐ Site council

_____

_____

☐ Schoolwide training efforts

_____

_____

☐ Parent–teacher organizations

_____

_____

☐ Professional learning teams

_____

_____

☐ Student advisory councils

_____

_____

☐ Student clubs

_____

_____

District-Level Policies and Practices

☐ District mission and vision statements

_____

_____

☐ District policies on equity, family engagement, or closing the achievement gap

_____

_____

☐ Human resources mission and vision statements

_____

_____

☐ District curriculum standards

_____

_____

☐ Building-level plans to address federal elementary and secondary education legislation, especially

- Title I—Improving the Academic Achievement of the Disadvantaged
- Title III—Language Instruction for Limited English Proficient and Immigrant Students
- Title VII—Indian, Native Hawaiian, and Alaska Native Education

_____

_____

☐ Districtwide equity teams or councils

_____

_____

☐ Textbook adoption committees

_____

_____

☐ Districtwide parent advisory councils

_____

_____

☐ District school board

_____

_____

☐ Teacher or administrative mentorship programs

_____

_____

- How does my current position and the "power" I hold situate me to lead the change to scale up the CRSB teaching practices within the school?
- What passion, skill, knowledge, and experience do I have in the area of CRSB teaching?
- How might I share my passion, skill, knowledge, and experience most effectively with my colleagues?

Snapshot 7.1 "Tulalip-Based Curriculum and Lushootseed Classes" is an example of an effort to connect the school culture and practices with the students' American Indian culture. The change began with one teacher in one fourth-grade classroom and has now been adopted school wide.

Snapshot 7.1

TULALIP-BASED CURRICULUM AND LUSHOOTSEED CLASSES

Tulalip Elementary School, Marysville, Washington

Grade levels: K–5

Subject areas: Reading, science, math, health, writing, and technology

Highlights: This whole-school focus integrates students' American Indian culture, language, and ways of knowing with interdisciplinary projects and units.

After the rumblings of an earthquake subside, teachers and students evacuate the school building, while administrators check to see that there is no damage to the building. Everyone is safe, and students—excited by this extra "recess"—begin chatting, wiggling, jumping, and playing clap-and-rhyme games while trying to remain in their classroom lines.

Surrounded by this commotion, one class of fourth- and fifth-graders stands out. Instead of giggling and gyrating, these kids are concentrating intently on their teacher, who is calling out words and phrases in the ancient language of Lushootseed.

"ey, s-YAH-yah," he prompts. Kids' hands shoot up. "Hello, friend!" a student responds. "us-CHAL chuwh," the teacher says. "How are you?" another student answers.

Eagerly, the youngsters volunteer English translations for words that were spoken for countless generations by the Tulalip Tribes that inhabited the evergreen forests and rocky beaches of east Puget Sound. The teacher even sneaks in a math problem, asking the students to estimate how long their arms and legs are in hweetl (a traditional Tulalip unit of measurement that is the distance from the middle finger to the thumb). Once again, nearly every hand shoots up to answer the question.

The reason for the children's enthusiasm is clear to teacher David Cort. At Tulalip Elementary School in the Marysville School District, he says, culture and curriculum are being thoughtfully integrated in ways that help students meet state academic standards. With the involvement of the Tulalip Tribal Cultural Resources Department (TCRD), students in each grade level are assured that they will have the opportunity to study Tulalip language and culture in the school.

The Tulalip-Based Classroom

Creating a Tulalip-Based Classroom (TBC) in the fourth grade was one of the first steps that Tulalip Elementary took in its journey to create a more culturally responsive curriculum. The classroom curriculum uses Tulalip language, literature, and culture to connect children with their culture and to satisfy all state standards. The TBC was a major outcome of a working document produced by a committee of tribal and school district staff who worked together for two years. Based on the premise that Native American children who feel positive about their culture perform better in school, the committee's vision was that schools in the Marysville School District would include more Tulalip language and culture in their curriculum.

Tulalip Elementary teacher David Cort worked with tribal language teacher Michele Balagot to develop the curriculum and teach the class in its first year. As Cort points out, it is a model that could be adapted for use with other languages, such as Spanish. The curriculum includes Tulalip content, such as Tulalip literature and the Lushootseed language, as well as Tulalip cultural knowledge and ways of thinking, such as traditional storytelling and methods of Tulalip measurement.

Study is student-centered in that it focuses on students' local environment and community, making learning relevant for them and building on their existing knowledge of the world. Traditional practices and beliefs are explored against the realities of current life. For example, a science unit focusing on the local saltwater ecosystem includes a study of the locals who fish and their families.

Reading in the TBC

The reading curriculum in the TBC uses traditional Tulalip stories as its basis. Before a story is used, Cort talks with elders in the community to make sure the school has permission to use it. Selected stories were made into books written in both Lushootseed and English. Students created the illustrations, modeled after the traditional Tulalip way of drawing or carving, which is realistic and natural compared to the stylized art that is commonly associated with northwest Native art.

Teacher David Cort recognizes the unique cultural perspectives about literacy that his Native American students bring to the classroom. He uses these perspectives to both affirm students' knowledge and background, and as a basis for understanding the values and skills required by the dominant culture. The curriculum emphasizes Lushootseed forms in the stories such as repetition (repeating words or ideas) and "circular figures" (repeating two ideas in reverse order). Cort says these forms lend beauty to the story and help listeners remember the story better and attend to the patterns within it. Historically, translators of Native stories sometimes viewed these features as tedious and therefore omitted them. The TBC teaches students to value, recognize, and appreciate these special features. Instruction also focuses on Tulalip ideas and beliefs behind storytelling. For example, Cort explains that traditional stories were told so that listeners would live their lives differently as a result of hearing the story. Stories were told again and again, allowing listeners to develop deeper insights with each hearing.

The Tulalip stories are referred to when reading other, predominantly Western, literature. For example, students might compare the similarities and differences between two characters from Tulalip and European stories.

(Continued)

(Continued)

Building a Whole-School Focus

After seeing the success of the TBC, the school began to include Tulalip language and culture in all grade levels. Teachers from the TCRD now teach daily 30- to 60-minute Lushootseed lessons in most classrooms. In Cheryl Moll's first- and second-grade class, TCRD teacher Natosha Gobin teaches students about the traditional naming ceremony, a northwest native tradition in which an individual receives an honored hereditary family name. In Tulalip culture, names are often given to children frequently around third to sixth grade. The two teachers culminate the three-month study with a mock ceremony in which students are given animal nicknames. Each child was responsible for a certain part of the ceremony, such as being floor managers or witnesses who tell Lushootseed sayings. In preparing for the ceremony, several of Gobin's coworkers visited the class to talk about ceremonies. Gobin also told traditional stories in Lushootseed about animal names.

Moll invites Gobin to participate in other class activities, thus the two teachers meet regularly to plan and coordinate their lessons. Recently, both teachers team-taught a unit on sea life, with Gobin teaching Lushootseed names for the animals and plants students were learning about in Moll's class.

Gobin has also worked with the school's music teacher, Sara O'Conner. O'Conner asked Gobin if she could use music class time for students to practice the Lushootseed songs Gobin was teaching them. O'Conner subsequently had students sing Lushootseed songs at the school's winter concert and summer barbecue.

Several teachers in the school have participated in college-level Lushootseed classes taught by the TCRD. Teachers comment that these classes have helped them to learn more about Native culture and to use Lushootseed with their students and their families.

Culture-Infused Technology Classes

While this effort was under way, the school secured funding for a technology coordinator and moved Cort into the position. Cort continues to integrate Tulalip culture into student projects in the weekly classes he teaches to all students in the school.

One such project is the CD-ROM "talking books" of Tulalip stories that students create. (See Figure 7.1, which was created by Nan McNutt & Shaun Peterson.) Using Macromedia Flash MX, a widely used website design tool, the project helps students develop and apply complex thinking skills in literacy, technology, art, language, and culture. One CD-ROM tells a traditional story in both English and Lushootseed, with information about the storyteller and an audio recording of the storyteller from the 1960s. Another CD-ROM focuses on a canoe story and includes students' written and oral essays on their personal experiences with the canoe culture (Figure 7.2). Students' enthusiasm for the project is

Figure 7.1　CD of "Talking Books"—Student Creative Tulalip Stories

Figure 7.2 Tulalip Canoes

apparent as they show visitors the witty animation and sounds they have created for these talking books.

The CD-ROMs were created originally for inclusion in take-home packets for prekindergartners attending the kindergarten registration. The Tulalip Tribes have given each family in the tribe a computer, so the CD-ROM is a software resource that provides young children at home with unique literacy and technology experiences and shows family members the skills children are learning in school.

Making Connections With
Children and Families

When describing the changes he has seen in children since the new curriculum was implemented, Cort states enthusiastically,

"Kids love learning about their culture. They feel pride; they see themselves as leaders. Culture motivates them to learn and to teach other kids."

Other teachers mention specific students whose behavior and grades improved after their culture became part of the curriculum. Sheryl Fryberg, Marysville School District Indian Education coordinator, comments, "We found that attendance improved. Students were working harder; they were excited to work on their projects since they were working on a real project in the real world. Test scores improved."

Teachers have seen several changes in the students as a result of learning a second language. For instance, it has stimulated students' thinking about language in both English and Lushootseed and

(Continued)

(Continued)

increased their understanding of the parts of speech and literary forms (such as passive voice, which is preferred in Lushootseed but discouraged in English). Teachers feel that young children learning the Lushootseed alphabet have an increased awareness of phonics. They also see evidence supporting research findings that studying a second language enhances problem-solving skills, flexibility in thinking, creativity, and the ability to see the world from different perspectives (Curtain, 1990).

Lines of communication between teachers and families have opened as children show their families what they are learning at school. "Some parents are really getting involved in this, and they ask questions about the language to teachers at school or when they see them in the community," says Gobin.

Cort concurs that parents are very enthusiastic, and that they enjoy seeing their kids learn the Lushootseed language. He comments, "The community wants their kids to do well in school, and it values its language and culture. We have a responsibility to give that to them, especially here at Tulalip, because we are a part of this history where education has been used to take away culture and language. It's extra work, but it can be done and it should be done."

Several lesson plans, including information on how lessons are aligned with state academic standards in reading, math, science, history, geography, music, health, and physical education, are described on the school's extensive website (www .msvl.k12.wa.us/elementary/tulalip/home .asp).

Collaborating With Other Teachers

In many schools, teachers who are doing unusual things are criticized, either overtly or covertly. New approaches can be threatening to others who have felt successful using strategies that are more typical. Supervisors can view the work as not covering the "basics" or not teaching the curriculum.

While keeping an open ear for constructive criticism, it is important not to let critical views stop you. Seek feedback and support from those who like your work, both within and outside the school building. Gaining feedback also can be a way of gauging interest in your work: when you hear a teacher wanting to learn more, invite that teacher to participate.

Teacher teaming is a way for like-minded professionals to work together. Begin by building a collaborative relationship. When two or more teachers collaborate using CRSB teaching practices, very powerful student learning and growth often occur (as was evidenced in Snapshot 1.1 "Project FRESA"). Teachers find the experience highly satisfying and energizing to their teaching, in addition to giving them the support they need when trying new ideas. Snapshot 7.2 "It's a Wild Ride" gives an example of a collaboration by three middle school teachers who teach different content areas.

Snapshot 7.2

IT'S A WILD RIDE: USING YOUTH CULTURE FOR HIGH-LEVEL LEARNING

O'Leary Junior High School, Twin Falls, Idaho

Grade level: 8

Subject areas: Math, science, and language arts

Highlights: Three teachers collaborate to develop an interdisciplinary project based on roller coaster design.

Years ago, as one strategy for addressing a host of problems at O'Leary Junior High, Principal Wiley Dobbs encouraged the formation of teaching teams empowered to create innovative curriculum. Teams were given a daily 85-minute joint planning period and encouraged to participate in professional development on teaming. Because of changes like these, the Idaho Department of Education now considers O'Leary to be a school of excellence, which is often hard to obtain for a school with a high percentage of students from low-income households (about 30 percent of their students are from low-income families).

Theresa Maves (science), Meile Harris (math), and Jill Whitesell (language arts) form a particularly dynamic team. All three began their careers in environments that included teams, and all have attended many workshops and conferences together. When designing a curriculum together, their first priority is to create synergy in learning: They want students to be able to see answers to the infamous question, "When are we ever going to use this?" They begin planning by looking at the district

curriculum and state standards, and by aligning concepts between content areas.

Together they created a project that would appeal to their students (that is, that would be responsive to youth culture), incorporate technology use, and provide opportunities for hands-on, meaningful, and higher-order learning. The students themselves worked in teams. Taking different roles—architect, public relations person, or engineer—they were asked to develop a detailed proposal for a new roller coaster at a local amusement park (Figure 7.3). During an eight-week period, students engaged intensely in investigating Newton's laws of motion, exploring careers, preparing proposals, keeping journals, using science probes and graphing calculators to collect and represent data, developing an electronic database, corresponding with an outside expert, and conducting self-assessments. Through the course of the project, more than 12 Idaho state science standards, 27 math standards, and 5 writing and researching standards were directly addressed. The culminating activity was a presentation from each group to "sell" its model.

(Continued)

(Continued)

Figure 7.3 Roller Coaster

"One of the biggest advantages to working on a team is just the support you get from the other team teachers . . . in terms of ideas about how to make your curriculum more meaningful," says Harris. "It is indisputable that teachers working together to develop meaningful instruction . . . during extended periods of time, carefully aligning multiple curriculum, instruction, and assessment, can accomplish astounding, yet measurable results."

For more information about this project, see http://www.netc.org/classrooms@work/classrooms/middleteam/index.html.

The Principal as Change Leader

Although principals are in a unique position to lead change, any principal who has actually tried to do so in a substantive way will tell you that it is a very difficult process. In her article, "Culturally Responsive Schools: Leadership, Language, and Literacy Development," Virginia Juettner (2003) describes her effort as a principal to promote schoolwide cultural responsiveness. Her journey reveals important areas to consider if you hope to create long-term change. She faced the challenge of bridging the cultural gap between white, middle-class teachers (teaching a predominantly white middle-class-focused curriculum) and the school's culturally and linguistically diverse students. With time, she learned that the principal must be an instructional leader who provides the opportunities and avenues for inviting the teaching staff, students, families, and community to share the responsibility of developing a culturally responsive school.

Being an effective leader of change can include

- creating culturally responsive policies for students, families, and community members;
- conducting program- and policy-building activities that involve both the staff and the community;
- fostering a schoolwide culture of respect, understanding for others, and responsibility for oneself and one's actions;
- encouraging a schoolwide knowledge and understanding of the languages and cultures represented in the community;
- promoting instructional strategies and curricula that are based on the students' languages and cultures as the foundation for learning;
- providing opportunities for continuous teacher research and the meaningful evaluation of student learning; and
- ensuring that the cultural and linguistic diversity of the students is evident throughout the school environment.

This principal's vision of what makes a culturally responsive school is in alignment with the five core beliefs and seven characteristics of exemplary schools that reach and teach all students, as developed by the National Center for Culturally Responsive Educational Systems (www.nccrest.org).

The five core beliefs of exemplary schools are

1. creating child- or learner-centered schools;

2. believing that all children can succeed at high academic levels without exception;

3. demanding that all children be treated with love, appreciation, care, and respect;

4. embracing the racial and ethnic culture of each child, including her or his first language; and

5. emphasizing that the school exists for and must serve the community.

The seven characteristics of exemplary schools are

1. a strong vision;

2. a loving and caring environment for children and adults;

3. a strong, collaborative "we are family" approach throughout the school;

4. an atmosphere of innovation, experimentation, and openness to new ideas;

5. a hardworking school staff (but not to the point of burnout);

6. an organizational culture that promotes the appropriate conduct of all members; and

7. a school staff that holds itself accountable, as a group, for the success of all.

Gathering Allies

Implementing culturally responsive activities and policies schoolwide is a collaborative effort among all the stakeholders of the school. Whether you are in the role of principal, teacher, or other staff member, you will need allies to successfully scale up your effort. Finding those allies can be a challenge. One of the best ways to promote schoolwide CRSB practices is to open the doors of your classroom to your professional peers, including sharing specific lesson plans and ideas. Seek out collaborative opportunities and invite other teachers, administrators, staff members, family members, or key members of the public such as business leaders, school board members, or politicians into the building to join you in the work you are doing. Share your experiences with building an inclusive culture in the classroom in ways that others can reflect on and possibly use. Help to "create a space" for discussions about the importance of embracing and representing cultural diversity in the classroom.

We can develop an understanding of our own and others' culture by creating spaces not only to recognize and value diverse culture but also to support the inclusion of new values and beliefs into our everyday lives and activities. To create opportunities to build on this understanding, try these suggestions from the National Institute for Urban School Improvement (White, Zion, & Kozleski, 2005):

- Learn about the lives of the teachers, administrators, and staff members in your building.
- Share with students stories about your own life.
- Promote time throughout the school year for the telling or portrayal of life stories.
- Help to create professional development opportunities such as professional learning teams.

Involving All Stakeholders: Families, Students, and Community

We all participate in a variety of cultural settings. The school is one of these settings that can be a source of strength and can promote a sense of belonging. In order to be as inclusive as possible, it is imperative to get direct input and involvement of all stakeholders from the beginning, including students, family members, and community members.

Students are often an untapped source of creative ideas for improving schools. Since they have a personal stake in the outcomes of all school improvement initiatives, they can offer unique recommendations for how to improve instruction and restructure the school to increase the level of student interest and participation. The act of listening to students requires risk-taking on the part of both the adults and the students. A commitment to this idea will take time, a lot of work, and the creation of communication feedback loops. Challenges include a shortage of time, unclear goals, and a lack of communication. Despite the challenges, though, finding strategies for engaging students in meaningful ways is worth the effort.

Setting an environment for open dialogue and active discussion in a classroom (as discussed in Chapter 4) allows student input in almost any subject. Expanding this to a schoolwide effort can take many forms, from providing input on student ideas and suggestions for everyday school issues to hard decisions affecting school-wide practices. Some ways to obtain student voice include student surveys, student-developed assessments of the school, suggestion boxes, student news reports broadcast to the school, student equity teams, and student councils. Promoting an open environment schoolwide takes leadership from both adults and students.

SEATTLE STUDENT EQUITY PROJECT

Seattle Public Schools is partnering with SoundOut to create, develop, and support student equity teams, focused on race relations, in high schools across the city.

The Seattle Student Equity Project focuses on three themes:

- Equity and race relations: Bringing communities together through open dialogue and honest reflection around what is meant by racism and the impact it has on our society and, more specifically, students
- Student voice: Engaging the perspectives and actions of young people in educational activities that partner students with adults to improve schools
- Service learning: Combining powerful opportunities to help others with substantial classroom learning goals

Every student equity team is invited to participate in a program that includes four components:

- Ongoing training for students and adults, focused on each project theme in order to increase the capacity through knowledge-sharing and skill-building activities
- Student-led evaluations of student perspectives about equity and race relations in Seattle Public Schools
- Service learning projects that are designed, implemented, and evaluated by students in response to student-led evaluations
- Cross-school collaborations through monthly meetings and training sessions that encourage students to share experiences and brainstorm responses

To learn more about the project, visit their website at http://www.soundout.org/features/SPS-SEP.htm

Bridging cultures, both in your classroom and schoolwide, is impossible without inviting families to be directly involved in the school. Many of the snapshots in this book involve families directly as a source of information, connection, strength, and education. For example, see the following: Snapshot 1.1 "Project FRESA," Snapshot 4.2 "Celebrating Differences—Achieving Results," Snapshot 5.2 "Collaborative Action Research Projects," Snapshot 5.3 "Family Maps," Snapshot 5.4 "Family Stories Books," Snapshot 5.5 "Fairy Tales, Folktales, and Family Stories," Snapshot 6.2 "Heritage Dolls," Snapshot 7.1 "Tulalip-Based Curriculum and Lushootseed Classes," and Snapshot 7.5 "Stories Project." All schoolwide CRSB practices benefit from the direct input of families and the community. Fostering this kind of family involvement requires two-way communication; inclusion of families as part of planning and decisionmaking groups; creation of an atmosphere of trust and respect among families, community members, and school staff; and the ability of the school to regard family members as experts in their own culture.

Begin by making a point of asking what the family and community members want for their children. Many activities (see, for example, Snapshot 7.1 "Tulalip-Based Curriculum and Lushootseed Classes" and Snapshot 7.5 "Stories Project" start with a classroom activity and grow schoolwide with help from family members and the community. Other activities integrate the local culture and school culture with schoolwide planning activities, as in Snapshot 4.2 about Arnaq School in Alaska, where the school staff led by the principal worked continually to bring the culture of the students into the school in a way that enhanced learning and self-identity. These efforts resulted in improved student test scores and increased student engagement in learning. Snapshot 7.3 "Culturally Responsive Discipline" shows how a middle school in Phoenix, Arizona, invites families into the daily setting of the school while promoting a positive school climate of respect and the expectation that all students can succeed.

Snapshot 7.3

CULTURALLY RESPONSIVE DISCIPLINE

Cordova Middle School, Phoenix, Arizona

Grade levels: 4–8

Subject areas: Focus on culturally responsive discipline practices

Highlights: A middle school with a diverse student population implements proactive, positive, and culturally responsive programs to reduce behavior referrals and increase student achievement.

Cordova Middle School (CMS) was recognized as an Arizona A+ Exemplary School (2004) and was one of only 20 K–12 schools nationally awarded a National School of Distinction in Leadership Excellence award by the Intel Corporation and Scholastic. The school's principal at that time, Karen Williams, was a National Distinguished Principal of the Year for 2004.

Serving close to 900 students in grades 4–8, CMS shares a campus with a primary K–3 school in an older, low-income neighborhood in West Central Phoenix, where housing includes federally subsidized single-family homes and high-density, low-income apartments. CMS's student body is culturally and linguistically diverse (CLD): approximately 83 percent Latino, 7 percent white, 5 percent black, 2 percent Native American, and 4 percent Asian or Pacific Islander. Of its more than 400 English language learners, 93 percent speak Spanish, but other languages represented include Vietnamese, Cantonese, Navajo, Yoruba, and French.

Prior to implementing culturally responsive discipline practices, CMS administrators were receiving 125 student office referrals per month for behavior issues. Many schools historically react to students' challenging behavior with detention, suspension, and expulsion, all of which punish students by excluding them from school and limiting their opportunity to receive positive support for behavior change. These punitive practices tend to be exclusionary and ineffective (Liaupsin, Jolivette, & Scott, 2005), and affect CLD students at disproportionately higher rates than cultural- and language-majority students (Skiba, 2001).

These CLD students are overrepresented in special education, where they have been placed based on behavior issues. Many of the CLD students who are referred for special education evaluation are diagnosed with Emotional/Behavioral Disorders (EBD) or else become part of a cycle of suspension that leads to a greater risk for school expulsion and school dropout. Furthermore, punitive and reactive disciplinary measures have been linked to the increased severity and incidence of the target behaviors (Turnbull et al., 2002). Fortunately, CMS administrators and teachers have taken a different approach. They decided to look at what the research said, and found that schools are encouraged to take a proactive approach to discipline based on the theoretical model that most behavior is learned, and that plans should be designed to promote children's social and behavioral development. In addition to being proactive, such approaches must simultaneously focus on students' cultural characteristics as well as on language needs (Osher et al., 2004).

A Culturally Responsive Approach to Discipline

At CMS, diversity does not correlate with low student achievement and increased behavioral and attendance problems. The school attributes this to the use of a combination of formalized, schoolwide, classroom, and individual student-focused approaches to promoting positive behavior. It also provides alternative supports for students who require specific social, behavioral, and emotional support, as well as varied opportunities for engagement in academic enrichment activities.

CMS's programs and practices are meeting the behavioral needs of students through positive intervention rather than punishment. Instead of using a prepackaged approach to proactive discipline, they have developed— *with the input of families*—various practices that they see as relevant for their own unique school community. This places important emphasis on culturally responsive discipline practices rather than on exclusionary practices that often are used with CLD students with social or emotional needs that affect behavior. In addition, CMS's programs and practices aim to alleviate the cultural conflict that can occur when educators do not fully understand and fail to integrate the cultures of their students into the school environment. Evidence of positive student outcomes supports these practices.

The school seems to be at the center of the community, with a parent volunteer room and meeting space on campus; language and parenting classes with childcare and Saturday classes for students and families; and an afterschool class for

(Continued)

(Continued)

students with limited English proficiency, which has been designed specifically for newly immigrated students. These Saturday Academic Academies often center on culturally based activities in order to promote parent and student involvement. One such example is a cooking class during which traditional Mexican food is prepared as a part of science and math lessons in which both students and parents lead and participate.

Other opportunities for parent and community involvement include the School Community Council, which meets once a month, and the CMS Booster Club, which is a parent organization that provides fundraising monies for extra- and co-curricular activities. The school provides meals throughout the summer, including school-sponsored volunteer luncheons with some food provided by teachers and other staff members. The recruitment of parent volunteers is coordinated by a parent- or community-volunteer coordinator, which is a paid, full-time position.

These resources complement the existing proactive discipline programs and practices, promote open communication, and help develop mutual respect among the students, faculty, parents, and community. They are culturally responsive in that they provide opportunities for parent and community presence and input in the school setting, and provide educational opportunities for parents based on their input on interest surveys and informal communication.

Both parents and students provide feedback, and the reviews have been positive, especially relating to student learning, teacher skill, respect for students, and high expectations for all students.

My son just graduated this year, and I'm very proud of him. I can honestly say that so much of it had to do with the teachers and their ability to show the students that they do count and that they can achieve as much as they

want in life. My son went on a lot of outings which were based on culture awareness. I personally feel that this interaction has opened my child's eyes to the possibilities that life has to offer him, and I know that he is able to become successful, however he chooses to be. Thank you, teachers, for taking the time to care and support our children.—A parent

Proactive and Alternative Support Practices

CMS programs and practices aim at building and strengthening the protective factors for students. These include a school culture of mutual expectations and respect, motivational systems that provide recognition for positive behavior, and relationships with caring adults in the school setting. They also focus on building behavioral skills such as conflict resolution, behavioral self-monitoring and evaluation, and identification of appropriate ways to express emotions and to generate solutions in frustrating circumstances. These programs and practices are grouped into two categories: proactive support and alternative support practices.

Proactive supports focus on preventing behavioral problems at the classroom and schoolwide level, or at the individual student level, and include the following two programs: (1) the Choose High Achievement, Citizenship, Homework and Attendance (CHA CHA) program, in which students discuss and evaluate their peers' efforts to treat others with respect, complete homework, and be present and punctual. Students earn rewards and help each other succeed. (2) There is also a Rights and Responsibilities program that builds teamwork and social-interdependence within classrooms by encouraging positive peer relationships, with members of the classroom encouraging each other to make wise socialization choices. Classes are rewarded with pizza and ice cream parties that they help plan. Teachers use a diversity self-assessment tool, which allows them to acknowledge and address their own beliefs, values, and biases related to students from diverse backgrounds.

The alternative support approaches are in response to individual students who display behavior difficulties. These students either are served individually or in small groups of students with similar areas of need. Supports include any of these:

- Mentoring: Individual students are matched with adult mentors from similar primary language and cultural backgrounds in the community.
- New directions: Staff-led groups help students build self-image, resist peer pressure, achieve goals, and negotiate teacher-student relationships.
- Peer mediation and counseling: Student-led groups are designed specifically for each student.

Results

The proactive discipline programs are working. Attendance has improved by 15 percent since the start of the program. In addition, the number of students qualifying for academic recognition has increased by 20 percent, and homework completion rates have increased from 60 to 95 percent. As a result of the positive interactions, student discipline referrals have dropped by 42 percent, decreasing the number of students visiting the office from the original 125 per month to about 25 per month, in a school of 900 students.

Analyses by ethnic or racial group demonstrate that CMS students achieve better than peers who attend other schools with similar demographics. CMS students exceed the national, district, and comparison-school averages in mathematics in all grades, and meet or exceed the comparison averages in reading and language—74 percent for CMS eighth-grade Latino students, compared to 47 percent for the Arizona state average. CMS students also meet or exceed reading standards—94 percent of sixth-grade Latino students meet or exceed writing standards, compared to 39 percent in the state. Another significant result is the impressive scores of those students who remain at CMS for more than one year. These students scored above grade level in all subject areas at all grades on the 2005 Stanford Nine Achievement Test.

Principal Barbara Marshall provided data that show 23 out of a class of 31 students stay after school for academic enrichment with their teacher. Marshall described a wide variety of academic activities in which students engage, including book clubs, quarterly Saturday Academic Academies for students and parents, as well as six new afterschool academic classes for students who were identified as "approaching the standard" on last year's Arizona Instrument to Measure Standards (AIMS) test in the area of reading or writing.

The school maximizes opportunities for academic engagement as a means for preventing negative behavior. CMS's dedication to academic success for all students and the efficacy of its practices are evidenced by high attendance and homework completion rates, as well as above-average standardized test scores as compared to national and state averages for schools with similar demographics.

To learn more about this school and its story, visit http://www.nccrest.org/.

Resource Development

The effort to take CRSB policies, practices, and teaching strategies schoolwide requires collaboration and a rich store of resources from which to draw. Often, this effort benefits from the deliberate documentation of the resources you gather and the processes by which you gather them.

Resource development is one of the first steps to becoming culturally responsive. For example, gathering information about the history of a community, interviewing elders, reading both fiction and nonfiction by authors from different cultures, and collecting cultural artifacts can all provide a deep well of material from which to create future activities. Along the way, you can create family maps—mapping the resources each family can provide—and collect family stories and photos that will provide wonderful details to embed in the learning activities. With time, these resources also provide future classes with a rich history of the students who came before them, and can help create a unified identity and sense of belonging at the school. Activities that can build from these resources include making a class quilt, developing a student bulletin board, sharing and documenting cultural celebrations, writing a community "memoir" with community members' help, and many others.

EFFECTIVE ONGOING PROFESSIONAL DEVELOPMENT

Scaling up CRSB teaching and learning ideas takes time and commitment from the entire staff. One way to help keep the momentum going is to adopt a professional development model that will ensure a positive structure for developing the CRSB vision of school change within a team approach. Professional development is fundamental to the process of developing a shared vision and building school support that promotes CRSB teaching. Professional development builds the foundation of cultural understanding and knowledge, supports CRSB curricular options across the continuum, and provides time for reflection. Tool 16, "Our Cultural and Educational Experiences," can be offered to school or district administrators as one such staff development activity. You can offer to facilitate the activity by yourself, with a colleague, or by using a staff development specialist.

One effective professional development strategy that many schools have adopted is the professional learning community approach. Working in professional learning teams, teachers use an inquiry cycle to engage in powerful conversations about best practices. Such reflective practice opens the door to both school improvement and improved teaching practices, while keeping staff members focused on high achievement for all students. This kind of ongoing, team-based, on-the-job professional development helps teachers increase their collaboration skills as they integrate new teaching strategies into their repertoire.

Effective professional development should include a continuum of activities, from workshops to study groups, in order to meet the varying learning needs of teachers. Traditionally, workshops are less effective than teacher networks and ongoing study groups. Professional development activities designed for teachers in the same school, grade, or subject area are particularly effective because staff members can collectively participate in and collaborate on the implementation of what was learned. These activities are more effective if the focus or content is on developing expertise in a subject, content, or pedagogical focus area that is targeted to a specific school and student context. Teachers need opportunities in their professional development to engage actively in the meaningful analysis of teaching and learning. This learning is more effective for teachers if it is longer, sustained over time, and intense. The culmination of the professional development learning is teacher coherence, communication among teachers, and activities that align with standards and assessments, teachers' goals, and school improvement efforts (Sather, 2009).

Other models of ongoing professional development that promote teacher collaboration include action research, lesson study, critical friends group, faculty study group, looking at student work, and data teams. A common element among these models is the need to examine teaching practice with an eye to improving student learning. Which of these models you choose depends on the goals of the group. Each can provide an avenue to create professional development opportunities using the tools from this manual to allow teachers to move closer to CRSB teaching, such as reflecting on their cultural heritage (memoir writing, artifact sharing, cultural celebrations, and other ways of knowing). Using one of these models can help start the schoolwide discussion about how to integrate cultural background—through storytelling, writing, speaking, drawing, and creating—into a curriculum. Topics for discussion could include how to build a sense of cultural awareness in the classroom, how to create an atmosphere of open dialogue, and how to recognize and address individual learning styles.

Resources on Creating Professional Learning Teams

Education Northwest (educationnorthwest.org/service/295)

Corwin Press (www.corwin.com/booksProdDesc.nav?prodId=Book232701)

Southwest Educational Development Laboratory (SEDL) (www.sedl.org/change/issues/issues61.html)

The SERVE Center at the University of North Carolina at Greensboro (http://www.serve.org/uploads/files/150%20PLCs.pdf)

TAKING CULTURALLY RESPONSIVE STANDARDS-BASED EFFORTS TO THE DISTRICT LEVEL

CRSB practices can be adopted on a wider scale, with the entire school district focusing on the concepts and essential elements of CRSB teaching. The district can provide supports such as guidelines, staff development, coaching, resources, access to expertise, curricular materials, and flexibility in scheduling. These are typically multiyear efforts, but can range from a major reform of all aspects of district operations to a single workshop presented and sponsored by the district. Following Tool 16 are Snapshot 7.4, "One District's Approach to Ensuring That all Students are Successful," on page 184 and Snapshot 7.5, "Stories Project," on page 186. These Snapshots are examples of two successful approaches: a comprehensive districtwide initiative in upstate New York and a Portland, Oregon, school district–sponsored photography and writing project that uses the home cultures of students and staff members as the basis for staff development, family partnership, and public engagement activities.

TOOL 16

OUR CULTURAL AND EDUCATIONAL EXPERIENCES

The purposes of this tool are

- to allow staff members to reflect on their own cultural and educational experiences and to consider how those experiences influence the way they view the world and the way they teach;
- to help staff members recognize and appreciate the diversity of life experiences among the staff and students in their school; and
- to help staff members get to know each other better.

Activities

- Discuss the meaning of culture.
- Interview each other in pairs, asking each other to share cultural and educational experiences.
- Introduce one another to the larger group, based on the interview questions.
- Discuss participants' cultural and educational experiences and reflect on how those experiences influence the way each person teaches.

Facilitating the Activity

This activity can be used at a gathering such as a staff meeting or an in-service day. Any staff member can guide the activity, but he or she should be a neutral facilitator and not a participant in the conversation. The facilitator should read the steps thoroughly prior to the activity, modifying them if necessary based on staff needs and experiences.

Things to Consider

Because an individual's culture and educational experiences are closely connected to his or her values and beliefs, facilitating a meaningful conversation about either can be tricky. To create a more comfortable environment during the activity, do the following:

- Explain to the staff that topics like culture, educational experiences, and culturally responsive teaching and learning are quite complex and sometimes difficult to talk about.
- Reassure them that today the group will try to explore the issues in a nonthreatening way. At the beginning of the activity, have the group set a few simple ground rules for discussion. Those rules might include showing mutual respect, recognizing that each person's experiences are true and valid for them and should not be debated, giving each person the right to pass, and ensuring confidentiality.

To be better prepared for facilitating steps 2 and 3, ponder the reflection questions on the handout before you present them to the staff and choose the questions that will be most important for your peers to address. Be willing to model high-quality discussion by sharing relevant experiences with the group.

Materials

- Handout (found on page 183): Reflection Questions on Our Cultural and Educational Experiences
- Flip chart and markers, or chalkboard and chalk

Time

At least one hour, though more time is preferable. (The times reflected in the parentheses below are just suggestions. Take as much time as you need within each step to fully explore each topic.)

Steps for the Activity

1. Set a positive tone for the activity: Welcome staff members, introduce yourself, explain the purpose of the activity, and set ground rules. (5 minutes)

2. Write the word "CULTURE" on the flip chart (chalkboard). Ask staff members to define culture. Record and validate all responses on the flip chart (chalkboard). Your list might include race, ethnicity, gender, religion, class background, sexual orientation, where you live, beliefs or values, and family structure. When done with the brainstorm, conclude by providing the following definition (both orally and in writing) and illicit feedback and thoughts on the definition. (10 minutes)

   Culture: The integrated pattern of human behavior that includes thoughts, communications, actions, customs, beliefs, values, and institutions of a racial, ethnic, religious, or social group.

3. Tell staff members that they will have an opportunity to get to know one another better through interviews. (15 minutes—allowing 3 minutes to introduce the activity and 12 minutes total for the pairs to interview each other). Have staff members pair up with someone they don't know well. Distribute the handout, "Reflection Questions on Our Cultural and Educational Experiences." (Note: There are many rich questions on the handout. You will want to select the key questions you want answered beforehand, depending on the amount of time you have.) Tell participants that after the interviews they will be responsible for introducing their partner to the group in the following way: their partner's name, grade level taught or role within the school, and something that stood out about their partner during the interview.

4. After the interviews, have the partners introduce one another to the rest of the team. (10 minutes)

5. Lead a discussion with the participants about the ways cultural heritage and educational experiences influence how people view the world and how teachers teach. To promote dialogue, ask the following questions: (20 minutes, or more if time permits)

   - What are some of your significant cultural experiences?
   - How does your cultural background or life experience influence your work?
   - In terms of culture, what do you need to know about your youth or students to create a rigorous and meaningful learning environment for them?
   - What type of staff interactions and program or classroom experiences do your youth or students need to be successful?

6. Ask staff members to think about one thing they can do to bring their students' home, family, or community culture into the classroom. Ask for volunteers to share their goal and the steps they need to take to achieve it. (5 minutes)

7. Thank staff members for being willing to share their life experiences and to learn from one another. Encourage them to continue their conversations about culture and being culturally responsive and to extend the conversations into their classrooms. (1 minute)

8. As appropriate and as time permits, use or share these creative extensions.

Creative Extensions

- Have a guest facilitator who is experienced in cultural or equity issues lead this conversation with you.
- Have staff members write a "teacher story" based on the interview questions.
- Have teachers find a creative way to display their writings (e.g., posting on a bulletin board at the school or district office or publishing in a school publication).
- During the interview, encourage staff members to use markers, paint, or crayons to express their cultural background and experiences. Ask them to display their art in their classrooms or to organize a group exhibit at school.
- Staff members can modify the reflection questions on the handout and do a similar "getting to know you" activity with students in their classrooms. Not only will the activity allow students to get to know each other better but it will also help staff members know their students better.
- Give the staff members disposable cameras and ask them to create a photographic or pictorial essay of their home culture, answering the following question: What people, activities, or objects make up their current cultural context? Then have them creatively display photos, drawn objects, pictures, words, and narratives to communicate their cultural framework within the larger group. Teachers could do a similar activity with students.

Handout: *Reflection Questions on Our Cultural and Educational Experiences*

- Introduce yourself. Share your name, the school or program you are with and your role within it, and what you hope to learn during the activity.

  _____

  _____

- Describe the cultural situation you grew up in. Think about where you lived, your class or socioeconomic status, ethnic or cultural background, religious or spiritual tradition, gender, and the ways that these factors have influenced you.

  _____

  _____

- What were your educational experiences as a youth? What were you successful at, and why? What did you struggle with, and why? As a youth, how did your home or family culture support your school success? Did your home or family culture ever clash with school culture? If so, how?

  _____

  _____

- Describe your cultural situation today. How do you identify racially or ethnically? Who is your family? What socioeconomic culture do you belong to? What spirituality do you practice? Where do you live and why? How do these aspects of your life influence your work?

  _____

  _____

- Think about the youth in your program or the students at your school. What do you know about their home, family, or community culture? What do you need to know to create a rigorous and meaningful learning environment for these young people?

  _____

  _____

- If you were a youth in your program or a student at your school, what type of staff interactions and program experiences would you need to be successful?

  _____

  _____

Snapshot 7.4

ONE DISTRICT'S APPROACH TO ENSURING THAT ALL STUDENTS ARE SUCCESSFUL

Ithaca City School District, Ithaca, New York

Grade levels: All

Subject area: Focus on equity and closing the achievement gap

Highlights: In 2003, the local school board challenged the Ithaca City School District to "eliminate race, class, and disability as predictors of student success." Since that time, the district—led by Superintendent Barry Derfel—has made an all-out commitment to cultural responsiveness, equity, and family engagement.

While he was a teacher in the district, Barry Derfel became aware that many of his students of color were not doing as well in his classes as his white students, although they were just as capable as their peers. Many were failing only because they didn't turn in their work. Rather than blaming students or parents, he took it upon himself to solve the problem. He adopted a policy of "no zeroes": getting a zero for not turning in work was not an option in his class. He did whatever it took to get the homework turned in: staying after school to help students, making phone calls, visiting the homes or workplaces of family members, or meeting them at coffee shops. Derfel sums up his philosophy like this: "Nothing about the kids and families are the problem: it's our practices." The no-zeroes policy was only the beginning.

As a white, male history teacher, Derfel was fully aware that he had to draw on the knowledge and experiences of students, families, and community members when dealing with subjects of race. One concrete thing he could do was to use inclusive and affirming language. Instead of saying, "Take this note home and get it signed," he would say, "Here's a note that needs be signed by an adult family member. Take more than one if you have family members in more than one house, apartment, or trailer." Instead of using the term "slavery," he used "enslavement." Instead of "disabled students" he said, "students with disabilities."

Derfel then took his commitment, caring, and expertise districtwide. The district gave support by creating an "Equity Mentor" position in each school. These mentors work an additional three hours per week outside the regular school day promoting equity. They are the point-persons with whom Derfel collaborates to ensure that culturally responsive practices permeate the district. He helps the mentors and the school staff "move beyond tolerating or celebrating differences to utilizing differences to grow the school."

Four years later, Derfel has put in place an impressive set of strategies and initiatives. He offers all staff members the "Equity Challenge of the Week." (For example: "Think of the three kids you know least about and have a conversation with each of them every day this week.") "I learned that I need to work with community members and families, so I do quite a bit of organizing and bringing groups together," says Derfel. His approach is to build the capacity of all stakeholders through training events, book groups, and forums on topics such as the experiences of African American students and rural white students in Ithaca, and

Web-based resources that include student-made videos and the many compelling concept papers that he has written. In addition, there are links to culturally responsive lesson plans, examples of "update letters" to share with families before each new topic is started, ways to engage students in self-evaluation of their work, and much more. He maintains a link to these resources at the bottom of his website in order to encourage all stakeholders to network with each other. Derfel actively invites critical feedback and is currently creating digital portfolios to document the impact of the district's equity work.

Family members actively participate in many of the district's equity projects, so Derfel proactively trains new teachers on effective ways to connect with families. He suggests that teachers have each student fill out a card with her or his phone number on it, and encourages staff members to make communications with families invitational, not just informational. "Make sure kids and families see themselves in the room," Derfel advises.

Derfel also emphasizes the importance of improving curriculum practices. He and his colleagues developed extensive resources for implementing and promoting "transformational pedagogy." Drawing on Dr. Martin Luther King Jr.'s 1967 book, *Where Do We Go From Here: Chaos or Community?*, they developed a framework for constructing transformational workshops and for helping teachers construct transformational lessons. As an example, below is an outline for a series of workshops that encourages teachers to use hip-hop to connect youth culture to academic content.

Essential Questions

- What is hip-hop?
- How are hip-hop and public education connected?

- How will student academic success and participation rates increase as educators incorporate hip-hop into their planning and teaching?

Major Understandings

- Students succeed and participate in schools when their cultural identity is affirmed.
- Educators need to confront our own deficit beliefs about hip-hop culture in order to effectively engage and affirm some students.
- Hip-hop education presents people of color and people without economic privilege as agents of history and resistance, and not as tokens, stereotypes, or passive victims.
- Hip-hop consists of at least five major elements.

The Student Will . . .

- Engage more consistently
- Broaden her writing style
- Exhibit excitement
- Exhibit increased enthusiasm for poetry
- Make and express connections between the classroom and his life
- Speak out
- Use writing to express herself
- Use writing to work for social justice in his life and in the community
- Think outside the box
- Reveal a broadened appreciation of hip-hop
- Express connections between hip-hop and other styles of music
- Exhibit increased self-esteem
- Communicate a belief that she is an agent of history and change
- Communicate his truths in ways that lead to positive results

Barry Derfel's website can be found at www.icsd .k12.ny.us/legacy/district/staffdev/bderfel.

Snapshot 7.5 "Stories Project" represents a very different type of districtwide effort. It is a part of a more comprehensive approach to achieving educational equity through cultural responsiveness. Portland (Oregon) Public Schools uses the visual arts to connect the entire school community in a visceral way.

Snapshot 7.5

STORIES PROJECT

Portland Public Schools, Portland, Oregon

Grade levels: Pre-K–12

Subject areas: All

Highlights: By combining art and literature, this district-sponsored project forms the basis for a wide variety of emotionally powerful staff development, family partnership, youth development, and community engagement activities.

What first captures your attention is a large black-and-white portrait of a young woman sitting in a wheelchair, twirling a baton in her hand. You view the next portrait and notice she has a twin sister, who also is in a wheelchair. Several other photographs capture the sisters in various parts of their lives: relaxing at home with their brother, studying in a classroom at school, and playing with a canary who is precariously perched on one of the twins' fingers. The narrative that accompanies the photos reads,

> Bryan, Angie, and Holly are teens that live with their stay-at-home mom, Colleen. Bryan is the oldest and Angie and Holly are new teens. All three face the excitement and challenge of adolescence. However, for the twins, entering the middle school experience with physical disabilities that require the use of wheelchairs makes going to school a different kind of challenge. In elementary school, Colleen provided a daily routine of lifting, dressing, and grooming and often walked the twins to school. She felt confident bringing the girls to teachers and a specialist who they

have known since the first grade. She relied on the trusting relationships that Angie and Holly developed with staff and peers. For Colleen, moving the twins into a middle school setting meant trusting new people with the care of her girls.

Looking at the next series of portraits you might first notice a striking pair of teenagers: a high school–age student with a dark-tinted pageboy haircut, and her boyfriend with an intense spiked red "do." Another picture depicts the young woman's family. Her brothers hang upside down from a huge oak tree in their yard while her mom and grandma lean against it. The narrative accompanying this group of photos speaks about how she lives with her mother, grandmother, two little brothers, and a houseful of assorted pets.

You move on to a third series of photographs depicting a Latino family. Their narrative reads, "Catalina speaks two languages. At home she speaks to her mother in Spanish and at school she talks with her teachers and friends in English. Her older sister comes to school meetings and conferences to translate school information for her mother. Her family and her teachers all work hard to communicate about homework expectations."

You continue to look at portrait after portrait until you have viewed all 65 powerful black-and-white and color photographs in the Stories Project exhibit, a collection of diverse students, families, and teachers who learn and teach in the Portland Public Schools family.

Today, this photo exhibit is the backdrop for a staff development session for teachers at Marysville Elementary School. The topic is "Race, Class, Culture, and the Dynamics of Difference in Education." The teachers take their time viewing each photograph, and then a facilitated conversation follows. Teachers are gently challenged to respond to questions like, Which of the photographs are you curious about? Which portraits most closely reflect your family? If you were to walk through the exhibit with your mother (or father, or other close relative), which photo would challenge them the most? What's your family story and what influence might this have on your teaching?

At other times, the exhibit is set up in a school library or staff lounge, and is used as a tool to promote conversation about family diversity, or appears in a session on "using family stories to promote literacy" at a national conference.

The exhibit—first and foremost—strives to honor the diversity of Portland Public School families and teachers, and the caring relationships that inspire an enduring love for learning. Their images speak to the complexity and importance of life both inside and outside the classroom walls, the value and challenges of school, and the potent and tender places where these worlds connect. Most of all, the portraits and their accompanying stories remind us that at the center of all success—emotional,

social, and academic—are trusting relationships: people who see us, people who know our strengths and our challenges, and people who are willing to stand by us, stand behind us, stand up to us, and stand up for us.

Shauna Adams, LCSW, the family involvement facilitator for the Portland Public School District and the creator of the Stories Project, chose photography to bring these diverse stories forward because pictures—like people—are simultaneously simple and complex. She believes that the power of photographs lies in their simple ability to make us curious, question, and take a closer look at ourselves and those we care for, educate, and support. She has learned that there is a story within every picture, and that there is a pool of knowledge contained in every story. When we take the time to stop, look, and listen, we find that these stories have the power to teach. Adams also knows that everyone has a story, and that by taking a closer look at someone else's story you might be inspired to share your own.

The Stories Project is a collaborative effort between the Portland Public School District's Title I Family Involvement Program and local photographer Kathleen Nyberg. The exhibit is used in a variety of ways to help teachers, administrators, students, families, and communities look at how they define family, diversity and equity, wellness, and success. It is often used to help teachers open the conversations about their own students' home learning environment and it encourages them to help their students uncover their own stories through photography and writing. This successful project inspired an offshoot: a Teachers' Stories Project. Here teachers share their own diverse families, opening their personal lives to the whole school community and connecting the circle to the families they serve.

STATEWIDE EFFORTS

Similar to districts, states may provide CRSB supports such as guidelines, staff development, coaching, resources, and curricular materials for schools.

One such effort is the Northwest Native American Reading Curriculum. The Washington State Office of the Superintendent of Public Instruction (OSPI) has published the Northwest Native American Reading Curriculum. The K–3 curriculum guide grew out of a research study, Reading and the Native American Learner, prepared by Magda Costantino and Joe St. Charles of the Evergreen Center for Educational Improvement at the Evergreen State College in Olympia, Washington.

The curriculum is designed to link reading and writing skills with subject matter that is relevant to Native American children. According to Denny Hurtado, director of Indian education at OSPI, "We wanted to do five things: Develop a Native American reading curriculum; encourage the use of technology; motivate Indian students; develop trust between tribes and schools; and embed the curriculum with an emphasis on involvement of tribal communities and families."

Washington's tribes, Indian educators, and specialists in culture, reading, and curriculum were involved in developing the three units: The Drum, The Canoe, and Hunting and Gathering. Native American authors and illustrators helped develop 22 original stories for the curriculum. Each unit is aligned with state standards with a particular focus on teaching compare/contrast and now/then skills.

The Alaska Standards for Culturally Responsive Schools are another statewide effort. The Alaska Native Knowledge Network—sponsored by the Alaska Federation of Natives, the University of Alaska, the National Science Foundation, and the Alaska Department of Education and Early Development—has published a series of culturally responsive standards and guidelines. The Alaska Standards for Culturally Responsive Schools were developed through regional and statewide meetings of Native educators and elders. They are not meant to displace other state content standards, but rather to complement them in an effort to promote the cultural well-being of Alaska Native students (see examples of some of the standards on page 98). Endorsed by the Alaska Department of Education and Early Development, the standards have been used as a model by indigenous groups worldwide. The Alaska Native Knowledge Network provides support to Alaska schools in implementing these standards and offers a repository of culturally based curricular information at www.ankn.uaf.edu.

In addition to the statewide work done by educational institutions, there also are statewide community organizations that have come together with educators to create unique learning opportunities for the students in their state. Snapshot 7.6 "Learning Through Laps, Legends, and Legacy" shows how the 500 Festival of the Indianapolis Motor Speedway® created an education program through an Indiana academic standards–based curriculum that offers a variety of interesting and thought-provoking lessons and projects.

Snapshot 7.6

LEARNING THROUGH LAPS, LEGENDS, AND LEGACY

Indiana Department of Public Instruction and the Indianapolis 500®, Indianapolis, Indiana

Grade level: 4

Subject areas: History and social studies, language arts, math, science, health, physical education, and visual arts

Highlights: The Indianapolis Motor Speedway uses the history and the social and economic significance of the Indianapolis 500 to provide a unique learning opportunity across seven subject areas.

For many students in Indiana, the Indianapolis 500 auto race and the month-long 500 Festival activities surrounding it are culturally significant events. The race is a source of pride for many people in the Indianapolis community and creates great interest and excitement across the state. Over time, the race has created a sense of shared experience and tradition.

Recognizing the unique and compelling educational opportunity that the event provides, staff members from the Indianapolis Motor Speedway have worked with educators to create a two-part program for all fourth-grade students in Indiana. This opportunity teaches students about Indiana history, the world of the Indianapolis 500 and the 500 Festival, and the cultural role of these events in the state of Indiana and its various communities. The program utilizes the historical, social, and economic significance of the Indianapolis 500 as a platform for creativity and learning across seven subject areas.

"This education program is not just designed to teach about the track and the festival—it teaches how to use math to solve real world problems and how to read to find facts and information and continually question what you

want to do," says James Carson, a teacher at Crooked Creek Elementary School. *"It takes the state standards and puts them into real world use in a friendly format that students are impacted by and learn from."*

"Kids get excited, and are motivated and enjoy learning more about their state through this terrific resource," adds Robert McLeaish, also of Crooked Creek. *"If we use this program along with whatever else we are using, we are really pushing our kids ahead and giving them a head start."*

The Indianapolis 500 Education Program was prepared by Indiana teachers for Indiana teachers. The two independent components of the educational program are an in-class curriculum and an optional onsite study trip to the Indianapolis Motor Speedway.

In-Class Curriculum

The in-class curriculum is free to all schools in Indiana. It provides eight lesson plans, a supplemental video, student reading

(Continued)

(Continued)

materials, and Indianapolis 500 learning materials. Teachers are encouraged to change and adapt the lessons—integrating them into their existing lesson plans as they see fit. Teachers are encouraged to make the lessons their own and to create plans that suit the individual needs of their students.

The eight lesson plans cover 33 Indiana Academic Standards: four in history and social studies, eight in language arts, eleven in math, four in science, three in health, one in physical education, and two in visual arts.

Dr. Suellen Reed, Indiana's Superintendent of Public Instruction, states, "It [the educational program] serves our accountability program well in offering challenging materials for continuous improvement."

Optional Study Trip

The second component of the education program is an optional study trip for students, teachers, and chaperones to the Indianapolis Motor Speedway. (Schools are not required to participate in the study trips to be enrolled in the program and receive the lesson plans.) During the study trip, students visit five education stations where they experience on-site programming and interactive lessons designed to incorporate the lessons learned in the classroom with real life scenarios.

To make the study trips possible for all schools in the state, the 500 Festival offers stipends to schools to offset their transportation costs. In addition, students, teachers, and chaperones are provided free admission to the Indianapolis Motor Speedway and the Hall of Fame Museum where they learn firsthand about one of Indiana's most widely recognized traditions.

"It was a worthwhile program. As we study Indiana history in fourth grade, we try to instill in our students pride in their state," asserts Jane Cumberworth of Rushville Elementary. *"Learning about (and visiting) Indianapolis Motor Speedway helps develop that pride."*

"Outstanding educational program," states Paula Jones, from the Metropolitan School District of Shakamak. *"Volunteers were courteous and informative. Track atmosphere—exciting. Students absolutely loved it."*

In the five years since the education program was launched, student enrollment has tripled, from serving 5,151 students in 2004 to serving 18,505 in 2009.

Source: Baugher, Joelle. *Learning Through Laps, Legends, and Legacy.* Indianapolis 500 Education Program, 500 Festival. Used with permission.

REFLECTION QUESTIONS

1. Where are you, your school, or your district in terms of CRSB teaching? Describe how far away or close you are to the goal of CRSB teaching.

2. Are there any structural aspects of your school (e.g., scheduling, use of staff, school policies, use of space) that need to be modified to support CRSB teaching?

3. What are some small ways you can integrate CRSB practices with what you're currently doing so it is not another add-on?

4. Who in your school or district is using CRSB practices? Who can you turn to in the school or community to develop, expand, or improve your practices? How can you learn from their experiences?

5. Which of your peers could be used as a trusted mentor to provide feedback to improve your skills and abilities (and remind you that you are not in this effort alone)? Who could *you* mentor?

6. Who could you collaborate with on an interdisciplinary project? What would you do? How could you get started?

7. In what ways can you adapt a current project or activity to include activities derived from local issues of concern (i.e., community-based learning or service learning)?

8. Thinking of the examples of David Cort and Barry Derfel, what things can you do to move some of your current practices to schoolwide practices or policies?

9. How could you use the staff development tool to help start conversations with colleagues and open up a dialogue about culturally responsive practices that are needed in your school?

10. How can you maximize professional development time to support teachers in implementing CRSB practices?

11. Are there any districtwide or state-level policies or practices that support and encourage your efforts?

8

Teachers Learning and Growing With Culturally Responsive Standards-Based Teaching

Teaching children with different cultural and language experiences kept pushing me toward the growing edge.

—Vivian Paley (1979)

The two reflections, the snapshot, and the review of field-test findings in this chapter provide deep insights into how different teachers at different levels have used the ideas contained in the first edition of *Culturally Responsive Standards-Based Teaching: Classroom to Community and Back*. Taken together, they give a picture of the many ways that teachers have challenged themselves to understand and implement CRSB teaching.

Lilia Doni, interviewed in the first reflection, is an experienced, highly skilled teacher of ESL elementary students. Doni is unique in that she has worked with

CRSB ideas for more than three school years. Her observations provide a wonderful portrait of how one teacher has evolved in her thinking and use of CSRB teaching. The interview also clearly reveals that the challenges as well as the rewards never go away—they just become more interesting.

The second reflection is a first-person essay by high school teacher Judy Kirkham. She writes eloquently of her experiences implementing an ambitious CRSB project for the first time—one that was based on a project she had done previously. Kirkham is an experienced, expert teacher who brings her formidable skills to the task yet still finds many challenges. These challenges—as well as her successes—are described in detail in her essay, particularly as she reflects on the experience and makes plans for the next year.

A snapshot about the work of Tania Harman, 2009 Indiana Teacher of the Year, follows Judy Kirkham's reflection. Although she did not use this publication to develop her CRSB teaching approach, she followed many of its tenets and its spirit in her work. Her evolution as a culturally responsive teacher and her advice for teachers new to the work are very helpful.

The fourth selection, a review of field-test findings, is an excerpt from a longer ethnography, conducted by Diane Dorfman, of the differing experiences of three teachers who learned and tried out the ideas in this publication during a yearlong field-test process. The three were involved in a multifaceted training course that included Web-based learning and support, as well as a number of on-site visits by a facilitator who provided technical assistance and additional training.

AN EXPERIENCED CRSB TEACHER REFLECTS: AN INTERVIEW WITH LILIA DONI

The following interview took place with Lilia Doni on June 15, 2005. Doni had been working with the first edition of *Culturally Responsive Standards-Based Teaching: Classroom to Community and Back* (hereafter *Classroom to Community and Back*) for nearly three years as an elementary ESL teacher at Whitman Elementary School in Portland, Oregon. She was involved in the original pilot study in 2002–2003; her project from that year is highlighted in this publication (Snapshot 5.5 "Fairy Tales, Folktales, and Family Stories"). She then continued on her own during the 2003–2004 school year, and again participated in the field test the following year. During 2004–2005, Doni developed an exceptional project where students wrote about a family member as a hero. During a week-long project, students read *The Color of My Words* by Lyn Joseph; learned interview techniques from a reporter; and created illustrated books that they read to many different classes in the school. The evolution of her thinking and work over several years provides an illustration of the value of persisting with CRSB teaching and its many powerful impacts.

Why is this type of teaching and learning important to you?

Parents are the first and primary and lifelong teachers of their children. They are the most important role models. They set the system of values and culture for their children that the children bring to the school. Children cannot verbally express these values, but it's very important for teachers to know what they are. The families are the source of this information. Whenever you meet with parents and [interact with them] through family projects, you need to find out what these values and cultural beliefs and practices are.

How has your work in this area changed over the years you've been involved with it?

I'm reminded of a joke my son told me. He likes to compose music so he likes this joke: An 18-year-old composer is asked, "Who is the greatest composer?" He says, "Me." He is asked again at 25 and he says, "Me and Mozart." At 40 he says, "Mozart and me." And at 60 he says, "Mozart." This is how I view the role of parents in teaching and learning. It's not me that has the most influence, it's the parents.

I used to think that the teacher is in charge. That's the system I came from [in Eastern Europe]. I first learned about the value of involving parents while working on an educational reform program in my home country, Moldova. It was an innovative, new idea for that school system. The teacher was seen as the only educator and the job of the teacher was to pour in knowledge. There was no value on the importance of home culture. But when we started to look at parents and looked at their values, we developed projects that would be based on family traditions.

When I came here, I saw the necessity of connecting schools and families. Here the students are much more multicultural than in Eastern Europe and I saw the gap between what the families know and do and what happens at school. My goal was to fill that gap by having much more communication with families, not only by opening the doors to parents, but by helping them understand how the system here works. I also found that I had to help mainstream teachers understand immigrant families—their beliefs about school based on their own experiences in their home countries.

At first my goal was to develop a multicultural curriculum to bring cultural diversity into the classroom. Then, through my initial involvement with *Classroom to Community and Back* three years ago, I realized that I should focus more on my student's home cultures; bring them into the curriculum. As a result of doing this I saw that my student's self-esteem rose and the families felt welcome in the school. It was successful, but not enough. The next step was not only to include their cultures and families on occasion or as part of a lesson, but to have it be the main overarching theme of my teaching. Now all my teaching is based on the families' culture, values, and practices. One example of the impact of this more comprehensive approach is a mother who responded to all the projects with high-quality poems and stories. In many of my units I ask students to have their parents dictate or write stories about their family history, interesting family members, routines and celebrations, and such. It was so amazing to have this high-quality and high-level response from this parent. She appreciated

(Continued)

(Continued)

the opportunity to use her writing talents. She bound the books and created a website for her and her family to display these stories. She sent me many notes. The other teachers would say how lucky I am to have such a parent. But I don't think I'm lucky; I worked hard to reach out to parents and give them an opportunity to show off their talents. In our very diverse and low-income school this response from a parent is rare, but this is as much because teachers don't expect it or ask for it, than because it's not there.

Of course it also hugely impacted her child, my student. This is a child with multiple physical, cognitive, and behavioral problems. He has great difficulty with reading and had many negative experiences in his previous school. He became proud of himself and his family. His amazing stories gave him a positive identity among his classmates and in the school. As he struggled to read these stories to himself and out loud, his reading improved a lot. He knew his reading was not good, but he was no longer embarrassed by it or afraid to try because he was so proud of the content.

What other impacts have you seen from your approach?

Now I see that learning became much more relevant to the students. These projects excite them and motivate them. Writing is a big challenge for them, so it really helps them to overcome this challenge when they want to write. Their self-esteem rose a lot. They became proud of their parents, and so became proud of themselves. They discovered what their parents valued and what their expectations are for them. For me, I found out that these parents have high expectations for their kids and value education a lot. This was very surprising to me. I had assumed from the low level of many of the kids' abilities and poor attitudes toward schoolwork that the families are busy and don't really care that much about their children's education.

This project helped me develop close relationships with some children. One boy, who hated to write, was motivated to write on his own about his favorite wrestler. He went on the Internet to find pictures and information. When we just started studying Native Americans, unprompted, he came to school the next day with all these pictures he found online and labeled them. He wrote on the paper, "to Ms. Doni, from Roger." Many children internalized the idea of interviewing their parents. One child who is Mayan interviewed her mother about the history of the foods they eat (she had been told by her that some foods, like chilies, go back to ancient times). She brought what she wrote to school the next day. This was not requested by me. They [the students] became famous in the school. They loved to read their stories to other classrooms. The power of this curriculum approach is to make them believe in themselves and to have high goals such as going to college.

Please talk about your experiences partnering with parents, particularly getting them directly involved at school.

In my first project in 2002, I spent a lot of time and work to get every parent to come to the school and read their folktale with their child to the class. I sent letters, made phone calls, made follow-up phone calls, caught them in the hall, had parents call other parents . . . it was a lot of work. Then they all came again for the final celebration. The results were great, though. I really got to know those families and they felt so good about their children and the school. They felt important and valued and felt proud of their families and heritage, even though they were low-income, immigrant families and even though they felt devalued by many other school activities and interactions. The children made good academic progress, too.

It was so much work, though, that I haven't done it again, especially as I know it would be even harder to do with the families I work with now. I connect with parents now mostly through the children. This is not as strong as having parents come to the school themselves, but it is better than no or almost no connection and I have seen some very positive impacts on families—as I talked about before. I would need much more support to more directly involve families—things like paid time to do home visits and make calls or someone to help make the calls and arrangements.

What are some of the problems and challenges for you with CRSB teaching?

It's a lot of work in that you need to create everything—there's not a set of curriculum activities to follow or adapt. I needed, and feel that I will always need, some assistance; someone to consult with me especially in helping to make sure that I'm teaching toward the standards and that the academic part is strong. It would work much better as a schoolwide effort with help from a Master Teacher and with collaboration within the school. When working alone, it's too hard. I also had problems coming up with ways to bring in families and culture that didn't involve writing. All my projects were basically writing projects. Because writing is particularly difficult for many of my students, some of them started to resist the activities because I did so many of them. Expanding into other curriculum areas is my next goal. If we used CRSB teaching schoolwide, I would get ideas from other teachers for different kinds of projects.

FAMILY FOLKTALE UNIT: A FIRST-PERSON ACCOUNT, BY JUDY KIRKHAM

I think we all know from our own educational experiences that the best teachers are often the best storytellers. No matter who we are or where we originally came from, exchanging stories is what could bring us all together. I hope my students saw that this year. Maybe some of them could become the storytellers of the future.

For the past several years, I have used a writing and speaking activity after teaching Greek mythology and a multicultural unit on folktales to sophomores [at Sheridan High School, Sheridan, Oregon]. Prior to writing their own stories in this imaginative genre, we talk about and review the different reasons why myths were developed and the different motifs for folktales and do a number of brainstorming activities. After reading folktales and myths, I had students write an original myth, folktale, fairy tale, or legend. I had encouraged them to ask their parents and/or grandparents for stories they heard as children and asked students to then "retell" them for this activity, but very few students actually took me up on this offer.

(Continued)

(Continued)

The ones I have gotten have usually been really good and I wanted to see more of these. This year, I decided to try to make it more culturally responsive, so before we even started reading the tales, I kept promoting the process we would be going through and the types of stories they would be writing. By the time we got to the reading, they wanted to know when they were going to write their stories. I took that as an encouraging sign.

We started this project at the beginning of April with a handout of anthropological questions that I had found in an English journal. I encouraged students to try to talk with family members over break and, using these questions, see if they could find someone in their family who might be familiar with either their family history or who might be able to tell them stories that they had heard as children from grandparents or great-grandparents. The problem was the questions were a little confusing. Some students in my classes said that I needed to put the questions into "plain" English because I had totally confused their parents! And, in looking at the questions again, maybe I did.

After break we started reading folktales from all over the world in regular English classes and were studying Middle Eastern literature in the honors course. I also assigned my honors students an outside reading book, *When the Legends Die* by Hal Borland (2001), so they could be reading about the possible consequences associated with losing one's cultural ties. I then gave all classes the outline of how I wanted them to proceed with this project by handing out "Folktale Unit Steps." This paper outlined the steps they were to take in preparing for this project and told them which steps would be graded.

By the second week in April, most students were planning their big project. This was also the end of the third grading period and the time for parent/teacher/student conferences. We usually get about a 75 percent turnout for this event, as parents are able to pick up their students' grades. I decided that I would talk to the parents of the students in my English 2 course about this project and enlist their help, and also use this time to explain the project and put things into more "plain" English. All the parents that I talked to were excited about this unit. As we were talking, they told their kids things like, "You know your grandma and her sisters all wrote out the stories of their lives"; "You know that your aunt has all the family genealogy written down"; or "We can talk to your grandfather this weekend." It was really pretty neat to watch parents and students interacting. I think that helped me later when students were getting stalled or needed encouragement. As one student said in a reflection, "When I learned that I was to find out about my family heritage, I just thought it was stupid and I blew it off. But my mom decided to help a little." He then became excited about the project and with some prodding by his parents finished the process.

Students Exploring Culture

Once we had finished all the reading and students had done initial interviews, we were ready to start researching. This is when I found out that many students really didn't know enough about their families to do a lot of quality research. When I do this project again, I will insert a step where they fill out a family tree so that we know family names. While this was a pretty confusing time in the computer lab, I could see that once students found a "lead," they became excited, shouting at me to come see what they had just found out about their last name, their grandparent, or someone with their last name in a part of the country or world that they knew their families had come from. It was interesting that those who weren't finding information were jealous of their classmates, asking them for more websites to search.

One of the students, who belongs to the Grand Ronde Tribe, asked if she could get a tribal storyteller to come and talk to us as her contribution to this project. She wasn't having much success tracing any family and thought of this as an alternative. Of course, I encouraged her excitedly, but she didn't have a lot of luck getting this to occur. I tried to contact one of her mentors to see if they could get an elder to come out and tell us some stories. She was pretty discouraged about what she saw as her failure, and I knew that I needed to make a mental note to formally contact the tribe the next time I did the project, so that we could listen to someone who was an experienced storyteller. In order to help her find a story, I remembered the American Indian Reading Series resource on the Education Northwest website (www.nwrel.org/indianed/indianreading/). The two of us looked at these and she found one that she liked to retell for this project. Most students, after a week of researching family history, were also ready to find stories from their cultural heritage. Students then brainstormed an original story using guidelines I gave them and came to an understanding that stories wouldn't be plagiarized.

Once students had a rough draft, they edited each other's stories, produced a final draft, and began to practice storytelling. Both the written story and the storytelling were tied to Oregon performance standards for 10th grade. Students followed the Oregon CIM [Certificate of Initial Mastery] writing and oral reporting guidelines as they wrote, reworked, and practiced telling their stories. We talked about how to use a more relaxed, informal, yet animated tone when telling their stories, similar to telling stories to a younger child.

We started the storytelling process and at first I was not feeling very positive, but as students became more comfortable and relaxed in the setting, their stories began to flow. The honors class blew me away with some of their stories and their storytelling skills. With all classes combined, I had about 79 percent of students participate, better than the usual 70 percent participation for speeches. I know that some students just really hate getting up in front of the class, and this more relaxed setting allowed some who had not done a speech all year to feel comfortable enough to tell their stories, which I felt was another positive aspect of this project.

Students were given a scoring guide to score each other's presentations based on topic, eye contact, voice, movement, and gestures. With this task, they seem to pay more attention and look for ways to improve their own speaking skills. Once students started the process, more volunteered, some even wanted to read each other's stories aloud, and one student even told his tale on "How the Moose Got His Hooves" to his own accompaniment on the guitar. Although he found accompanying himself to be more difficult than he originally thought, it was fun for his audience, and I'm considering offering musical accompaniment to students next year as an option. Students' written stories were scored based on performance standards including ideas/content, organization, voice, word choice, sentence fluency, and conventions. Many students met these standards, but there were also some who did not. Some of those students still need writing or communication samples for their portfolios, and I may offer them the chance to re-edit or re-present their tales if time permits.

Interesting and Diverse Stories

While the writing would take more editing for a display or publication, the range and creativity expressed within the stories were impressive. Many male students stuck with violence and blood and supernatural creatures, which is pretty typical (after all, we have to get Star Wars and Lord of the Rings fans from somewhere) of what I have seen in the past. Because we have so many people in this area whose families emigrated from the British Isles, we also had a lot of leprechauns jumping about and causing mischief. I did learn about some new

(Continued)

(Continued)

creatures called Boggarts, who are little creatures who live in homes in England and if the human family doesn't take care of them they will cause all kinds of destruction.

Some of the more interesting tales came from students who had really delved into their family backgrounds and who came from non-European backgrounds. One that combined both was "Joseph and Octavia." This was a story that actually came from one of the anthropological questions about taboos. This student found that one of her grandmothers had come from England and "horrified" her family by marrying an "Indian" when she got to America. She wrote the story of their courtship and marriage in the face of family disapproval on both sides. A couple of other students went back to the days of the "Wild West" and based their tales on family stories, composing tales like "The Legend of John Mitchell, Horse Thief," and "My Adventure With Jesse James"—just how many people are related to that guy? Others based stories in the Northern European tradition, writing stories like "The Little Nut Twig," "Two-Eyes," and "The Frog Prince."

Several students from Mexico and Central and South America also wrote some interesting tales. One young man, who was adopted from Guatemala along with his twin sister, wrote a Mayan-based tale about "The Origin of Jaguar." A really good story was written by a girl who claims Chile as one of her homes (her parents have been missionaries, and she is of Central American/Mexican heritage). Her story was "Demon-Dragon" and was full of great images and mystical elements. Another great story was written by a young lady, named Rosa, who worked her life and emigration from Oaxaca into a story. When we had been doing research, she was quite discouraged and became sad because her parents are still there, and she is here. When she was writing about her cultural background, she talked about the difficulty of even communicating with her parents now as they speak Mizteca, and she is slowly losing her ability to speak it although she can still understand some of what they say. This story was her way of combining the two cultures, and she titled it "No Matter the Distance."

Our only Asian American student wrote a tale based on her South Korean background, which had a rural setting, where families were raising rice and helping each other in difficult times. I also had students who were quite resistant to investigating their family heritage and writing these tales. One, in particular, said he was American and that was good enough! He did write a semi-humorous satirical tale about family heritage. I think he may have learned more than he really would admit as he says toward the end of his story, "The moral of the story is to know your own heritage but don't let it change you."

In the honors class, we were also finishing *When the Legends Die* as the last of the students were telling their tales. In a final discussion on the book, I tried to tie together the two assignments by giving them a quote from the author, Hal Borland, in reference to the heritage of America: "Memories should endure. Unless we know where we came from, something about the road we traveled as a people, how can we know who we are and where we are going?" [See Wagner, 1987.] That opened up quite a discussion (the young man who was "American and that's good enough" was in this class) and was a good wrap-up in that class to this whole process of looking at family heritage.

Improvements

I did enjoy learning more about students through their stories and family history summaries, but I was quite frustrated at times with the slow pace of the research. Students need more time to digest the materials they are finding as they research. In the future, I will definitely divide this project into four major pieces across the four quarters—research, writing, storytelling, and publication, and have a process grade for each quarter. I'd include more outside resources in the research quarter—like the historical society, consulates, genealogical groups or the tribe, and include a family tree for students to use. During fall parent/teacher/student conferences, I can gain parental help, one of the really positive aspects of this year's project. I also could have students work letter writing into this first quarter by asking them to contact one outside source for possible information. If I start this project at the beginning of the year, students might also be studying the different waves of immigration into the United States, and I could utilize the history teachers to help with this research. I think a culminating short paper, similar to what I asked for in the initial steps, would be a good final grade for this step.

When it comes to the writing portion, I may have to rearrange the order of the world literature we study, so that students could have read folktales prior to beginning the writing process. I really need to make sure they are doing their own brainstorming and writing as we begin this part of the process. Once they have rough drafts, we need to spend lots more time editing. I think we could start with peer editing, but it was very obvious from reading the final tales that I also need to do one-to-one conferencing with students to point out the common errors they are making but not catching. With the time crunch I was under to finish up this project, I didn't take that time with them. I think a final typed tale, following the guidelines outlined, would be the final grade for this part of the process.

For the storytelling section, I need to make a lot more community connections and get some "professional" storytellers in to show students how to teach others through this oral tradition. Long before second semester, I will need to make formal arrangements with people to come to our classes. Rather than relying totally on students for this, I need to also make the requests from the school. Since our cultural studies teacher will be on a Fulbright exchange to Mexico for the first few months of the school year, I might also be able to use the cultural expertise of her exchange teacher, who will be teaching in her place and would be a good resource for our students whose families come from Mexico. Maybe he will also be a good storyteller!

Prior to class presentations, students need outlets to practice. We didn't do enough of this formal preparation, and I think students would feel more comfortable with their material if we did more of this ahead of time. We will have done a number of other speeches prior to this one as part of the ongoing curriculum, but I would like students to feel comfortable enough with their stories to be able to tell them without just reading their papers. The final storytelling would be their grade this quarter.

If students work on-and-off all next school year on this project, they should certainly be rewarded by seeing their projects in some sort of printed or published form that they could keep. I think it is also at this point that I might be able to utilize the skills of the art teacher and her students for illustrations of stories and printing/binding ideas.

Next year, our high school will be participating in a Comprehensive School Reform grant process. I think culturally responsive projects, such as the one I made a first attempt at this year, certainly fit into the goals of the No Child Left Behind Act and Oregon standards in a way that would help us as a school to begin to fuse all facets of our school community into a more cohesive, better functioning unit. As part of the committee that will be leading the grant implementation, I will certainly try to raise awareness about the possibilities of using culturally responsive curriculum as a way to bring our subgroups up to what would be considered an acceptable level by both the federal government and the state.

(Continued)

(Continued)

"A life without stories would be no life at all. And stories bound us, did they not one to another, the living to the dead, people to animals, people to the land?" This quote in Alexander McCall Smith's book, *In the Company of Cheerful Ladies* (2005), beautifully sums up the point I was trying to make with my students when we were doing our Family Folktale Unit. I wanted them to see the connections all around them—to the past, to their families, to their cultures, to their land, and to each other. I'm not sure whether I made as eloquent a point with all my students as Smith did in his book, but I did get them interested in their family histories and cultures.

Tania Harman from South Bend, Indiana, is another experienced, passionate teacher who has implemented CSRB teaching for many years. The story of her journey, captured in Snapshot 8.1 "Tania Harman's Journey to Promote CRSB Teaching Practices," is both instructive and inspiring. She offers useful advice for teachers starting to do this work.

Snapshot 8.1

A JOURNEY TO PROMOTE CRSB TEACHING PRACTICES

"Is that how you do things in your home?"

Warren Primary School, South Bend, Indiana

Grade level: 1 and 2

Subject areas: Social studies, literacy

Highlights: Tania Harman's journey promoting CRSB teaching began with a "wake-up call" from her young students about how different their world was from her own. She now trains other teachers and, as the 2009 Indiana Teacher of the Year, has a platform to convey her message on the vital importance of connecting curricula with students' lives.

Tania Harman, the 2009 Indiana Teacher of the Year, started her journey toward culturally responsive teaching when she taught first grade in a South Bend inner-city school. Out of the 20 students in the class, 17 had one or more parents who were incarcerated. During sharing time, they would often talk about the toys they played with at the prison. She witnessed two boys fighting over who had "real" jail boots. The one with black boots insisted his were real, while the one with brown boots countered that he had the real ones. As it turned out, their fathers were in different jails that had different uniforms and they were both correct. This started on her journey to understand and empathize with the particular lives, issues, and values of her students, which were very different from her own.

Harman is an ESL teacher in a bilingual first- and second-grade classroom at Warren Primary in South Bend. She expertly incorporates the cultures of the children throughout the curriculum. She starts by not assuming that she knows her students, but works to find out about their home lives or, in Harman's words, "what they bring to the table." Do any have gay or lesbian parents, incarcerated parents, grandparents who are the primary caregivers, multiple families living in the same house, or families with unique cultural or religious practices?"

When Harman teaches timelines as part of the social studies curriculum, she has her students create personal timelines. These timelines "come alive" when they bring in artifacts from home connected to key events in their lives. For example, students sometimes bring in items related to their communion, since there are many Catholic families in the school community. This becomes an opportunity for the whole class to learn about and appreciate different traditions and religious practices. This information also is used in lessons in other content areas such as graphing in math. They create bar graphs from the data on how many students are from a particular country or continent, how many people live in their home, and other family customs.

Appreciation for diversity then moves beyond the classroom. "Writing lessons draw from literature with characters that my kids can connect with," states Harman. They read about children from many different cultures so they can do character studies and make comparisons to their own lives and to those of their classmates.

Harman knows she is successful when she hears her students asking each other about their lives and families. They seek, on their own, more information—they are curious and caring.

As the 2009 Indiana Teacher of the Year, Harman works with other teachers, where she has found new challenges. She understands when some of the teachers she works with are resistant to incorporating culturally responsive practices into the curriculum: this is not how they were taught to teach, it seems like extra work, it can open up sensitive topics, such as religion, that are taboo in public schools and difficult to explain to young children, and so on. In response, Harman suggests, "Start small and don't expect to have expertise 'overnight.' There is a continuum of progress—keep moving until things become natural, second nature. Enhance what you're already doing. Collaborate with other teachers; go to the media/library specialist for help finding a new book rather than one you've been using, a book that shows life from a different angle that shows diversity, and is more connected to the lives of your students. Pick one lesson, then one unit, then one subject." Harman recommends that when you hear or read about a family routine or tradition, simply ask the class, "Is that how you do things in your home?"

REVIEW: HOW DOES CLASSROOM TO COMMUNITY AND BACK AFFECT TEACHER THOUGHT AND PRACTICE?

Notes From the 2004 Field-Test Participants, by Diane Dorfman

After reading *Classroom to Community and Back*, receiving training and technical assistance, and implementing its lessons, what changes occur? Are teachers more culturally responsive? Are curricula transformed? Are students achieving more? While we cannot answer those questions definitively, we can glimpse some significant effects of the publication on teacher thought and practice by looking briefly at three participants.

First is a middle school health/physical education teacher who began with a basic knowledge of cultural responsiveness, who responded positively to the readings, but who regularly displayed impatience with his Native American students' inability to behave according to his

(Continued)

(Continued)

expectations. This participant created an admirable final project combining standards and a culturally responsive curriculum in an innovative, sustainable gym course that holds the promise of building more community involvement as well as continuing to engage students. The project was developed in conjunction with ongoing professional development at the district level on Native American culture, which reinforced *Classroom to Community and Back*'s teaching. The most effective element in transforming his understanding, according to the participant, was implementation of the curriculum. "Seeing these tools at work with our Native games was an 'aha' in itself. I had students participating who have not participated in my class all year." For someone with little knowledge at the outset, the interplay of all factors—mutually reinforcing lessons from more than one source and the evidence of practice—was effective.

A second participant's progress poses more questions than answers on *Classroom to Community and Back*'s impact. The second participant, a middle school science teacher, entered with a fairly sophisticated understanding of not only the importance of cultural responsiveness in the abstract but also of its impact on student achievement. Even so, her curriculum project showed almost no influence of the publication's lessons. The critical issue here is that understanding the lessons of the publication and the importance of culturally responsive teaching to student achievement does not guarantee implementation—a key hurdle all teachers must overcome in order to realize the myriad benefits of the publication's lessons.

Writing about bringing families into the classroom and advocating for a better understanding of cultural diversity schoolwide, this participant said, "I have been studying and doing research on differentiated instruction. My goal is to integrate the strategies I'm learning from that research with the skills and strategies I'm learning from [*Classroom to Community and Back*]." She produced an excellent continuum with compelling elements of a culturally responsive curriculum and assessment. But, she also wrote, "The challenges I face in my classroom are time and curriculum related. We have an overwhelming responsibility to accommodate a variety of activities going on in our building and district (testing, etc). Sometimes this makes it very difficult to take the time to add one more thing. I do active teaching almost 90 percent of the time and my prep time is used to help individual students who are falling behind. My specific goal is to integrate the culturally responsive strategies into my science curriculum with the intent to reach all."

The constraints on her had an unfortunate consequence. Although this participant had a well-developed sense of how crucial culturally responsive strategies are to affecting real learning, her project included almost no such strategies. She reproduced an experiment on paper towel absorbency as she had done it previously, adding only the element of asking students how paper towels are used in their homes. The absorbency experiments were then based on those uses. Challenged by the field-test facilitator to recognize the project's failure to connect with the community, the students, or any sociocultural themes, the participant did reflect on the gap between her considerable knowledge and the work she was doing in the classroom: "I feel that this particular project was not exactly a good example of bringing in culturally, economically, and linguistically diverse backgrounds. Although it did seem to bring in lots of discussion of home environments in the way paper towels were used differently. About two-thirds of the way through this process I discovered that my reference of 'culture' was a bit narrow, however. *This occurred after my meeting with the facilitator* [emphasis added.]. I feel that now I can tie my relevant 'community' culture into my science curriculum as opposed to focusing only on individualized families." She goes on to describe ideas to link the experiments with research on the local environment, pollutants, and the impact on water levels and quality.

Although more community based, the ideas still are not culturally responsive. Perhaps this participant shows that teachers working through *Classroom to Community and Back*, able to understand and even embrace its lessons, must recognize that the time they invest in developing culturally responsive curriculum is not extraneous, but is essential to teaching. In this case, personal contact with a facilitator shed the light that a strong background, reinforced by the publication, somehow did not. One assumes that more intensive facilitation earlier in the process would have been effective in helping this teacher to better implement CRSB practices, but it may be that the numerous constraints on her and her particular learning style require a long timeline to move from theory to practice.

A third participant taught kindergarten. For her, the publication deepened, expanded, and strengthened an already highly developed understanding of the power and pedagogical importance of culture. She found in *Classroom to Community and Back*'s lessons ways to rethink strategies, and she learned that simpler was often more effective. She wrote,

> Our cultures are a large part of our knowledge. If teachers ignore cultures, they will see fewer 'aha!' moments—those times when students make that wonderful connection and understand—in their classrooms. . . . Culture colors our learning. My culture influences how I teach and learn. My students' cultures influence how they learn and teach me and other students. Our cultures influence how we act and feel about learning as well as how we behave in school. . . . Each day my students and I are creating the culture of our classroom. I believe it is open, accepting, and evolving. My hope is that my students feel that it is open, accepting, and evolving.

Her progress through the year demonstrated a commitment to engaging all her students, involving their families, and expanding the understandings and strategies schoolwide. Her Family Maps Project—an extension of a unit on Lewis and Clark—linked a variety of content standards to stories and maps of the students' families' migration from their ancestral homes, engaging their families as well as her colleagues. We see here that advanced teachers also profit from the publication's lessons and hands-on approaches. From her solid base of knowledge, she could refine classroom practice and focus on scaling up the work to the building level and possibly to the district level.

These three examples of the impact of *Classroom to Community and Back* on teacher thought and practice are not exhaustive. They merely offer a glimpse into the widely varying positions from which teachers first encounter the publication, and some critical factors affecting their success in realizing its concepts and strategies. While a basic knowledge of how students' culture influences learning is helpful, it does not guarantee success without a commitment to incorporating that culture into the curriculum and making it a priority among so many other competing priorities. Facilitation or training in the publication's use can make the difference for teachers who find the concepts difficult either to grasp or to put into practice. Conversely, teachers with little knowledge who are supported by simultaneous professional development activities or other building- or district-level mentoring can make tremendous progress with little facilitation. The publication is a resource and guide for those with advanced knowledge as well, allowing them to see that culturally responsive teaching is not overly time-consuming or unnecessarily complicated. With some thought, effective strategies can be incorporated easily into almost any lesson plan. Moreover, readers can find in the publication strategies for inviting other teachers, administrators, and students' families to participate in culturally responsive teaching and learning.

CONCLUSION

The two reflections, the snapshot, and the review of field-test findings provide insights into the complexities of effectively implementing CRSB, as well as the potential for great impacts on student learning. Each teacher's journey is unique, and where she starts is not necessarily a good predictor of where she'll end up. Some who started with negative views of their students' cultures developed empathy and created effective lessons. Some who were (or appeared to be) quite sophisticated in their understanding of the impacts of culture on teaching and learning developed lessons that were clearly not culturally responsive.

Below are additional insights gleaned from the experiences of the teachers in these selections:

- Some students will resist CRSB strategies for various reasons, and some will have difficulty because of a lack of knowledge of or shame about their own cultures. Not all students will benefit immediately or easily. However, teachers have found that almost all these students eventually have positive or growth-enhancing experiences. They also found that generally, across the whole class, participation and engagement in learning increases in CRSB lessons as compared to other, similar lessons.

- Teachers who viewed CRSB teaching as both integral to creating effective lessons and necessary for engaging diverse students tended to be more successful than teachers who did not hold this view.

- A number of successful teachers started in CRSB teaching by using a lesson or project they already had done successfully and were comfortable with, and to which they added a cultural element.

- Learning to teach using CRSB teaching is a long, ongoing process requiring commitment and persistence. It can eventually become second nature and can yield many rewards for teachers, students, and families. However, even very experienced teachers with great expertise in CSRB teaching had many challenges.

- Multiple constraints and pulls on teachers' time and efforts impacted their ability to implement CRSB teaching.

- Teachers who struggled with basic teaching skills such as group management or organization and who lacked a working knowledge of the standards in the subjects they taught had difficulty implementing CRSB teaching.

- Nearly all teachers who implemented CRSB teaching felt that it was worth the effort and plan on continuing. They all had some pleasant surprises regarding the positive impacts of their CRSB lessons.

- It is helpful, perhaps essential, to have peer, expert, and administrative support along with specific resources for CRSB teaching. A schoolwide and even districtwide approach would make implementation much easier.

- Teachers can use CRSB teaching as a mechanism to engage families—including many families who are not typically involved with their child's school or learning—in unique, positive, and powerful ways since it does not necessarily entail direct, in-school involvement.

It's as true for teachers as it is for students that, as Plutarch said, "A mind is not a vessel to be filled, but a fire to be kindled."

REFLECTION QUESTIONS

1. How do you define "dominant U.S. culture"? How does this view impact you and your students?

2. When was the first time you "encountered" race or culture (for example, when was the first time you were the only one of your race, gender, or class in a group)? What happened? What can you take from that experience that could help you build empathy with your students?

3. Describe an encounter with a student in which you learned that assumptions you had about that student were wrong. What advice would you give to other teachers based on that experience?

4. Are there aspects of your culture(s) that could clash with some of your students' cultures or get in the way of connecting with them?

5. What is your personal vision of CRSB teaching?

6. What do you believe about how your students learn and about their ability to learn? What influences your beliefs? What could change those beliefs?

7. Envision some of your struggling students as successful in the future. What are they doing, in your vision? What realistic role models of success exist for your students in their own communities?

9

Background Research and Theoretical Base

Culturally responsive pedagogy validates, facilitates, liberates, and empowers ethnically diverse students by simultaneously cultivating their cultural integrity, individual abilities, and academic success.

—Geneva Gay (2000)

A culturally responsive standards-based (CRSB) curriculum is critical to achieve the ultimate goal of all schools—high achievement for all students, particularly those who have been labeled least likely to succeed. An assumption behind *Culturally Responsive Standards-Based Teaching: Classroom to Community and Back* is that low school performance is in part due to the lack of congruence between the cultures of the families and communities and the cultural norms embedded in the expectations, policies, procedures, and practices of schools. Examples of this are well documented in the literature from the perspectives of many different cultural groups and on many different aspects of schooling, including the early identification of learning problems, student attendance, test scores, homework completion, and engagement in learning (Bensman, 1999; Bowman & Stott, 1994; Cummins, 1986; Delpit, 1995; Entwistle, 1995; Ladson-Billings, 1995). In this chapter, we review the research that provides evidence that a culturally responsive curriculum is one of the most effective ways to reach all students and raise achievement.

CRSB teaching is effective because it integrates elements proven effective in engaging students in authentic learning and enabling them to succeed in school. These elements and the way they are integrated are graphically displayed in the diagram in Figure 9.1. This integration of standards-based practices, culturally responsive teaching practices, and school-family-community partnerships in education can lead to student achievement and youth success by (1) enhancing engagement and motivation in learning, (2) creating academic rigor and challenging curriculum, and (3) improving partnerships with families.

Figure 9.1 CRSB Teaching

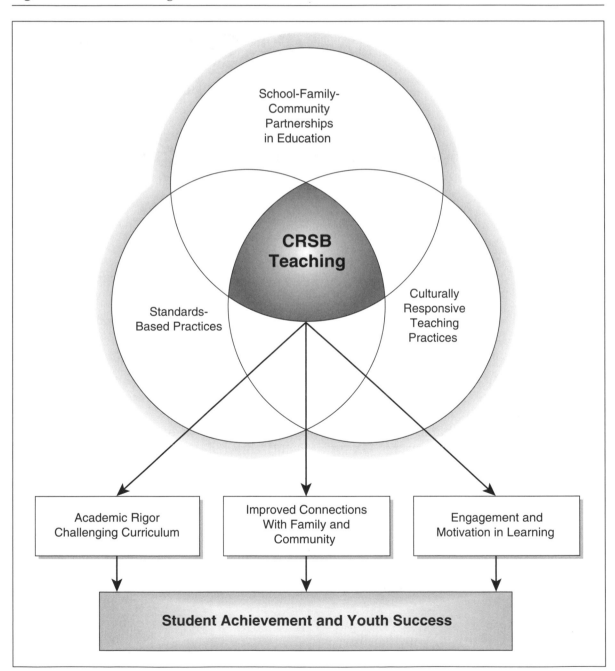

ENHANCING ENGAGEMENT AND MOTIVATION IN LEARNING

What is the often-held belief as to why students do poorly? School staff members name behavior issues within the classroom as one of the primary reasons for low achievement. Teachers usually turn to behavior management strategies to bring their students into line, often overlooking the link between students' behavior problems and their lack of engagement in learning. Teachers can affect change by using CRSB teaching as a way to create a meaningful curriculum that engages students and motivates them to learn and participate, thus promoting high achievement and reducing negative behaviors.

There is evidence to indicate that high motivation and engagement in learning have consistently been linked to reduced dropout rates and increased levels of student success (Blank, 1997; Dev, 1997). Engaged students make a psychological investment in learning: they are motivated to learn from a desire for competence, understanding, or simply a love of learning, rather than a desire for good grades, the teacher's approval, or acceptance to a good college. Engagement also promotes a higher quality of learning—not just rote learning, but learning that includes greater creativity and cognitive flexibility (Voke, 2002). Engagement is an essential prerequisite for the development of understanding—an understanding of the material in a way that allows students to incorporate and internalize it into their lives.

Students are most likely to be engaged in learning when they are active and given some choice and control over the learning process—and when the curriculum is individualized, authentic, and related to their interests. Authentic, challenging, intellectual learning—as opposed to basic skill learning—has been shown to improve student scores on conventional standardized tests. Unfortunately, the reality is that many classroom practices and much instruction emphasize student passivity, rote learning, and isolated skill training (Goodlad, 1984; Newmann, Bryk, & Nagaoka, 2001; Yair, 2000).

Some research also tells us that the teachers who are most successful in engaging students develop activities with students' basic psychological and intellectual needs in mind. Students need work that develops their sense of competency, allows them to develop connections with others, gives them some degree of autonomy, and provides for originality and self-expression (Ames, 1992; Anderman & Midgley, 1998; Strong, Silver, & Robinson, 1995).

"Doing well in school requires the belief that school achievement can be a promising basis of self-esteem, and that belief needs constant reaffirmation, even for advantaged students," writes Steele (1992). Creating schools that help children foster a positive self-image is even more critical for children from cultural groups that may suffer from low expectations, prejudice, and discrimination. Dawn Smith, principal of Warm Springs Elementary School on the Warm Springs Indian Reservation in Central Oregon, credits the inclusion of language and culture with improving students' self-esteem. "In the past several years, we've seen how the more the kids believe in themselves and their abilities, the more they feel comfortable with themselves, the easier it is to engage them in learning," she observes (Briggs & Carter, 2001).

Learning is the act of making meaning out of experience. In light of this fact, it is reasonable to say that no learning situation is culturally neutral. A culturally responsive approach to teaching includes real-life ways of integrating and organizing cultural, social, scientific, and civic learning across subject areas. It deepens the meaning of learning and cognitive value of learning because students can make authentic connections to their experiences, frames of reference, and interests (Ginsberg & Wlodkowski, 2000).

Community-based learning makes school relevant to students by connecting academic concepts to real-life applications, and makes students active learners who are responsible for their own learning. While many community-based learning programs include academic learning as an outcome, it is usually approached as a way to reinforce the basic concepts learned in school. Motivation to learn the basics and the ability to apply them to real-life situations are the unique additions of community-based learning.

The outcomes of community-based learning cover the full range of knowledge, skills, and attitudes needed to be an effective citizen, worker, and lifelong learner. Articles and research reports across the various categories of community-based learning suggest five major outcome areas: (1) intellectual development and academic learning, (2) career and vocational, (3) personal–social development, (4) service and work values, and (5) understanding and use of community resources (Conrad & Hedin, 1989; Owens & Wang, 1996).

CREATING ACADEMIC RIGOR AND CHALLENGING CURRICULA

In a review of the research on culturally responsive teaching, Geneva Gay found that when a curriculum had even minimal cultural content it resulted in "improved student achievement, according to a variety of indicators, across ethnic groups, grade levels, and subject or skill areas. The multiple achievement effects include higher scores on standardized tests, higher grade point averages, improved student self-concepts and self-confidence, and greater varieties and levels of student engagement with subject matter" (Gay, 2000, p. 146).

Determining the effects of standards-based curricula is complex. In a review of research related to literacy and math, Apthorp and colleagues (2001, pp. 177–178) found that certain teaching practices had more impact on student learning to standards than others did. The standards themselves do not result in improved learning or achievement, but provide appropriately high expectations. Good teaching is required to implement the standards.

The practices Apthorp and colleagues identified include these:

- Using a curriculum that adheres to the standards
- Imparting higher-order knowledge and skills
- Individualizing to meet students' needs through ongoing assessment
- Using knowledge of students' backgrounds, interests, and prior knowledge to individualize instruction
- Individualizing instruction by using knowledge of each student's level of understanding, progress made, what each can do and learn on her own, and what she needs
- Intervening early when a student is in danger of falling behind
- Managing classrooms effectively

Students are better able to comprehend new information when it builds on what they already know. For example, referring specifically to reading, Cleary and Peacock (1998) write, "Teachers can help students see the meaning in the act of reading by providing them with meaningful texts, texts connected with their own experience, or by helping them find relevance in texts they must read by helping them search for the universals in human experience." The Center for Research in Education, Diversity, and Excellence (CREDE) also cites contextualization as one of the key components in its Five Standards for Effective Pedagogy (http://gse .berkeley.edu/research/credearchive/standards/standards.html).

IMPROVING PARTNERSHIPS WITH FAMILIES AND THE COMMUNITY

Culturally responsive teaching reaches out to the experiences of students, which includes their families and communities in every aspect of the educational process. This is a very deep and effective form of family involvement. Educators and researchers confirm that families and community members play a vital role in ensuring student success. Regardless of the economic, racial, or cultural background of the family, when parents are partners in their children's education, the results are improved student achievement, better school attendance, reduced dropout rates, and decreased delinquency (Clark, 1993; Comer & Haynes, 1992; Epstein, 1991; Griffith, 1996; Henderson & Berla, 1994; Thorkildsen & Stein, 1998).

There is ample evidence that bridging the cultural gap through intensive and comprehensive school, family, and community partnerships is achievable and that it results in significant gains in student learning (Braxton, 1999; Cummins, 1986; Epstein, 1995; Ladson-Billings, 1995; Osborne, 1996; Snow, Burns, & Griffin, 1998; Tabors & Snow, 1994; Valdés, 1996). The benefits include better parent–child relations, more funds coming into schools, community services that are more effective, and lower dropout rates (Ballen & Moles, 1994; Comer, 1993; Cummins, 1986; Epstein, 1995; Fruchter, Galletta, & White, 1992).

A list of resources is provided in the next section to help you begin thinking and talking about these issues. The mounting evidence that connecting to students in culturally responsive classrooms enhances both teaching and learning is a great support as you embark on this critical, challenging work.

Resources

The following resources are categorized by topic and broken out by websites—listed first in alphabetic order—and print materials (books, journal articles, etc.)—listed next in alphabetic order.

Assessment

Burke, K. (1994). *The mindful school: How to assess authentic learning*. Palatine, IL: IRI/Skylight.

Wiggins, G., & McTighe, J. (2005). *Understanding by design*, 2nd ed. Alexandria, VA: Association for Supervision and Curriculum Development.

Community-Based Learning

Haas, T., & Nachtigal, P. (1998). Place value: An educator's guide to good literature on rural lifeways, environments, and purposes of education. Charleston, WV: ERIC Clearinghouse on Rural Education and Small Schools. (ERIC Document Reproduction Service No. ED420461)

Knapp, C. E. (1996). Just beyond the classroom: Community adventures for interdisciplinary learning. Charleston, WV: ERIC Clearinghouse on Rural Education and Small Schools. (ERIC Document Reproduction Service No. ED388485)

Miller, B. A., & Hahn, K. J. (1997). Finding their own place: Youth in three small rural communities take part in instructive school-to-work experiences. Charleston, WV: ERIC Clearinghouse on Rural Education and Small Schools. (ERIC Document Reproduction Service No. ED413122)

National Service-Learning Clearinghouse. ETR Associates, Scotts Valley, CA. www.service learning.org

Critical Thinking

Foundation for Critical Thinking. Dillon Beach, CA. www.criticalthinking.org

Gardner, H. (1999). *Intelligence reframed: Multiple intelligences for the 21st century*. New York: Basic Books.

Culture and Multicultural Curriculum

Cooper, P. (1993). *When stories come to school: Telling, writing, and performing stories in the early childhood classroom*. New York: Teachers & Writers Collaborative.

Freedom Writers (with Gruwell, E.). (1999). *The freedom writers diary: How a teacher and 150 teens used writing to change themselves and the world around them*. New York: Doubleday.

Kovacs, E. (1994). *Writing across cultures: A handbook on writing poetry and lyrical prose. From African drum song to blues, ghazal to haiku, villanelle to the zoo.* Hillsboro, OR: Blue Heron.

Manley, A., & O'Neill, C. (Eds.). (1997). *Dreamseekers: Creative approaches to the African American heritage.* Portsmouth, NH: Heinemann.

Osterling, J. P. (2001). Waking the sleeping giant: Engaging and capitalizing on the sociocultural strengths of the Latino community. *Bilingual Research Journal, 25*(1/2), 1–30.

Pierce, M., & Brisk, M. E. (2002). Sharing the bilingual journey: Situational autobiography in a family literacy context. *Bilingual Research Journal, 26*(3), 575–597.

Reese, L. (2002). Parental strategies in contrasting cultural settings: Families in Mexico and "el norte." *Anthropology and Education Quarterly, 33*(1), 30–59.

Romo, H. D. (2002). Celebrating diversity to support, student success. *SEDLetter, 14*(2), 18–24. Southwest Educational Development Laboratory, Austin, TX. Retrieved December 15, 2009, from www.sedl.org/pubs/sedletter/v14n02/4.html

Rothstein-Fisch, C., Greenfield, P. M., & Trumbull, E. (1999). Bridging cultures with classroom strategies. *Educational Leadership, 56*(7), 64–67.

Saldaña, J. (1995). *Drama of color: Improvisation with multiethnic folklore.* Portsmouth, NH: Heinemann.

Teaching Tolerance. Southern Poverty Law Center, Montgomery, AL. www.tolerance.org/

Trumbull, E., Rothstein-Fisch, C., & Greenfield, P. M. (2000). *Bridging cultures in our schools: New approaches that work [Knowledge brief].* San Francisco, CA: WestEd. (ERIC ED440954)

Wang, M. C., Haertel, G. D., & Walberg, H. J. (1993/1994). What helps students learn? *Educational Leadership, 51*(4), 74–79.

Weatherford, J. (1991). *Native roots: How the Indians enriched America.* New York: Crown.

Curriculum Development

Armento, B. J. (n.d.). The framework for curriculum development. Evergreen State College, Washington Center, Olympia, WA. Retrieved December 15, 2009, from www.evergreen.edu/washcenter/resources/FrameworkCurriculum.htm

Ethnomathematics Digital Library. Pacific Resources for Education and Learning, Honolulu. www.ethnomath.org

Indian reading series: Stories and legends of the northwest. (n.d.). Education Northwest, Portland, OR. http://educationnorthwest.org/resource/1112

Johnson, E. B. (2002). *Contextual teaching and learning: What it is and why it's here to stay.* Thousand Oaks, CA: Corwin.

Kemple, M., Kiefer, J., & Skelding, M. (2001). *Living traditions—A teacher's guide: Teaching local history using state and national standards.* Montpelier, VT: Common Roots Press.

Rethinking Schools. Milwaukee, WI. www.rethinkingschools.org

Spicer, J. (n.d.). *Mathematics of world cultures = a world of possibilities.* Columbus, OH: Ohio State University, Eisenhower National Center for Math and Science Education.

Tharp, R. G., & Gallimore, R. (1988). *Rousing minds to life: Teaching, learning, and schooling in social context.* New York: Cambridge University Press.

Zaslavsky, C. (1996). *The multicultural math classroom: Bringing in the world.* Portsmouth, NH: Heinemann.

Engagement and Motivation

Brewster, C., & Fager, J. (2000, October). Increasing student engagement and motivation: From time-on-task to homework. Northwest Regional Educational Laboratory, Portland, OR. Retrieved December 16, 2009, from http://educationnorthwest.org/webfm_send/452

Bryk, A. S., Nagaoka, J. K., & Newmann, F. M. (2000). *Chicago classroom demands for authentic intellectual work: Trends from 1997–1999.* Consortium on Chicago School Research, Chicago, IL. (ERIC ED470295)

Home–School Connection

Ban, J. R. (1993). *Parents assuring student success (PASS): Achievement made easy by learning together*. Bloomington, IN: National Education Service.

Edwards, R. (Ed.). (2002). *Children, home, and school: Regulation, autonomy, or connection?* New York: RoutledgeFalmer.

Finn, J. D. (1998). Parental engagement that makes a difference. *Educational Leadership, 55*(8), 20–24.

Kyle, D., & McIntyre, E. (2000). Family visits benefit teachers and families—and students most of all (CREDE Practitioner Brief No. 1). Center for Research on Education, Diversity & Excellence, Santa Cruz, CA. Retrieved December 15, 2009, from http://gse.berkeley .edu/research/credearchive/research/sfc/pb1.shtml

National PTA. (2000). Building successful partnerships: A guide for developing parent and family involvement programs. National Education Service, Bloomington, IN. (ERIC ED442910)

Zellman, G. L., & Waterman, J. M. (1998). Understanding the impact of parent school involvement on children's educational outcomes. *Journal of Educational Research, 91*(6), 370–380.

Projects

Chard, S. C. Project Approach. University of Alberta, Edmonton, Alberta, Canada. www.proj ectapproach.org/

Edwards, K. M. (2000). *Everyone's guide to successful project planning: Tools for youth*. Portland, OR: Northwest Regional Educational Laboratory.

Schuler, D. (2000). The project approach: Meeting the state standards [Entire issue]. *Early Childhood Research and Practice, 2*(1). Retrieved December 15, 2009, from http://ecrp.uiuc .edu/v2n1/schuler.html

Standards

Content Knowledge (4th ed.) Mid-continent Research for Education and Learning, Aurora, CO. www.mcrel.org/standards-benchmarks/

Hurt, J. (2003). *Taming the standards: A commonsense approach to higher student achievement, K–12*. Portsmouth, NH: Heinemann.

Lachat, M. A. (1999). Standards, equity, and cultural diversity. Education Alliance, Northeast and Islands Regional Educational Laboratory at Brown, Brown University, Providence, RI. Retrieved December 15, 2009, from www.alliance.brown.edu/pubs/standards/ StEqDiv.pdf

Youth Development

Developmental Asset Tools. Search Institute, Minneapolis, MN. www.search-institute.org/ assets/

Positive Youth Development. National Clearinghouse on Families and Youth, Silver Spring, MD. www.ncfy.com/pyd

Center for Youth Development and Policy Research. (1996). *Advancing youth development: A curriculum for training youth workers*. Washington, DC: Academy for Educational Development.

Glossary of Terms

Assessment: An exercise—such as a written or verbal test, portfolio, or demonstration—that seeks to measure a student's skills or knowledge in a subject area, or more globally (such as with IQ or SAT tests). Assessments are usually either criterion-referenced (the score is determined by how well a student does according to a set of criteria or a rubric) or norm-referenced (the score is determined by how well a student does as compared to other students).

Asset mapping: A process of creating a map of your (school) community that tells you what, where, and who the assets are of your school community. It helps everyone involved to learn about what they and their community have to offer the school.

Authentic assessment: An assessment strategy that asks students to demonstrate abilities through performance-based tasks within real-world situations. Taking a driving test behind the wheel of a car to get a license is a classic example of an authentic assessment.

Benchmark: A description of student knowledge expected at a specific grade, age, or developmental level. Benchmarks often are used in conjunction with standards.

Community-based learning: A broad set of teaching strategies that links learning activities in classrooms with a full range of experiences available in the community. This includes project-based learning, service learning, experiential learning, cooperative education, school-to-work programs, youth apprenticeship, lifelong learning, and many others. It provides learners of all ages with the ability to identify what they wish to learn and opens up an unlimited set of resources to support them.

Contextual teaching and learning: A conception of teaching and learning in which subject matter and content relate to real-world situations. Contextual teaching and learning motivate students to make connections between knowledge and its applications to their lives as family members, citizens, and workers.

Critical thinking: A process that stresses an attitude of suspended judgment, incorporates logical inquiry and problem solving, and leads to an evaluative decision or action (from the National Council of Teachers of English Committee on Critical Thinking and Language Arts).

Cultural competence: A set of congruent behaviors, attitudes, and policies that comes together in a system, agency, or among professionals, and enables them to work effectively in cross-cultural situations. Five essential elements contribute to the ability of a system, institution, or agency to become more culturally competent:

1. Valuing diversity

2. Having the capacity for cultural self-assessment

3. Being conscious of the dynamics inherent when cultures interact

4. Having institutionalized culture knowledge

5. Having developed adaptations to service delivery reflecting an understanding of cultural diversity

These five elements should be manifested at every level of an organization, including policy making, administration, and practice. Furthermore, these elements should be reflected in the attitudes, structures, policies, and services of the organization.

Culture: The integrated pattern of human behavior that includes thoughts, communications, actions, customs, beliefs, values, and institutions of a racial, ethnic, religious, or social group.

Curriculum (plural: curricula or curriculums): A plan of instruction that details what students are to know, how they are to learn it, what the teacher's role is, and the context in which learning and teaching will take place.

Evaluation: How well a program, curriculum, school, or district is teaching individuals to master skills or knowledge. Evaluation usually is based on gathering the assessment information from a number of individuals served by that program or school.

Experiential learning: Education that stresses hands-on experience and is accomplished by field trips, internships, or activity-oriented projects, as opposed to traditional classroom learning.

Higher-order thinking skills: The ability to view a problem or situation from multiple perspectives and to analyze it deeply, to understand complex concepts, and to apply sometimes conflicting information to address a problem that may have more than one correct answer.

Integrated curriculum: A meaningful way of organizing a curriculum that removes the boundaries between subject areas. Such a curriculum is based on the interdependence of concepts and knowledge and allows for faculty collaboration.

Learner-centered classroom: A classroom in which students are encouraged to choose their own learning goals and projects. This approach is based on the belief that students have a natural inclination to learn, that they learn better when they work on real or authentic tasks, that they benefit from interacting with diverse groups of people, and that they learn best when teachers understand and value the difference in how each student learns.

Learning style: The unique and idiosyncratic way each person learns. It may include how a person processes experiences (whole vs. part), the person's level of tolerance for accepting things that differ from the "norm," the degree to which a person reflects or acts impulsively, how a person categorizes information (broadly vs. narrowly), a person's level of persistence, a person's level of anxiety to perform, and a person's locus of control (internal vs. external). Another way of conceptualizing learning style is based on Howard Gardner's multiple intelligences theory.

Multicultural education: An educational approach that looks beyond curricula's content and strategies from the white, Western European tradition. The goal usually is to broaden students' perspectives and understandings to encompass one or more cultures that are different from their own. Some multicultural education models highlight subjects from diverse cultural, ethnic, racial, and gender perspectives. Others represent an immersion in one culture, ethnicity, or race.

Multiple intelligences: Howard Gardner's theory, which states that people are "smart" in different ways. The multiple intelligences are linguistic, logical-mathematical, spatial, bodily kinesthetic, musical, interpersonal, intrapersonal, and naturalist. An understanding of these intelligences can help teachers reach students and help students make learning connections.

Outcomes-based education: An integrated system of educational programs that aligns specific student outcomes, instructional methods, and assessment; also an education theory that guides curriculum by setting goals for students to accomplish. Outcomes-based education focuses more on these goals, or outcomes, than on "inputs," or subject units.

Positive youth development: An approach to working with children and youth that recognizes the developmental needs of young people and provides the supports, services, and opportunities they need to grow up healthy, caring, and responsible.

Project-based learning: A student-centered instructional strategy that engages students in long-term projects (usually in groups) that integrate several content areas and result in a product or report. It encourages students to play an active role in the creation of assignments and activities and, as a result, to help develop their collaboration, critical thinking, and problem-solving skills.

Reflection: Activities that are designed to encourage the self-analysis of learning experiences and to help set meaningful goals. Reflection usually involves some "evaluation" of those experiences and one's role in them (in order to improve in the future), but it can also involve reflecting on the context of the experiences, the relationship between the experiences and other events, or individual values and beliefs. Reflection can be organized as a group discussion, journal writing, role-play, media-based project, survey, or questionnaire, or it can involve the use of a more formal assessment tool.

Rubrics: Specific criteria or guidelines used to evaluate students' work.

Service learning: Combining service with learning activities to allow students to do work in the community that meets human needs or improves the community. Service-learning activities are integrated into the academic curriculum and provide students with the opportunity to use skills and knowledge they acquire in school in real-life situations to make a positive contribution. Students also apply the skills and knowledge they acquire in service learning to their schoolwork.

Standards: Statements of what students should know and be able to demonstrate. When—and to what degree—students should know something are benchmarks. Subject-matter standards form the bases to measure students' academic progress according to benchmarks. Curriculum standards drive what students learn in the classroom. Various standards have been developed by national organizations, state departments of education, districts, and schools. There is national debate on how to implement such standards: how prescriptive they should be, and whether they should be national or local, voluntary or mandated.

Teaching: Both what is taught (curriculum) and how it is taught (instructional practices).

Transferable skills: Skills that are interchangeable from one job or workplace to another. For example, the ability to handle cash is a skill transferable from restaurant cashier to bank teller. Some skills, such as the ability to function as a team member, are transferable to almost any job.

Transformational teaching and learning: Teaching practices that seek to create deep changes in students. These may involve changes in values, beliefs, attitudes, or behaviors and practices. Whereas most teaching seeks more superficial, though important, changes—such as improving reading, boosting test-taking ability, or imparting knowledge of history—transformational teaching seeks to improve students' lives and their relationships with others.

References

Adams, S., Edwards, K., & Dirks, P. (2003). *Beyond the Oregon Trail: Oregon's untold history.* Portland, OR: Oregon Uniting.

Ahearn, C., Childs-Bowen, D., Coady, M., Dickson, K., Heintz, C., Hughes, K., et al. (2002). *The diversity kit: An introductory resource for social change in education* (Pts. 1–3). Providence, RI: Brown University, Education Alliance, Northeast and Islands Regional Educational Laboratory at Brown.

Ames, C. (1992). Classrooms: Goals, structures, and student motivation. *Journal of Educational Psychology, 84*(3), 261–271.

Anderman, L. H., & Midgley, C. (1998). *Motivation and middle school students* [ERIC digest]. Champaign, IL: ERIC Clearinghouse on Elementary and Early Childhood Education. (ERIC ED421281)

Apthorp, H. S., Dean, C. B., Florian, J. E., Lauer, P. A., Reichardt, R., Sanders, N. M., et al. (2001). *Standards in classroom practice: Research synthesis.* Aurora, CO: Mid-continent Research for Education and Learning.

Argyris, C., Putnam, R., & Smith, D. M. (1985). *Action science: Concepts, methods and skills for research and intervention.* San Francisco: Jossey-Bass.

Ballen, J., & Moles, O. (1994). *Strong families, strong schools: Building community partnerships for learning.* Washington, DC: U.S. Department of Education.

Banks, J. A. (2008). *Teaching strategies for ethnic studies* (8th ed.). Boston: Pearson/Allyn & Bacon.

Bateson, G. (1979). *Mind and Nature: A Necessary Unity (Advances in Systems Theory, Complexity, and the Human Sciences).* Hampton, VA: Hampton Press.

Bensman, D. (1999, April). Open doors, closed doors: Home-school partnerships in a large Bronx elementary school. Paper presented at the annual meeting of the American Educational Research Association, Montreal, Quebec, Canada. (ERIC ED430695)

Blank, W. (1997). Authentic instruction. In W. E. Blank & S. Harwell (Eds.), *Promising practices for connecting high school to the real world* (pp. 15–21). Tampa: University of South Florida. (ERIC ED407586)

Boethel, M. (with Averett, A., Buttram, J., Donnelly, D., Jordan, C., Myers, M., et al.). (2003). *Diversity: School, family, & community connections* [Annual synthesis]. Austin, TX: Southwest Educational Development Laboratory.

Borland, H. (2001). *When the legends die.* New York: Dell Laurel-Leaf.

Bottoms, G., & Webb, L. D. (1998). *Connecting the curriculum to "real life."* Reston, VA: National Association of Secondary School Principals.

Bowman, B. T., & Stott, F. M. (1994). Understanding development in a cultural context: The challenge for teachers. In B. L. Mallory & R. S. New (Eds.), *Diversity and developmentally appropriate practices: Challenges for early childhood education* (pp. 119–133). New York: Teachers College Press.

Braxton, B. (1999). Philip's transformation. *Rethinking schools, 13*(2), p. 11.

Briggs, K., & Carter, S. (2001, December 9). Tribes racing to save dying languages. *Oregonian,* pp. A1, A13.

Bronfenbrenner, U. (1985). The three worlds of childhood. *Principal, 64*(5), 7–11.

Brooks, J. G., & Brooks, M. G. (1993). *In search of understanding: The case for constructivist classrooms.* Alexandria, VA: Association for Supervision and Curriculum Development.

Burke, K. (1994). *The mindful school: How to assess authentic learning.* Palatine, IL: IRI/Skylight.

Christensen, L. (2000). *Reading, writing, and rising up: Teaching about social justice and the power of the written word.* Milwaukee, WI: Rethinking Schools.

Chubb, J. E., & Loveless, T. (Eds.). (2002). *Bridging the achievement gap.* Washington, DC: Brookings Institution Press.

Clark, R. M. (1993). Homework-focused parenting practices that positively affect student achievement. In N. F. Chavkin (Ed.), *Families and schools in a pluralistic society* (pp. 85–105). Albany: State University of New York Press.

Cleary, L. M., & Peacock, T. D. (1998). *Collected wisdom: American Indian education.* Boston: Allyn & Bacon.

Coerr, E. (2004). *Sadako and the thousand paper cranes.* New York: Penguin Modern Classics.

Comer, J. P. (1993). *School power: Implications of an intervention project* (2nd ed.). New York: Free Press.

Comer, J. P., & Haynes, N. M. (1992). *Summary of school development program effects.* New Haven, CT: Yale Child Study Center.

Conrad, D., & Hedin, D. (1989). *High school community service: A review of research and programs.* Madison, WI: Wisconsin Center for Educational Research, National Center on Effective Secondary Schools. (ERIC ED313569)

Cross, T. (1995–1996). Developing a knowledge base to support cultural competence. *Family Resource Coalition Report, 14*(3/4), 2–7. (ERIC ED393594)

Cross, T. L., Bazron, B. J., Dennis, K. W., & Isaacs, M. R. (1989). *Towards a culturally competent system of care: Vol. 1. A monograph on effective services for minority children who are severely emotionally disturbed.* Washington, DC: Georgetown University Child Development Center, CASSP Technical Assistance Center. (ERIC ED330171)

Cuban, L. (1988). A fundamental puzzle of school reform. *Phi Delta Kappan, 69*(5), 341-344.

Cummins, J. (1986). Empowering minority students: A framework for intervention. *Harvard Educational Review, 56*(1), 18–36.

Curtain, H. (1990). *Foreign language learning: An early start* [ERIC digest]. Washington, DC: ERIC Clearinghouse on Languages and Linguistics. (ERIC ED328083)

Delisio, E. R. (2008). *Home visits forge school, family links* (Updated ed.). Wallingford, CT: Education World. Retrieved December 9, 2009, from http://www.educationworld.com/a_admin/admin/admin342.shtml

Delpit, L. (1995). *Other people's children: Cultural conflict in the classroom.* New York: New Press.

Derman-Sparks, L., & the A. B. C. Task Force. (1989). *Anti-bias curriculum: Tools for empowering young children.* Washington, DC: National Association for the Education of Young Children.

Dev, P. C. (1997). Intrinsic motivation and academic achievement: What does their relationship imply for the classroom teacher? *Remedial and Special Education, 18*(1), 12–19.

Dorfman, D. (1998). *Mapping community assets workbook. Strengthening community education: The basis for sustainable renewal.* Portland, OR: Northwest Regional Educational Laboratory. (ERIC ED426499)

Entwistle, D. R. (1995). The role of schools in sustaining early childhood program benefits. *Future of Children, 5*(3), 133–144.

Epstein, J. L. (1991). Effects on student achievement of teachers' practices of parental involvement. In S. B. Silvern (Ed.), *Advances in reading/language research: Vol. 5. Literacy through family, community, and school interaction* (pp. 261–276). Greenwich, CT: JAI Press.

Epstein, J. L. (1995). School/family/community partnerships: Caring for the children we share. *Phi Delta Kappan, 76*(9), 701–712.

Fletcher, R. (2003, June 17). *Deepening the reading/writing connection.* Workshop presented at Northwest Educational Service District, Hillsboro, OR.

Fruchter, N., Galletta, A., & White, J. L. (1992). *New directions in parent involvement.* Washington, DC: Academy for Educational Development.

Fullan, M. (2007) *The new meaning of educational change* (4th ed.). New York: Teachers College Press.

Gay, G. (2000). *Culturally responsive teaching: Theory, research, and practice.* New York: Teachers College Press.

Ginsberg, M. B., & Wlodkowski, R. J. (2000). *Creating highly motivating classrooms for all students: A schoolwide approach to powerful teaching with diverse learners.* San Francisco: Jossey-Bass.

Gonzalez-Mena, J. (2005). *Diversity in early care and education: Honoring differences* (4th ed.). Boston: McGraw-Hill.

Goodlad, J. I. (1984). *A place called school: Prospects for the future.* New York: McGraw-Hill.

Greenspan, S. I. (with Benderly, B. L.). (1997). *The growth of the mind and the endangered origins of intelligence.* Reading, MA: Addison-Wesley.

Griffith, J. (1996). Relation of parental involvement, empowerment, and school traits to student academic performance. *Journal of Educational Research, 90*(1), 33–41.

Haycock, K. (2001). Closing the achievement gap. *Educational Leadership, 58*(6), 6–11.

Henderson, A. T., & Berla, N. (Eds.). (1994). *A new generation of evidence: The family is critical to student achievement.* Washington, DC: National Committee for Citizens in Education.

Henderson, A. T., & Mapp, K. L. (2002). *A new wave of evidence: The impact of school, family, and community connections on student achievement* [Annual synthesis]. Austin, TX: Southwest Educational Development Laboratory, National Center for Family & Community Connections with Schools.

Howard, G. R. (2003). *Speaking of difference: Reflections on the possibility of culturally competent conversation.* Retrieved December 9, 2009, from New Horizons for Learning website: http://www.newhorizons.org/strategies/multicultural/howard.htm

Hurt, J. (2003). *Taming the standards: A commonsense approach to higher student achievement, K–12.* Portsmouth, NH: Heinemann.

Jensen, E. (1998). *Teaching with the brain in mind.* Alexandria, VA: Association for Supervision and Curriculum Development.

Johnson, D. W., Johnson, R. T., & Stanne, M. B. (2000). *Cooperative learning methods: A meta-analysis.* Minneapolis: University of Minnesota. Retrieved December 9, 2009, from http://www.co-operation.org/pages/cl-methods.html

Johnson, R. T., & Johnson, D. W. (1994). An overview of cooperative learning. In J. S. Thousand, R. A. Villa, & A. I. Nevin (Eds.), *Creativity and collaborative learning: A practical guide to empowering students and teachers* (pp. 31–44). Baltimore: P. H. Brookes. Retrieved December 9, 2009, from http://www.co-operation.org/pages/overviewpaper.html

Johnston, R. C., & Viadero, D. (2000, March 15). Unmet promise: Raising minority achievement. *Education Week, 19*(27), 1, 18–19.

Jones, E., & Nimmo, J. (1994). *Emergent curriculum.* Washington, DC: National Association for the Education of Young Children.

Juettner, V. (2003). Culturally responsive schools: Leadership, language, and literacy development. *Talking Points, 14*(2), 11–16. Urbana, IL: National Council of Teachers of English.

King, Martin Luther Jr. (1967). *Where do we go from here: Chaos or community?* Beacon Press: Boston.

Klug, B. J., & Whitfield, P. T. (2003). *Widening the circle: Culturally relevant pedagogy for American Indian children.* New York: RoutledgeFalmer.

Knapp, M. S. (with Adelman, N. E., Marder, C., McCollum, H., Needels, M. C., Padilla, C., et al.). (1995). *Teaching for meaning in high-poverty classrooms.* New York: Teachers College Press.

Kyle, D. W., & McIntyre, E. (2000). *Family visits benefit teachers and families—and students most of all* (Practitioner Brief No. 1). Santa Cruz, CA: Center for Research on Education, Diversity & Excellence.

Ladson-Billings, G. (1994). *The dreamkeepers: Successful teachers of African American children.* San Francisco, CA: Jossey-Bass.

Ladson-Billings, G. (1995). But that's just good teaching! The case for culturally relevant pedagogy. *Theory Into Practice, 34*(3), 159–165.

Liaupsin, C. J., Jolivette, K., & Scott, T. M. (2005). Schoolwide systems of behavior support: Maximizing student success in schools. In R. B. Rutherford, Jr., M. M. Quinn, & S. R. Mathur (Eds.), *Handbook of research in emotional and behavioral disorders* (pp. 487–501). New York: Guilford Press.

Lyman, L., & Foyle, H. C. (1988). *Cooperative learning strategies and children* [ERIC digest]. Urbana, IL: ERIC Clearinghouse on Elementary and Early Childhood Education. (ERIC ED306003)

Marzano, R. J., Pickering, D. J., & Pollock, J. E. (2001). *Classroom instruction that works: Research-based strategies for increasing student achievement.* Alexandria, VA: Association for Supervision and Curriculum Development.

McBrien, J. L., & Brandt, R. S. (with Cole, R. W.). (1997). *The language of learning: A guide to education terms.* Alexandria, VA: Association for Supervision and Curriculum Development.

McCombs, B. L. (2000). Reducing the achievement gap. *Society, 37*(5), 29–36.

McCunn, R. L. (2004). *Thousand pieces of gold.* Boston: Beacon Press.

Mitchell, R., Willis, M., & Chicago Teachers Union Quest Center. (1995). *Learning in overdrive: Designing curriculum, instruction, and assessment from standards: A manual for teachers.* Golden, CO: North American Press.

Morefield, J. (1996). *Recreating schools for all children* (Rev. ed.). Seattle, WA: New Horizon for Learning. Retrieved December 9, 2009, from http://www.newhorizons.org/trans/morefield.htm

Moursund, D. (2002). *Project-based learning using information technologies* (2nd ed.). Washington, DC: International Society for Technology in Education.

Nadelson, L. (2000). Discourse: Problem solving and project-based learning in high school mathematics. *Northwest Teacher, 1*(1), p. 20. Retrieved December 10, 2009, from http://educationnorthwest.org/webfm_send/349

Nave, G., & Ko, L. (2004). *Assessing school preparation for new and diverse students.* Portland, OR: Northwest Regional Educational Laboratory. (ERIC ED484555)

Newmann, F. M., Bryk, A. S., & Nagaoka, J. K. (2001). *Authentic intellectual work and standardized tests: Conflict or coexistence?* Chicago, IL: Consortium on Chicago School Research. (ERIC ED470299)

Nieto, S. (2003). *What keeps teachers going?* New York: Teachers College Press.

Noguera, P. A. (2003, August 13). Taking on the tough issues: The role of educational leaders in restoring public faith in public education. *In Motion Magazine.* Retrieved December 21, 2009, from http://www.inmotionmagazine.com/er/pn_leaders.html

Northwest Regional Advisory Committee. (2005). *A report to the U.S. Department of Education on educational challenges and technical assistance needs for the Northwest Region.* Washington, DC: U.S. Department of Education.

Novick, R. (2002). *Many paths to literacy: Language, literature, and learning in the primary classroom.* Portland, OR: Northwest Regional Educational Laboratory. (ERIC ED467518)

Ogbu, J. U. (1993). Differences in cultural frame of reference. *International Journal of Behavioral Development, 16*(3), 483–506.

Osborne, A. B. (1996). Practice into theory into practice: Culturally relevant pedagogy for students we have marginalized and normalized. *Anthropology and Education Quarterly, 27*(3), 285–314.

Osher, D., Cartledge, G., Oswald, D., Sutherland, K. S., Artiles, A. J., & Coutinho, M. (2004). Cultural and linguistic competency and disproportionate representation. In R. B. Rutherford, Jr., M. M. Quinn, & S. R. Mathur (Eds.), *Handbook of research in emotional and behavioral disorders* (pp. 54–77). New York: Guilford Press.

Owens, T. R., & Wang, C. (1996). *Community-based learning: A foundation for meaningful educational reform* (SIRS Topical Synthesis No. 8). Portland, OR: Northwest Regional Educational Laboratory.

Paley, V. G. (1979). *White teacher.* Cambridge, MA: Harvard University Press.

Paul, R., & Elder, L. (2001). *The miniature guide to critical thinking: Concepts and tools.* Dillon Beach, CA: Foundation for Critical Thinking.

Perkins, D., & Tishman, S. (2000). *Patterns of thinking.* Cambridge, MA: Harvard Graduate School of Education, Project Zero. Retrieved December 10, 2009, from http://www.pz.harvard.edu/Research/PatThk.htm

Phillips, C. B. (1988). Nurturing diversity for today's children and tomorrow's leaders. *Young Children, 43*(2), 42–47.

Planty, M., Hussar, W., Snyder, T., Kena, G., KewalRamani, A., Kemp, J., et al. (2009a). Indicator 7: Racial/ ethnic enrollment in public schools. In *The condition of education 2009* (NCES 2009–081). Washington, DC: U.S. Department of Education, National Center for Education Statistics. Retrieved December 21, 2009, from http://nces.ed.gov/programs/coe/2009/pdf/7_2009.pdf

Planty, M., Hussar, W., Snyder, T., Kena, G., KewalRamani, A., Kemp, J., et al. (2009b). Indicator 8: Language minority school-age children. In *The condition of education 2009* (NCES 2009–081). Washington, DC: U.S. Department of Education, National Center for Education Statistics. Retrieved December 21, 2009, from http://nces.ed.gov/programs/coe/2009/pdf/8_2009.pdf

Powell, R. R., Zehm, S., & Garcia, J. (1996). *Field experience: Strategies for exploring diversity in schools.* Upper Saddle River, NJ: Prentice Hall.

Sather, S.E. (2009). *Leading professional learning teams: A start-up guide for improving instruction.* Thousand Oaks, CA: Corwin.

Singleton, G., & Linton, C. (2006). *Courageous conversations about race: A field guide for achieving equity in schools.* Thousand Oaks, CA: Corwin Press.

Skiba, R. (2001). When is disproportionality discrimination? The overrepresentation of Black students in school suspension. In W. Ayers, B. Dohrn, & R. Ayers (Eds.), *Zero tolerance: Resisting the drive for punishment in schools* (pp. 165-176). New York: New Press.

Smith, A. M. (2005). *In the company of cheerful ladies.* New York: Pantheon Books.

Snow, C. E., Burns, M. S., & Griffin, P. (Eds.). (1998). *Preventing reading difficulties in young children.* Washington, DC: National Academy Press.

Steele, C. M. (1992). Race and the schooling of Black Americans. *Atlantic Monthly, 269*(4), 67–78.

Strong, R., Silver, H. F., & Robinson, A. (1995). What do students want (and what really motivates them)? *Educational Leadership, 53*(1), 8–12.

Tabors, P. O., & Snow, C. E. (1994). English as a second language in preschool programs. In F. Genesee (Ed.), *Educating second language children: The whole child, the whole curriculum, the whole community* (pp. 103–125). New York: Cambridge University Press.

Thorkildsen, R., & Stein, M. R. S. (1998). *Is parent involvement related to student achievement? Exploring the evidence* (Research Bulletin No. 22). Bloomington, IN: Phi Delta Kappa Center for Evaluation, Development, and Research.

Turnbull, A., Edmonson, H., Griggs, P., Wickham, D., Sailor, W., Freeman, R., et al. (2002). A blueprint for schoolwide positive behavior support: Implementation of three components. *Exceptional Children, 68*(3), 377–402.

Valdés, G. (1996). *Con respeto: Bridging the distances between culturally diverse families and schools, an ethnographic portrait.* New York: Teachers College Press.

Voke, H. (2002). *Motivating students to learn: Student engagement* (ASCD InfoBrief No. 8). Alexandria, VA: Association for Supervision and Curriculum Development.

Wagner, K. (1987). *When the legends die: Reproducible activity book.* Logan, IA: Perfection Form.

Wheatley, M., & Frieze, D. (2006). *Using emergence to take social innovations to scale.* Provo, UT: Margaret J. Wheatley. Retrieved December 21, 2009, from http://www.margaretwheatley.com/articles/emergence.html

White, K. K., Zion, S., & Kozleski, E. (2005). *Cultural identity and teaching.* Tempe, AZ: Arizona State University, National Institute for Urban School Improvement.

Wiggins, G., & McTighe, J. (1998). *Understanding by design.* Alexandria, VA: Association for Supervision and Curriculum Development.

Wirt, J., Choy, S., Rooney, P., Hussar, W., Provasnik, S., & Hampden-Thompson, G. (2005). *The condition of education 2005.* Washington, DC; U.S. Department of Education, National Center for Education Statistics. Retrieved December 10, 2009, from http://nces.ed.gov/pubsearch/pubsinfo.asp?pubid=2005094

Yair, G. (2000). Reforming motivation: How the structure of instruction affects students' learning experiences. *British Educational Research Journal, 26*(2), 191–210.

Index

CORWIN

A SAGE Company

The Corwin logo—a raven striding across an open book—represents the union of courage and learning. Corwin is committed to improving education for all learners by publishing books and other professional development resources for those serving the field of PreK–12 education. By providing practical, hands-on materials, Corwin continues to carry out the promise of its motto: **"Helping Educators Do Their Work Better."**

CREATING STRONG
SCHOOLS & COMMUNITIES

Education Northwest, formerly known as the Northwest Regional Educational Laboratory, is a nonprofit organization dedicated to transforming teaching and learning. We work with educators, administrators, policymakers, and communities across the country. Headquartered in Portland, Oregon, our mission is to improve learning by building capacity in schools, families, and communities through applied research and development. More information about Education Northwest is available at educationnorthwest.org.